Catherine Breillat

Manchester University Press

FRENCH FILM DIRECTORS

DIANA HOLMES and ROBERT INGRAM *series editors*
DUDLEY ANDREW *series consultant*

FRENCH FILM DIRECTORS

Catherine Breillat

DOUGLAS KEESEY

Manchester University Press
MANCHESTER AND NEW YORK

distributed exclusively in the USA by Palgrave Macmillan

Published by Manchester University Press
Oxford Road, Manchester M13 9NR, UK
and Room 400, 175 Fifth Avenue, New York, NY 10010, USA
www.manchesteruniversitypress.co.uk

Distributed exclusively in the USA by
Palgrave, 175 Fifth Avenue, New York, NY 10010, USA

Distributed exclusively in Canada by
UBC Press, University of British Columbia, 2029 West Mall, Vancouver, BC, Canada V6T 1Z2

British Library Cataloguing-in-Publication Data
A catalogue record for this book is available from the British Library

Library of Congress Cataloging-in-Publication Data applied for

ISBN 978 0 7190 7530 8 *hardback*

First published 2009

18 17 16 15 14 13 12 11 10 09   10 9 8 7 6 5 4 3 2 1

Mixed Sources
Product group from well-managed
forests and other controlled sources
www.fsc.org Cert no. TT-COC-2082
© 1996 Forest Stewardship Council

Typeset in Scala with Meta display
by Koinonia, Manchester
Printed in Great Britain
by Cromwell Press Ltd, Trowbridge

Contents

List of plates

Series editors' foreword

To an anglophone audience, the combination of the words 'French' and 'cinema' evokes a particular kind of film: elegant and wordy, sexy but serious – an image as dependent upon national stereotypes as is that of the crudely commercial Hollywood blockbuster, which is not to say that either image is without foundation. Over the past two decades, this generalised sense of a significant relationship between French identity and film has been explored in scholarly books and articles, and has entered the curriculum at university level and, in Britain, at A-level. The study of film as art-form and (to a lesser extent) as industry, has become a popular and widespread element of French Studies, and French cinema has acquired an important place within Film Studies. Meanwhile, the growth in multi-screen and 'art-house' cinemas, together with the development of the video industry, has led to the greater availability of foreign-language films to an English-speaking audience. Responding to these developments, this series is designed for students and teachers seeking information and accessible but rigorous critical study of French cinema, and for the enthusiastic filmgoer who wants to know more.

The adoption of a director-based approach raises questions about auteurism. A series that categorises films not according to period or to genre (for example), but to the person who directed them, runs the risk of espousing a romantic view of film as the product of solitary inspiration. On this model, the critic's role might seem to be that of discovering continuities, revealing a necessarily coherent set of themes and motifs which correspond to the particular genius of the individual. This is not our aim: the auteur perspective on film, itself most clearly articulated in France in the early 1950s, will be interrogated in certain volumes of the series, and, throughout, the director will be treated as one highly significant element in a complex process of film production and reception which includes socio-economic and political determinants, the work of a large and highly skilled team of artists and technicians, the mechanisms of production and distribution, and the complex and multiply determined responses of spectators.

The work of some of the directors in the series is already well known outside France, that of others is less so – the aim is both to provide informative and original English-language studies of established figures, and to extend the range of French directors known to anglophone students of cinema. We intend the series to contribute to the promotion of the formal and informal study of French films, and to the pleasure of those who watch them.

DIANA HOLMES
ROBERT INGRAM

Acknowledgements

I am grateful to Matthew Frost at Manchester University Press for his belief in me and this project from its inception and for his unfailingly helpful advice throughout its various stages. I would also like to thank series editors Diana Holmes and Robert Ingram for their valuable feedback on the proposal and for their wonderfully thorough reading of the draft typescript. My thanks to Linda Halisky, Dean of the College of Liberal Arts at Cal Poly, and to David Kann, Chair of the English Department, for providing travel and research funds enabling me to attend screenings of *Une vieille maîtresse* and Q&As with Catherine Breillat at the 2007 New York Film Festival, and additional thanks to Jim Dee, owner of the local Palm Theatre, for putting me in touch with IFC for advance information about the Festival. I would like to thank Richard Rushton for inviting me to present a paper at the 2008 Catherine Breillat conference held at London's Institute of Germanic and Romance Studies. I very much appreciate the prompt advice and expert research assistance provided by Howard Mandelbaum, Ron Mandelbaum, Derek Davidson, Cory Plowman and S. Victor Burgos at Photofest. Katie Tool, Connie Davis, Kathy Severn and Sue Otto gave me outstanding encouragement and technical support, and the superb staff at Kennedy Library – Karen Beaton, Judy Drake, Sharon Fujitani, Linda Hauck, Jan Kline, Heather Lucio, Holly Richmond and Janice Stone – came through time and time again for me; their assistance was absolutely vital to the completion of this book. I am grateful to John Harrington who has helped me with film teaching, film scholarship and so much else besides, and to Sheila Gold who first introduced me to the delights of French literature and film. Finally, I am profoundly grateful to my wife, Helen Bailey, without whose critical eye and compassionate ear this work would not even have been possible. This book is dedicated to her.

Introduction

The movie trailer for Catherine Breillat's *Romance* (1999) advertises the film as 'choquant, provoquant, sexuel, pervers, troublant, lucide, sincère, sexuel, cruel, érotique, cru, excitant, agressif, tendre, libre, interdit'[1] (Wilson 2001: 157). This kind of sensationalistic marketing has expanded Breillat's viewership, but it has also fed her reputation as being 'the auteur of porn', an 'art-porn provocateur', a purveyor of 'arthouse smut' and 'French Skinema'. These epithets are ironic given that Breillat has devoted her cinematic career to fighting pornography's objectification of women as mere flesh for male consumption. Breillat has often said that the subject of her films is not 'sexuality', but women's 'sexual identity' and particularly the way in which patriarchal society makes women feel ashamed of their bodies and their desires (Breillat 2006a: 106). Under the male gaze, a woman is not allowed to develop her own identity as a physical and spiritual being but instead she is 'cut in two', her body severed from her soul, as she is forced into a stereotyped gender role – either the asexual 'good girl' (virgin, wife, mother) or the hypersexual 'bad girl' (mistress, whore).

In Breillat's film *A ma sœur!* (*Fat Girl* (2001)), two sisters watch a rebroadcast of a 1960s' TV interview with actress and singer Laura Betti (who also appears in a bit part elsewhere in the film). In the face of the male interviewer's lascivious questioning, Betti insists that 'dans ma spectacle, il y a des "problèmes sexuels", si vous voulez, il n'y a pas de "sexe", c'est différent'[2] – a point that Breillat herself has made

---

1 'shocking, provocative, sexual, perverted, troubling, lucid, sincere, sexual, cruel, erotic, crude, exciting, aggressive, tender, free, forbidden' (Wilson 2001: 157).

2 'my show is about "sexual problems", if you like, it's not about "sex", that's

in many TV interviews about her own work. Betti goes on to mention a 1959 essay by Simone de Beauvoir on actress Brigitte Bardot (also known as BB or bébé), whose sexual independence in *Et Dieu créa la femme (And God Created Woman)* (1956) had provoked much social criticism: 'To say that "BB embodies the immorality of an age" means that the character she has created challenges certain taboos accepted by the preceding age, particularly those which denied women sexual autonomy. In France, there is still a great deal of emphasis, officially, on women's dependence upon men' (Beauvoir 1972: 36). Beauvoir argues that Bardot's active claim to her own identity, her 'haughty shamelessless', posed a challenge to the either/or categories (object of lust or worship) in which men tried to place her: 'nothing can be read into Bardot's face. It is what it is. It has the forthright presence of reality. It is a stumbling-block to lewd fantasies and ethereal dreams alike. Most Frenchmen like to indulge in mystic flights as a change from ribaldry, and vice-versa. With BB they get nowhere' (Beauvoir 1972: 23, 23–4). Just as Beauvoir saw the problem of woman's sense of self as being explored through the female characters played by Bardot, so Breillat views the heroines of her own films as undertaking 'une quête, la recherche d'une identité sexuelle'[3] (Hecquet 2000).

And the chain of references here – the Breillat, Betti, Beauvoir, Bardot 'sisterhood' – also shows that Breillat is conscious of making her films within a sociocultural context. This point is worth emphasising, because Breillat's nearly total creative control over her films and her increasingly tight focus on a narrow range of characters and locations (*Anatomie de l'enfer* (2003) is about a man and a woman in a room) have led some commentators to view her work as entirely personal and closed off from outside influences. According to Claire Clouzot, author of a recent volume on Breillat in Cahiers du cinéma's 'Auteurs' series, 'C'est une auteur autiste. Elle n'entend que ce qui la concerne. D'une œuvre à l'autre, elle ressasse l'aventure de ses pulsions, de ses obsessions. Elle est sourde au monde, au social, au sociétal'[4] (Clouzot 2004:

---

different.' Here and throughout this book, quotations without parenthetical attribution are from dialogue in the particular film being discussed at the time. All translations from the French are mine, except in cases where an English translation is credited in the footnotes.

3 'a quest, the search for a sexual identity'.

4 'This is an autistic auteur. She hears only what matters to her. From one work to the next, she takes up again the adventure of her drives, her obsessions. She is deaf to the world, to the social, the societal'.

11). This statement is consistent with the 'genius against the world' tendency of some French auteurist criticism, but my approach will be one that considers Breillat not as somehow monolithically rising above her social and cultural contexts, but instead as interacting and negotiating with them. A director's family and friends form one key context for her work, and I will examine Breillat's relation to some of the most important women in her life, including her mother, her sister, and fellow director Christine Pascal, whom she considered to be a kind of second sister. I will study the impact of a gender-conservative family environment and a strict religious upbringing, and then the counter-vailing influence of the Women's Liberation Movement on Breillat when she moved from the provinces to Paris. My discussion of Breil-lat's films will connect them to feminist writings by Beauvoir, Hélène Cixous, Claire Duchen, Juliet Mitchell, Anita Phillips and Susan Bordo as well as to male gender studies by Elisabeth Badinter, Pierre Bourdieu and Daniel Welzer-Lang. I will also explore the extraordinarily varied cultural context of Breillat's work, including the literature, films, paint-ings, photos and pop music that have influenced her films. Special attention will be devoted to discussion of the complex relation between Breillat's films and patriarchal pornography.

Catherine Breillat was born on 13 July 1948 – thirteen months after her sister Marie-Hélène – in Bressuire, a provincial town near Niort in western France. Her father was the town doctor and her mother a housewife. The two sisters received a repressive education at a Catholic boarding school where, Breillat recalls, when another girl got her first period, she was separated from the others and labelled a slut (Breillat 2006a: 21). When Catherine and Marie-Hélène reached puberty, their parents pulled them out of school and confined them to home where they could be kept under strict supervision. The girls' developing bodies were regarded with grave suspicion and they were made to feel ashamed of their own desires. Luckily, the young Breillat was able to escape via trips to the municipal library, these being among the only outings that she was permitted. Once she had finished with the children's books, she started on the adult section and discovered a whole series of scandalous authors who were not afraid of intellectual or sexual expression, including François Rabelais, the Marquis de Sade, the Count de Lautréamont, Fyodor Dostoyevsky and Jacques Audiberti. A young girl reading Sade? Antony Copley can give us some sense of why Breillat might have been drawn to such an author: 'one has the impression that his writing on sexual affairs was but an excuse for his endless forays against catholic morality. How to explain this fury? Was it a rebellion against his catholic upbringing? ... Against the piety of his parents? Or, as seems most probable, anger at a catholic morality that condemned his sexuality?' (Copley 1989: 49). Unfortunately, while the young Breillat found inspiration in these taboo-breaking texts, she also found herself internalising the fear and loathing of the female body expressed by some of these male authors: 'Ce sont des choses que j'ai lues dans mon enfance et que j'ai faites miennes. C'est d'une misogynie! ... Les écrivains qui l'ont écrit avec toute leur âme et d'une manière sublime ont écrit leur horreur des femmes! Leur désir de meurtre sur les femmes! ... en tant que filles, on est nourries de ce discours terrifiant des hommes sur les femmes'[5] (Clément 2002: 286–7). Women's struggle to throw off this internalised sense of shame and to adopt an affirmative view of their own sexuality would become the subject of many Breillat films.

It was one film in particular, Ingmar Bergman's *La Nuit des forains* (*Sawdust and Tinsel*) (1953), that first inspired Breillat to become a director when she saw it at the local ciné-club. The heroine of this film is seduced and abandoned by an actor, but she is able to fulfil her desire through the affair, and her passion is so sublime that it raises her above humiliation and degradation, enabling her to withstand and defy the actor's cruel treatment. Breillat saw in this heroine a potential model for herself, a way beyond self-loathing and internalised shame, a validation of her sex despite patriarchal disparagement: 'Ce film-là, quand je l'ai vu, j'ai décidé immédiatement d'être cinéaste. Pas par amour de cinéma. Par nécessité. Pour me sauver. ... Ce film m'a inventée quand j'avais 12 ans. Il m'a fait naître à moi-même'[6] (Breillat 2003: 67). One week later, Breillat saw Luis Buñuel's *Viridiana* (1961) in which a young woman, on the verge of taking her nun's vows, is almost molested by her uncle and then attacked by a tramp, and yet despite these assaults upon her honour she remains both

5 'These are things that I read in my childhood and that I made mine. They had such misogyny! ... The authors who wrote this with all their soul and in such a sublime manner wrote about their horror of women! Their murderous desires toward women! ... as girls, we are nourished on this terrifying discourse by men about women'.

6 'This is the film that, when I saw it, I immediately decided to become a director. Not out of love for the cinema. By necessity. To save myself. ... This film invented me when I was 12 years old. It enabled me to be born to myself'.

proud and spiritually strong, not defiled or self-despising. Breillat superimposed the two heroines of these films in her mind and made them the prototype of her own female characters – 'Ces jeunes filles irradiées, marmoréennes, complètement sculpturales, froides et en même temps fiévreuses, orgueilleuses, se brûlant dans des désirs de culpabilité, s'abaissant dans des choses qui pourtant ne les abîment pas'[7] (Breillat 2006a: 127).

At age sixteen, Breillat eagerly departed the provinces in order to make a life for herself in Paris, where she frequented the Cinémathèque française and the movie theatres on the Champs-Elysées. Determined to become a director, she applied to IDHEC (the Institut des hautes études cinématographiques) but was told that only men could enrol in the directors' training programme. Undaunted, she tried her hand at writing in the hope that, if her book got noticed, she might be asked to turn her fiction into a film, as had happened for Alain Robbe-Grillet. Breillat's first novel, *L'Homme facile* (*A Man for the Asking*) (1968), certainly brought her attention from a public scandalised by the fact that such a boldly sexual book had been written by an angel-faced young woman. Indeed, if the book had been published in the year that she wrote it, she would have been too young to be allowed to buy it: 'Ma première expérience de la loi et de la censure, c'est l'écriture de mon premier livre, à 17 ans. Le livre a été censuré "interdit aux moins de dix-huit ans". J'étais ainsi interdite à moi-même. Je pouvais écrire un livre, mais je n'avais pas le droit de le relire'[8] (Breillat 2006b: 69). While waiting for her chance to direct, Breillat also dabbled in acting alongside her sister Marie-Hélène, who had made this career her profession. As fate would have it, Breillat made her acting debut in a landmark film that would greatly influence her own work, Bernardo Bertolucci's *Last Tango in Paris* (1972), in which she and her sister appear as clothes shop assistants fitting a young bride for a wedding dress. The bride (Maria Schneider) is torn between the roles of wife and 'whore', between marrying her conventional fiancé and having passionate sex with an anonymous man (Marlon Brando) whom

7 'These young girls who are radiant, marmoreal, completely sculptural, cold and at the same time feverish, proud, burning with guilty desires, abasing themselves in things which still do not defile them.'

8 'My first experience of the law and of censorship was the writing of my first book, at age 17. The book was censored as "forbidden to those under the age of eighteen". I was thus forbidden to myself. I could write the book, but I didn't have the right to reread it'.

she meets for illicit rendezvous. In real life, Breillat herself made an unconventional marriage (with a homosexual), a union which did not last but which resulted in a child. (In subsequent years, she would have two more children, each with a different man.)

In 1976, Breillat did finally get to direct a film (*Une vraie jeune fille*) based on one of her books (*Le Soupirail*), but the producer went bankrupt and the movie was not released. (This intensely autobiographical film about a young girl's exploration of her body and the physical world would not see theatre screens until 2000, after the international success of *Romance*.) Following the false start of *Une vraie jeune fille*, Breillat tried again with *Tapage nocturne* (1979), but this film about a 'liberated' woman's troubled relationships with multiple men was neither a commercial nor a critical success. The fact that the film was forbidden to those under eighteen hurt its box office, and Breillat was hurt when reviewers compared her work unfavourably to that of male directors: 'Catherine Breillat a réussi aussi bien (sans le talent et avec quel simplisme en sus!) que Jean Eustache dans ses films, à donner une image méprisante et misogyne des relations amoureuses entre homme et femme. Et cette fois, c'est le point de vue d'une femme: bravo Catherine!'[9] (Audé 1979: 79). Such stinging criticism made Breillat doubt whether she was cut out to be a director, and it would be nine years before her next effort, *36 fillette* (1987). This film, which could be described as *Lolita* told from the girl's point of view, received some savage notices in the French press – one critic charged that it would 'provoquer la bête vaguement pédophile qui sommeille en tout spectateur adulte'[10] (Godard 1988) – but the movie was picked up for the New York Film Festival and became the first film to bring Breillat some international attention. After *Sale comme un ange* (1991), her distinctly female take on the 'polar' ('police film') which fared well with critics if not at the box office, the French public turned out in greater numbers for *Parfait amour!* (1996), an intimate detailing of the events leading up to the brutal murder of an older woman by her younger male lover.

But it was the combined public and critical furore over *Romance*

9 'Catherine Breillat has succeeded as well (without the talent and with oversimplification to boot!) as Jean Eustache in his films, in giving a contemptuous and misogynistic image of amorous relations between man and woman. And this time, it's from a woman's point of view: bravo Catherine!'

10 'provoke the latent paedophile beast that slumbers within every adult viewer'.

that finally gained Breillat her worldwide reputation. The story of a woman's search for fulfilment of body and soul, *Romance* challenged and scandalised audiences in being both highly intellectual and sexually graphic. No one knew quite what to make of the film, but everyone had an opinion. On the one side, there were those who focused obsessively on the casting of porn star Rocco Siffredi and whether he was really having sex on camera with lead actress Caroline Ducey. On the other side, there were viewers who thought the film was overly cerebral and pretentious: 'Only in a French movie would a woman embrace sexual experimentation merely to attain an enormous *pensée*. ... pornographic but unarousing, ... the movie feels like a third-rate Left Bank novel from fifty years ago' (Denby 1999). A point that often seemed to be missed was that Breillat had deliberately introduced hardcore elements (erections, penetration, ejaculation) into a mainstream art film in order to reunite the body and the head, sex and sentiment, and to defy the conventional separation between feelings (elevated into 'art') and the flesh (relegated to 'pornography'). The film's explicit sex scenes ran afoul of the censors, whose job it is to maintain the very distinction between art and porn that Breillat was deconstructing. In Japan, certain body parts were masked with optical fogging. Australia's ratings board refused to classify *Romance*, effectively banning the film, until a public and media outcry led to the ban's being overturned. In the UK, *Romance* can be credited with having contributed to a quiet revolution at the British Board of Film Classification, which surprisingly passed the film uncut as an '18' rather than slapping it with an 'R18' and restricting it to being shown only in sex shops or specially licensed cinemas. In addition to struggles with censorship, *Romance* also met with ideological protests, particularly from feminists disturbed by the film's representation of its female character as a sexual masochist. For example, a group of Swedish feminists chained themselves to a theatre door to prevent the film from being shown in Stockholm. Breillat has often drawn criticism from those who would have her promote the feminist cause by presenting more positive images of women, but her great subject is women's attempt to confront and work through the negative images of themselves that they have internalised: 'My own position is that a woman must be a militant feminist in life, but when she is making a work of art, things are different. Real life is confused. As a feminist artist, it is difficult to take responsibility for feelings such as unease, confusion, shame, self-destruction, sado-masochism – all these are human feelings you can claim as an individual, but as a feminist they are obviously not the ones you can easily highlight' (Breillat in Vincendeau 1989: 41).

Breillat's next film after *Romance* was *A ma sœur!* which performed well on the arthouse circuit and became her most critically acclaimed work to date. This film, in which a girl watches while her sister is seduced and abandoned by an older boy, also pushed the limits of mainstream cinema with scenes of anal intercourse and child rape. In Canada, the Ontario Film Review Board banned the film, but when the distributor filed a suit (supported by directors Atom Egoyan and David Cronenberg), the film was granted a rating and finally released. The widespread public interest in this film led Breillat to make a movie about the making of *A ma sœur!* called *Sex Is Comedy* in 2002. Between these two films, Breillat directed *Brève traversée* (2001), which reverses the male predator/female sufferer dynamic with its story of an older woman who seduces and abandons a young male virgin. In 2003, Breillat released *Anatomie de l'enfer*, the film that represents her most radical attempt to exorcise the demons of shame and to bless female sexuality as something sacred rather than cursed. Ironically (given Breillat's attempt to unite skin and spirit), the lead actress insisted that a body double be used for the vaginal close-ups. The film's controversial subject matter limited its audience, but it was appreciated by aficionados and selected by a number of critics for their lists of the year's best films. Most recently, this most contemporary of directors surprised everyone by making a costume drama, *Une vieille maîtresse* (2007), which though set in the nineteenth century does still deal with Breillat's characteristic conflict between a conventionally spiritual wife and a demonically passionate mistress. The film was nominated for a Palme d'or at Cannes.

As Anne Gillain has noted, 'Catherine Breillat is an author in all the New Wave splendor of the word. The sharpness of her polemical gift brings to mind the young Turks confronting the old order in the 1960s. Like them, Catherine Breillat bases her work on a personal, autobiographical vision; like them, she writes her own scripts and dialogues' (Gillain 2003: 205). It is not unusual for Breillat herself to choose the costumes (the red dresses worn by so many of her female characters), to do the decor (Robert's *Romance* chinoiserie came from her own apartment), to find the props (the wall crucifix in *Anatomie de l'enfer*) or to occupy herself with the actors' make-up. But even an auteur is dependent on the creative contributions of her cast and crew. Agnès Guillemot, veteran editor of films by Jean-Luc Godard and François Truffaut, helped Breillat to develop her now-signature style of uninterrupted takes and pregnant pauses to convey the characters' emotions and interactions in *Sale comme un ange*, *Parfait amour!* and *Romance*. Theodoros Angelopoulos' great cinematographer, Yorgos Arvanitis, has found the spiritual light in female characters' faces during their moments of sexual ecstasy in *Romance*, *A ma sœur!*, *Anatomie de l'enfer* and *Une vieille maîtresse*. First assistant director Michaël Weill (affectionately known as 'Miko') has worked with Breillat on every one of her films since *Romance* and is often asked to play out 'intimate' scenes with the director so that she can work out their choreography, as Léo does for Jeanne in the metacinematic *Sex Is Comedy*. Producer Jean-François Lepetit has provided unfailing financial support for Breillat's films even in cases (such as *Anatomie de l'enfer*) where a big return on the investment seemed unlikely. The contribution made by Breillat's lead actresses is incalculable, for she demands a great deal from them both physically and emotionally, and in most instances a film's success or failure depends almost entirely on their performance. Roxane Mesquida, who has starred in three Breillat films (and played a young woman who loses her virginity in each one), was pushed to do twenty takes of the (simulated) sodomy scene in *A ma sœur!* (Breillat used the last take.) As Mesquida has said about working with Breillat, 'Cela m'apprend à découvrir mes émotions, au risque d'en être submergée. Mais c'est si bon! J'ai tellement confiance en elle que je me laisse complètement faire, parce que je sais très bien qu'elle ne m'abandonnera pas'[11] (Flach Film 2007). In interviews, Breillat has been generous in acknowledging all that her collaborators have brought to her work.

This book discusses Breillat's films in thematic groupings. Chapters 1 and 2 consider her three female coming-of-age films – *Une vraie jeune fille*, *36 fillette* and *A ma sœur!* – with *Sex is Comedy*, a movie about the making of *A ma sœur!*, paired with that film in chapter 2. In chapter 3, I study Breillat's three movies about masculinity in crisis – *Sale comme un ange* (with a look at its early avatar, *Police*), *Parfait*

---

11 'That teaches me to discover my emotions, at the risk of being submerged by them. But it's so good! I have such confidence in her that I completely let myself go, because I know very well that she will not abandon me'.

amour! and *Brève traversée*. Chapter 4 examines *Tapage nocturne*, *Romance* and *Anatomie de l'enfer*, the three films that Breillat has made about the sexual odysseys of adult women. In the book's conclusion, I look at Breillat's relation to and influence on other contemporary directors before turning to a discussion of her latest film, *Une vieille maîtresse*.

References

Audé, Françoise (1979), '*Tapage nocturne*,' *Positif* 224, 79.

Beauvoir, Simone de (1972), *Brigitte Bardot and the Lolita Syndrome*, trans. Bernard Fretchman, New York, Arno Press.

Breillat, Catherine (2003), 'Le Film qui m'a inventée', *Cahiers du cinéma* 582, 66–7.

Breillat, Catherine (2006a), *Corps amoureux: Entretiens avec Claire Vassé*, Paris, Denoël.

Breillat, Catherine (2006b), 'La Censure, pour se cacher de soi-même ... ', in Eric Alt (ed.), *Le Sexe et ses juges*, Paris, Syllepse, pp. 69–73.

Clément, Jérôme (2002), 'Catherine Breillat', *Les Femmes et l'amour*, Paris, Stock, pp. 267–300.

Clouzot, Claire (2004), *Catherine Breillat: Indécence et pureté*, Paris, Cahiers du cinéma.

Copley, Antony (1989), *Sexual Moralities in France, 1780–1980*, London and New York, Routledge.

Denby, David (1999), '*Romance*', *New Yorker*, 4 October.

Flach Film (2007), Dossier de presse: *Une vieille maîtresse*, Paris, Flach Film.

Gillain, Anne (2003), 'Profile of a Filmmaker: Catherine Breillat', in Roger Célestin, Eliane DalMolin and Isabelle de Courtivron (eds), *Beyond French Feminisms: Debates on Women, Politics, and Culture in France, 1981–2001*, New York, Palgrave Macmillan, pp. 201–11.

Godard, Colette (1988), *Le Monde*, 30 March.

Hecquet, Céline (2000), 'Catherine Breillat donne sa langue au Chat', *Inrockuptibles*, 19 May.

Vincendeau, Ginette (1989), 'The Closer You Get ... ', *Monthly Film Bulletin* 661:56, 41–2.

Wilson, Emma (2001), 'Deforming Femininity: Catherine Breillat's *Romance*', in Lucy Mazdon (ed.), *France on Film: Reflections on Popular French Cinema*, London, Wallflower Press, pp. 145–57.

Female virgins and the shaming gaze

Une vraie jeune fille (A Real Young Girl)

Given Breillat's efforts over the years to distance her work from mere pornography, there is some irony in the fact that her first directing opportunity was partly owing to the popularity of pornographic films. After the abolition of censorship in 1974 and the box-office success of *Emmanuelle*, the tide of pornographic films rose in France, amounting to almost half of all French film production in 1974 and 1975. In line with this trend, producer André Génovès offered Breillat the chance to make her first movie: 'Il désirait un porno soft réalisé par une femme'[1] (Ciment 1988: 3). Not knowing the rules or norms and having no one to guide her, Breillat took a three-person crew from the porn industry, with herself serving as writer, director and production designer, and made her first film in four weeks, shooting without sound and with only one take per shot. The result – not a softcore porn film, but instead what Breillat has called 'a kind of underground, "wild" movie' (Vincendeau 1989: 41) – would have made a striking directorial debut, but due to a fateful turn of events *Une vraie jeune fille* would not be released for another twenty-four years.

First, in December 1975 the government re-imposed a kind of censorship on pornographic films by increasing the tax on their production and distribution and by subjecting them to an X classification. When Génovès viewed the rushes of Breillat's film, he thought it would be branded with an X, so he lost faith in it and reduced her already meagre financing. Then Génovès' production company went

---

1 'He desired a softcore porn film directed by a woman'.

bankrupt, and *Une vraie jeune fille* was consigned to judicial limbo. There was thus a sense in which Breillat's film, explicit but not pornographic, was nevertheless blotted out by the anti-porn crusade. As she sees it, her 'film was "censored", even though it wasn't physically censored, because there was a compulsion in society that was saying that films that talked about sexuality *should* be banned. Distributors, newspapers, critics – everybody thought it was a horrible pornographic film. So as a fact, it was censored' (Wiegand 2001). It was only after the international success of Breillat's *Romance* that her very first film, *Une vraie jeune fille*, would finally see the screen in 2000.

Like many other neophyte directors, Breillat included a number of autobiographical elements in her first feature. Alice, the eponymous heroine of *Une vraie jeune fille*, is fourteen verging on fifteen years of age during her summer vacation in the early 1960s (TV broadcasts in the film put the date at 1963), and Breillat was born on 13 July 1948. This means that Alice is still a minor, the age of consent in France being fifteen back then as well as now. Like Alice, Breillat was subject to a strict Catholic upbringing, which included close supervision by the nuns at a girls' boarding school and rigid control by her parents at home and on vacation. The Landes region in southwest France where Alice spends her family vacation is the same area that Breillat used to pass on the way to summer break with her parents. Like Alice, the young Breillat matured early, getting her first period at age nine and developing full breasts by age twelve, and she was similarly subjected to her parents' vociferous disapproval of her womanly body, with her mother even calling her a 'pute' ('whore') (Clouzot 2004: 16). (It is interesting to note that, in post-synching the film's sound, Breillat had her own mother dub the voice of Alice's mother, while Breillat's sister dubbed Alice's dialogue.) Both Alice and Breillat suffer the disparagement directed at their bodies by their parents, the nuns and the local townsfolk (the people of 'Aupom' for Alice, Niort for Breillat), and both girls experience this adult disapproval as a kind of anti-education or un-birth: 'Je n'ai pas été très bien élevée, je suis très mutilée'[2] (Clouzot 2004: 171); 'Ce ne sont pas mes parents qui m'ont fait exister, ni la ville de Niort. Eux faisaient tout pour que je n'existe pas. C'étaient des bourgeois puritains et censeurs'[3] (Breillat 2006: 16).

2 'I was not very well brought up, I was very mutilated'.
3 'It wasn't my parents who made me exist, or the village of Niort. They did everything so that I would not exist. They were puritanical and censorious bourgeois'.

Alice's first thoughts in the film, conveyed as a voice-over interior monologue, are 'Je m'appelle Alice, Alice Bonnard, du nom de mon père et de ma mère. Je n'aime pas les gens. Ils m'oppressent'.[4] The heaviness and heat of the summer weigh on Alice like the stifling feeling that she is expected to become just like her mother, a 'grosse vache', 'frigide mesquine et ménagère', one of those 'femmes que la vie, la fatalité et la pesanteur ont beaucoup abîmées'[5] (Breillat 1974: 51, 15, 52). The mother's first words to Alice in the film are 'ma fille', claiming her as her daughter, her girl. At night she turns out the light in her daughter's bedroom in order to stop Alice from writing in her diary, much as the dorm supervisor at her Catholic boarding school would remove Alice's hand from between her legs and shush her to sleep. In these ways, her mother and the nuns stifle Alice's literary and sexual self-expression. When Alice applies lipstick and mascara to go to the fair, her mother interrogates her from the other side of the bathroom door, and when Alice daydreams about kissing a boy, her mother throws cold water from wet laundry onto her daughter's bikini top and accuses Alice of being 'encore habillée comme une pute'.[6] Horrified to learn from the village grocer lady (a petty, spiteful woman) that Alice has been roaming the countryside on her bicycle, her mother panics at the thought that Alice might get pregnant and shuts her up within the narrow confines of the house and grounds.

While the mother may sometimes seem like a wicked witch from a fairytale (particularly as the film is very much told from young Alice's perspective), it's important to understand the mother's repressive and overprotective behaviour within the context of that time. As Breillat has said about her own mother, who in the early 1960s was hypervigilant regarding Breillat's and her sister's sexuality and who curtailed their freedom through a similar home confinement, 'A l'époque, la pilule n'existait pas, il n'y avait rien pour réparer les dégâts si dégâts il y avait, et l'avortement était un crime. La seule chose que les parents croyaient pouvoir faire, c'était d'enfermer leurs enfants, de les

---

4 'I'm called Alice, Alice Bonnard, after the name of my father and mother. I don't like people. They oppress me'.

5 'fat cow' ... 'a frigid, petty housewife' ... 'women that life, fatality and gravity have mostly destroyed'. *Le Soupirail* is the novel by Breillat on which she based her screenplay for *Une vraie jeune fille*.

6 'once again dressed like a whore'.

enfermer sous clé'[7] (Breillat 2006: 13). Contraception did not become legally available in France until 1967, and women were not granted the right to abortion until 1975. Only 'bad girls' had premarital sex and got into trouble. 'Good girls' or 'vraies jeunes filles' were expected to abstain until they were properly wed, with their virginity as guarantee that they were viable commodities on the marriage market. Indeed, for Breillat, 'la "vraie jeune fille" fait référence à la virginité comme valeur établie et presque "marchande"'[8] (Breillat 2006: 12).

And once married, women were expected to be 'good' wives and mothers, to keep house and bear children who would grow up to be 'good girls' and do likewise. Even though French women were given the right to vote in 1944, pro-natalist propaganda by the postwar government discouraged women from seeking independent careers and instead promoted 'la femme au foyer' ('the homemaker') as the ideal woman: 'Women's world was still defined as private, as domestic; women's fulfilment was still thought to be wrapped up in house and home; women's biology was still destiny. A good woman was a good mother; a good mother was a wife and a housewife; and, for at least fifteen years after the war, no vision of fulfilled femininity involving anything other than domesticity and motherhood was readily available to women' (Duchen 1994: 64). When Alice's mother criticises one of Alice's schoolgirl friends for wanting to be a pilot, she is merely expressing the then-common view that any role for women besides that of 'mère-ménagère' ('housewife and mother') is presumptuous and selfish. Near the end of the film, we learn that Alice's mother may have given up several lovers and a more independent life in Paris to settle for domestic life in the provinces with Alice's father. Like most women of that time, she is entirely dependent on her husband for both love and money, a fact she begins to rue when he becomes a philanderer and his business shows signs of impending failure. Even though she slaves away at home, he is contemptuous of her housework, saying that she has never had the audacity to do anything but darn stockings and be frugal, that she has never earned anything. Yet her life has been subject to the

7 'At that time, the pill didn't exist, there was nothing to repair the damage if damage occurred, and abortion was a crime. The only thing that parents believed they could do was to confine their children, to confine them under lock and key'.

8 '"vraie jeune fille" makes reference to virginity as an established and almost "market" value'.

prevailing division of labour whereby man is the breadwinner and woman the homemaker. In fact, until 1965 married women in France did not have the right to get a job, open a bank account or dispose of their own property without their husbands' permission, and despite women's marital dissatisfaction it was not until 1975 that divorce by mutual consent became legal.

In the face of her mother's attempts to confine her to home and to the role of 'good girl' and future homemaker, Alice looks for freedom wherever she can find it. Turning to the 'chansons yéyé' ('pop songs') she hears on the radio and to the 'copains' and 'copines' ('male and female pop star pals') she sees on TV, Alice finds cultural forms and role models that both express and give shape to her new sexual feelings. (It is interesting to note that, when Breillat was young, she not only wanted to be a writer and director but also entertained the notion of becoming a singer or actress.) As Alice listens to a song on the car radio, we see her framed from below with her eyes half-closed and then with the sun shining on her face as she looks up. Alice worships the female singer for transporting her to another world of the music's making: 'Ecoute ça. Je ferais n'importe quoi pour cette femme'.[9] Later, Alice's face lights up as she watches a TV performance by the same female pop star, who is dressed in a frilly blouse while coyly holding a daisy as she sings, 'Suis-je une petite fille / je ne sais pas / je ne sais pas / ou bien une grande fille / vous le savez bien pour moï'.[10] These lyrics seem to express Alice's self-doubt regarding her transitional state, but they also embolden her with their suggestion that girls on the verge of change can be seductive. Indeed, as Alice stands in her parents' kitchen taking in the pop star's 'little girl' act, Alice's pink headband and blue shirt with white polka dots are in provocative contrast to the black bikini with red fringe that she is wearing underneath. Soon thereafter, Alice is listening to the same 'little girl' song on the radio while stretched out in her sexy bikini on the lawn, as if she were the nymphet Sue Lyon sunning herself in Stanley Kubrick's *Lolita* (1962). (The 'Suis-je une petite fille' ditty even has a teasing sound like the 'ya ya / ya-uh ya-uh / ya ya' song that Lolita listens to on her radio.) Alice's radio tune prompts her to have an erotic fantasy in which she is lying, coyly seductive, on the sand and attracts the attentions of a playfully

9 'Listen to that. I would do anything for that woman'.
10 'Am I a little girl / I don't know / I don't know / or a big girl / only you can know for me'. All the lyrics to the songs in the film were written by Breillat.

aggressive beach boy, as in a rock-and-roll beach-party movie.

Popular culture also shapes Alice's masculine object of desire – the sexualised male as 'bad boy' – much as songs and images had lent a form to her desiring self – the 'naughty girl'. Again in the kitchen with her parents, Alice's eyes open wide as she watches a male rock star belt out a tune, his hair in a pompadour, his lips snarling and his hips gyrating like Elvis's. As Susan Weiner has noted about France's own answer to Elvis, Johnny Hallyday, 'When Johnny first appeared on the TV show "L'Ecole des vedettes" in 1960 at the age of seventeen, clad in tight black leather pants, to sing "T'Aimer Follement", his French version of Elvis Presley's "Makin' Love", he became notorious overnight. ... Parents were horrified; teenagers were thrilled' (Weiner 2001: 146). As the rock star on Alice's TV sings about a tumultuous love affair ('je vivais sur un volcan'),[11] Alice may imagine herself as his fiery lover, and when he screams that he doesn't give a damn about the 'petite amie' who left him, that he just wants to ride around in his sports car and pick up lots of girls, Alice may dream of being the one girl so passionate she will make him care. Later, Alice goes to a bar where rock music is on the jukebox, and flirts with a boy who's playing the tough guy with slicked-back hair and a leather jacket. He may callously trade queens in a card game with his buddies, but he ends up following Alice out the door and chasing after her on his motorbike. Still later, when Alice is in the car with Jim – a James Dean look-alike who smokes cigarettes and sports an arm tattoo – the voice of a male rock singer on the soundtrack seems to be telling her just what she wants to hear from Jim, that only her love can tame this bad boy: 'si ... on objecte / que je ne suis qu'un voyou / aucune loi ne m'arrête / je m'arrête à tes genoux / ... je ne demande / que de t'aimer à la folie'.[12]

'Naughty girls' may get to play with 'bad boys', but they are still 'naughty': her parents' repression of her sexually developing body, their looks of disapproval, make Alice feel ashamed of herself. As Breillat has said, 'on vous enferme et on vous suspecte. Mais de quoi peut-on suspecter une petite fille? J'ai intégré la haine et la honte que l'on m'a inculquées si fortement à un âge où l'on est si faible'[13] (Guilloux

11 'I was living on a volcano'.
12 'if they object / that I'm only a lout / no law stops me / I stop at your knees / ... the only thing that I ask / is to love you like crazy'.
13 'they confine you and they suspect you. But what is there to suspect about a

1999). In one scene, while having tea and jam with her parents, Alice drops a spoon under the table and then surreptitiously slips it inside her panties. Editing in the scene shows that the spoon, sticky with Alice's secretions, is connected in her mind to the viscous jam and the tacky flypaper with its dirty, dying flies: 'je me livrais encore et encore à une inquisition naturelle de mon vagin cramoisi, inspectant sans fin ses secrets ... car il était important de savoir que j'avais cela même lorsque j'étais habillée et que je marchais entre mon père et ma mère et qu'en cela j'étais incurable'[14] (Breillat 1974: 173–4). Psychologist Silvan Tomkins has argued that 'when the self feels ashamed, it is felt as a sickness within the self', and that the 'necessity of hiding shame and its sources enormously increases the stress of adolescence. When the increase in the strength of the sex drive evokes guilt ... , the adolescent feels she must hide both her sex drive and her ... shame ... lest she increase her and her parents' humiliation, and thus forfeit the love and respect of her parents who would be shocked by the disclosure' (Sedgwick and Frank 1995: 136, 173; pronouns changed to the feminine). In another scene, Alice walks through a trash-strewn field dragging her panties which are down around her ankles, then squats to urinate in the dark outside her house like some filthy animal. She can see her mother just inside moving about in the light, keeping a clean house. The shame induced by her parents makes Alice view her body's secretions as dirty secrets to be kept hidden, the terrible truth about herself: 'ses règles témoignaient de la purulence de son âme ... elle sue elle suinte elle crachote elle chie elle urine elle s'enfoutre s'ensanglante elle pourrit'[15] (Breillat 1974: 106, 129–30).

Sometimes Alice seems to take perverse pleasure in her illicit liquids and forbidden orifices, in covert or open defiance of her parents who would have her be ashamed of these things. When her father tells her that she is a danger to herself and that he should have locked her up after her first period, she uses her finger to dig at earwax in her ear, thus blocking him out and rooting around in her

---

little girl? I internalised the hatred and the shame that they inculcated in me so strongly at an age when I was so weak'.

14 'I engaged again and again in a natural inquisition of my blushing vagina, ceaselessly inspecting its secrets ... because it was important to know that I had "that" even when I was dressed and when I was walking between my father and my mother and that for that reason I was incurable'.

15 'her period bore witness to the purulence of her soul ... she sweats she oozes she spits she shits she urinates she buggers herself bloody she rots'.

own 'filth'. Later, since she has been ordered to preserve her virginity, Alice 'obeys' by violating another orifice, buggering herself with a bottle of tanning oil. In another scene, when she is expected to feed the chickens and collect their eggs like a good mother-to-be, Alice deliberately breaks an egg, letting its yolk run through her fingers, and then looks up defiantly at her mother. Alice's transgressive play with liquids is reminiscent of Simone's in Georges Bataille's surrealist novel *Histoire de l'œil* (*Story of the Eye*) (1928), a major influence on Breillat. For sexual excitement, Simone sits in a saucer of milk and then stands up, letting the white liquid drip from her thighs; she urinates on cracked eggs in the bidet; and she inserts a man's severed eye, thinking of it as an egg, into her vagina and anus. The more shameful, perverse and blasphemous the act, the more erotic it is for Simone who, like Alice, thrills at being a good girl gone bad: 'The significant thing about Simone is precisely that she is not a whore but a "young girl from a good family", a virginal-looking adolescent who ... experiences sex as profoundly scandalous' (Suleiman 1990: 82).

The extremity of Alice's revolt against repression can tend toward nihilism, resulting in thoughts of befouling or murdering a 'holier than thou' world that makes her feel dirty because of her desires, or of committing suicide because she is so mortified by her shameful sexuality: 'j'ai des impulsions terribles. Me détruire. Détruire. Salir'[16] (Breillat 1974: 135). There are times when Alice strongly resembles the antihero of Lautréamont's *Les Chants de Maldoror* (1868), a fiction which had a formative influence on Breillat when she was young. Much as Maldoror claims to be expressing the true nature of his sinful self and this fallen world by committing terrible – and often obscenely sexual – acts as he wanders the earth, so Alice feels an 'indomptable désir ... de retrouver la lande et la passion secrète car malsaine qui les lie', and it is on the arid moor or deserted dunes that Alice explores the region between 'ses cuisses, comme milieu elles aussi d'un paysage au partage secret'[17] (Breillat 1974: 59, 34). Self-loathing can lead Alice's thoughts to turn morbid, as when she associates the stickiness of her vagina during masturbation with the sticky innards of a chicken being gutted by her mother, as if the punishment for

16 'I had terrible urges. To destroy myself. To destroy. To dirty'.
17 'indomitable desire to find again the moor and the passion – secret because unhealthy – which links them' ... 'her thighs, themselves being also like a landscape with a secret opening'.

pleasuring herself were disembowelment. This scene is based on a most disturbing passage in *Les Chants de Maldoror* where a 'jeune fille' becomes a 'poulet vidé', stabbed in her sex with a knife and gutted 'par l'ouverture épouvantable'[18] (Lautréamont 1973: 132).

However, like Maldoror, Alice also finds a strange peace in her sinful kinship with fallen nature. As she stands on the moor with her panties down around her ankles and with her sex exposed, 'le vent passait sur ses lèvres son sourire glacial' and she seems able to 'se dessaisir d'elle-même'; she feels 'une joie honteuse' and she can 'imaginer l'infini en son universalité morbide'[19] (Breillat 1974: 67–8). Later on the dunes, Alice drops her panties on the carcass of a dead dog and then sits in the surf, letting the ocean surge up between her legs. To Alice, the ocean represents 'la mort et la fascination morbide de la Faute', and initially she fears being overrun by this 'grand monstre ... rampant and animé de ce mouvement perpétuel d'orgasme telle-ment terrible', but eventually she finds that an 'équilibre des forces s'établit' between the sea and herself, and 'elle reprit confiance, alors elle imagina de s'offrir'[20] (Breillat 1974: 117–18). The ocean and the wind may be violent as rape and cold as death, but at least Alice feels physically connected to them, feels herself to be akin to a force of nature and not so weak and alone. Maldoror too has such moments of feeling strangely related to the wildness of nature: 'je rôde autour des habitations des hommes, pendant les nuits orageuses, les yeux ardents, les cheveux flagellés par le vent des tempêtes ... Réponds-moi, océan, veux-tu être mon frère? ... Déroule tes vagues épouvant-ables, océan hideux, compris par moi seul, et devant lequel je tombe, prosterné à tes genoux'[21] (Lautréamont 1973: 29, 36–7).

18 'young girl' ... 'gutted chicken' ... 'the hideous hole' (Lautréamont 1978: 129). When Breillat edited *Le Livre du plaisir* (Breillat 1999: 237–8), she included this particular passage by Lautréamont as among those sexual writings that most influenced her.

19 'the wind passed over her lips, her glacial smile' ... 'let herself go' ... 'a shameful joy' ... 'imagine infinity in its universal morbidity'.

20 'death and the morbid fascination of Sin' ... 'great monster ... rampant and animated with this perpetual motion of so terrible an orgasm' ... 'equilibrium of forces established itself' ... 'she regained confidence, then she imagined offering herself'.

21 'on stormy nights I prowl around the habitations of men, my hair lashed by the wind of tempests, my eyes aflame. ... Answer me, ocean, will you be my brother? ... Unroll your frightful waves, hideous ocean, whom I alone understand, before which I fall, prostrate, at your knees' (Lautréamont 1978: 40, 46).

Alice views the natural world as wild and threatening because that is the way she has been taught to feel about her own physical nature, and her sense of being at one with such a fallen world can seem despairing and suicidal, as when she imagines, 'je puis ... accepter la débâcle et m'y confondre'[22] (Breillat 1974: 138–9). However, Alice may also be looking for a more positive reflection of her physicality in the world around her, a more welcoming response to her expressions of sexuality that would in fact ratify them as 'natural'. In this 'quête, la recherche d'une identité sexuelle'[23] as Breillat has called it (Hecquet 2000), writing and mirrors are important modes of self-discovery. Emblematic of this quest is the scene in her Catholic boarding school where, after the dorm supervisor has stopped Alice from masturbating and speaking, Alice uses the vaginal secretions on her finger to write her name on a mirror. Alice's desire for self-recognition and acceptance of her sexuality is in conflict with the negative view of herself that she has internalised, the disapproving look that prompts her to hide her sex as a shameful secret. At home on vacation in her parents' house, Alice keeps the hallway dark as she walks to her bedroom, and when she undresses in front of the mirror, she prudishly takes off only one piece of clothing at a time, with the camera framing only parts of her body: 'je n'aime pas me voir autrement que par petits morceaux'.[24] Even these glances are too much for Alice as, repelled by her own image, she backs away from the mirror and falls onto her bed. Then, as a light bulb glares down at her and an overbearing and repetitious theme churns on the soundtrack, Alice vomits in disgust at her body.

Yet it is this very sickness of self-loathing that prompts Alice's dawning realisation that it is not her body, but others' negative view of it, that is unnatural and obscene. 'Le dégoût me rend lucide',[25] thinks Alice, and this is the moment she begins to write in a diary about the conflict within her between desire and disgust. Opening her Catholic school notebook and writing in red ink using the pen she got for her first communion, Alice challenges her repressive religious upbringing and expresses her physicality as if she were writing in menstrual blood. 'C'est beau d'écrire avec de l'encre', Breillat has

22 'I can ... accept the disaster and lose myself in it'.
23 'quest, the search for a sexual identity'.
24 'I don't like seeing myself except in tiny bits'.
25 'Disgust makes me lucid'.

noted, 'ça remplit la pensée de quelque chose de sensuel, fluide et liquide. ... Ce qui sort alors de votre plume, c'est comme du sang, c'est votre sang qui s'épand, le sang de la pensée en fait'[26] (Breillat 2006: 249). The credits at the beginning of *Une vraie jeune fille*, including 'écrit et réalisé par Catherine Breillat',[27] appear over the same open school notebook as that used by Alice, and the semi-autobiographical film we are seeing is like Breillat's diary, her cinematic version of 'écriture féminine' ('feminine writing'). Hélène Cixous might almost have had Alice/Breillat's story in mind when she wrote: 'J'ai plus d'une fois été émerveillée par ce qu'une femme me décrivait d'un monde sien qu'elle hantait secrètement depuis sa petite enfance. Monde de recherche, d'élaboration d'un savoir, à partir d'une expérimentation systématique des fonctionnements du corps, d'une interrogation précise et passionnée de son érogénéité. Cette pratique, d'une richesse inventive extraordinaire, en particulier de la masturbation, se prolonge ou s'accompagne, d'une production de *formes*, d'une véritable activité esthétique'[28] (Cixous 1975: 39). When Alice faces the mirror again in an effort to see whether she is the 'putain' ('whore') her mother accuses her of being, Alice dabs red ink on her pubis and nipples, nearly swooning from the intense feelings this brings on. Still unable to stand the sight of her sexuality for long ('je ne peux pas admettre la proximité de mon visage et de mon vagin'),[29] Alice is at least beginning to express her sensuality, to 'write' her body out of repression and to awaken her libidinal zones: 'Ecrire, acte, qui non seulement "réalisera" le rapport dé-censuré de la femme à sa sexualité, à son être-femme, lui rendant accès à ses propres forces; qui lui rendra ses biens, ses plaisirs, ses organes, ses immenses territoires corporels tenus sous scellés; qui l'arrachera à la structure surmoïsée

26 'It's beautiful to write with ink' ... 'it fills your thought with something sensual, fluid and liquid. ... What comes out of your pen, it's like blood, it's your blood that spreads out, the blood of your thought, in fact'.

27 'written and directed by Catherine Breillat'.

28 'I have been amazed more than once by a description a woman gave me of a world all her own which she had been secretly haunting since early childhood. A world of searching, the elaboration of a knowledge, on the basis of a systematic experimentation with the bodily functions, a passionate and precise interrogation of her erotogeneity. This practice, extraordinarily rich and inventive, in particular as concerns masturbation, is prolonged or accompanied by a production of forms, a veritable aesthetic activity' (Cixous 1980: 246).

29 'I can't accept the proximity of my face and my vagina'.

dans laquelle on lui réservait toujours la même place de coupable'[30] (Cixous 1975: 43).

In a final scene of writing and self-reflection, Alice uses her pen to make a red stain on her nightgown near her sex, and this time she is able to look steadily and unflinchingly at herself in the mirror. She drips hot wax from a candle onto her hand where it burns only slightly, while she thinks, 'les symboles ne me font pas peur'.[31] In this scene, the candle and hot wax symbolise the phallus and ejaculation, while the red-stained nightgown signifies the loss of her virginity. These symbols enable Alice to imagine sexuality as something other than the unknown, threatening thing she has been taught to fear. They make sex visible, bearable, even potentially pleasurable. Alice thinks next about trying the hot wax/semen in her mouth, and then her thoughts turn to her would-be lover, Jim. As Breillat has explained, '*Une vraie jeune fille* a pour démarche de matérialiser les interdits ... qui amène au rite ... une volonté d'exorcisme ... Se mettre en face de sa peur et la dépasser vous impose le rite, le symbolique'[32] (Clouzot 2004: 174).

Alice uses her imagination in an attempt to exorcise her fear of Jim's penetrating eyes and phallic dominance. While she desperately wants to be seen by him as more than just a 'petite fille', she is also afraid of being brutalised or violated. When she first meets Jim in her father's office, Jim looks up and down her bikini-clad body, causing her to squirm and glance nervously over at her father, as if she were still daddy's little girl. Later while Jim is working at the sawmill, Alice sneaks a glance at the crotch of his blue jeans and licks her lips, but then she runs and hides behind a pile of lumber. Jim is often associated in Alice's mind with virile dominance – smoking a cigarette, holding a board at crotch level or working a machine that looks like a cannon protruding from his waist. Alice entertains fearful fantasies

30 'To write. An act which will not only "realize" the decensored relation of woman to her sexuality, to her womanly being, giving her access to her native strength; it will give her back her goods, her pleasures, her organs, her immense bodily territories which have been kept under seal; it will tear her away from the super-egoized structure in which she has always occupied the place reserved for the guilty' (Cixous 1980: 250).

31 'symbols don't scare me'.

32 '*Une vraie jeune fille* has as its project to give a form to forbidden things ... which leads to a ritual ... a willed exorcism ... Positioning yourself to face your fear and overcome it requires you to perform a symbolic ritual'.

of Jim's phallus cutting through *her*, of watching him 'diriger la scie sans s'émouvoir comme s'il n'était pas sensible à son tranchant', the blades that 'ouvrent les jambes fraîches et nacrées du bois'[33] (Breillat 1974: 172–3, 87). Alice also fantasises that she is naked and spread-eagled on the ground, bound by barbed wire, while Jim attempts to stuff an earthworm into her vagina, then stands there towering over her, snickering. In this daydream, Alice gives a form to her fear of the male sex as ugly, invasive and deadly (worms are traditionally associated with corpses). Intercourse is imagined as a grotesque act where she is pinned down, exposed and humiliated. What pleasure there is is masochistic, and the scene is reminiscent of the erotic fantasies of Séverine (Catherine Deneuve) in Luis Buñuel's *Belle de jour* (1967). Séverine is a repressed bourgeoise who can only think of pleasure in connection with punishment, as when she gets excited by the thought of being tied to a post and having mud thrown at her while being called a whore.

But the symbols in Alice's later fantasy show her to be working through her shame and humiliation toward a sense of sex as potentially liberating and empowering. First, Alice pictures herself as clucking like a 'poule' ('chicken' but also 'prostitute') and crawling around with her skirt hiked up and feathers stuck in her rear end, while Jim stands above her in a phallically dominant position, urinating. However, Jim then drops to his knees, bringing himself down to her level, and plucks a feather from her bottom as she yelps. The taking of her virginity is thus figured as a brief, almost comical pain – a strong contrast with the horribly gutted chicken she had earlier imagined herself as being. Alice lies down on top of Jim, using a kiss to take the feather back from his mouth to hers, as they begin a playful game in which the roles of dominant and submissive, having and losing, move back and forth between them. Like a gentleman suitor, Jim picks a flower and presents it to her, but when she reaches for it, he stands and holds it up beyond her grasp, as if he wants her to grovel for it, which she does, her face near the crotch of his jeans. However, in the next shot he is suddenly the romantic lover again, adorning her hair with flowers, and then he is on his back with a flower in his mouth, while she wriggles her body on top of his, rubbing her hair on his chest.

33 'direct the saw without feeling, as if he were unmoved by its cutting' ... 'open the fresh and pearly legs of the wood'.

In this fantasy, Alice imagines a deflowering in which she is not the loser. What is taken from her – the flower, the feather, her integrity, her dignity – are things that he gives back (romantically) or that she reclaims for herself. At the end of her fantasy, she rolls off Jim and they masturbate separately, after which he (callously?) wipes his semen on her shirt. She watches him deflate – 'je regardais son vit agonisant comme un poisson mort'[34] – and then she stands up and walks off, telling him to go away. Why does the fantasy end this way? Perhaps Alice fears that Jim is a cad simply using her for sex, and so she imagines using and dumping *him* first. Perhaps she thinks that his romantic behaviour hides a desire for dominance, so she asserts her superiority before he can claim his. What is certain is that Alice's fantasy has taken her from a fear of phallic dominance to a sense that she can not only survive sex but rise up as stronger in the end. It is the male organ that deflates and 'dies' – 'est-ce que ce sexe qui fait leur puissance n'est pas un sexe trop petit, trop court, trop faible? C'est eux, en fait, le sexe faible'[35] (Breillat 2006: 52–3) – while she imagines herself sexually satisfied and triumphant.

Alice may live out an entire relationship with Jim in her mind, using fantasy to overcome the obstacles to her desires, but what happens in reality would seem to be quite different. Just as her mother is turning out the light in Alice's bedroom to stop her from writing in her diary, the sound of a shot is heard in the night. On the next morning, it is discovered that Jim was killed by her father's shotgun, which had been rigged to blast wild pigs trying to ruin the corn. Jim had been going through the cornfield on his way to a rendezvous with Alice, who had been planning to give him her virginity that very night. It would appear that Alice's parents have succeeded in preventing a marauding male from ruining her honour. But from Alice's perspective, they have extinguished her sexual- and self-expression, keeping her confined to their house and trapped in the role of the 'good little girl'. At first glance, Alice's plight would seem similar to that of the title character in Robert Bresson's *Mouchette* (1967). In Bresson's film, a gamekeeper fights with a poacher over a woman (compare Alice's father, Jim and Alice), and one of the men ends up dead. Mouchette is a fourteen-year-old girl (like Alice) who is frightened

---

34 'I looked at his cock flopping like a dead fish'.
35 'this sex which gives them their power, is it not a sex that is too small, too short, too weak? It's they, in fact, who are the weaker sex'.

by but strangely attracted to the poacher (Jim). At the end of the film, Mouchette witnesses a hare being shot (compare Jim, or Alice's own sexual desire), and she commits suicide.

But here is where the comparison ends, for as Alice stands looking out her window at Jim's dead body, she almost seems to be smiling. Does Alice harbour a secret wish, as in her earlier fantasy, to see Jim's penetrating eyes turned sightless and his hard body flopped down dead on the ground? Indeed, as Alice moves away from the window and turns to pick up her diary, we wonder if Jim's death *is* a fantasy, something Alice scripted to prove herself alluring but to save herself from being dominated. After all, it was Alice who refused to have sex with Jim in his car and who enticed him to come to her that night through the booby-trapped cornfield. Thus, unlike Mouchette who is raped by the poacher before she commits suicide, Alice survives Jim with her dignity intact. She packs her diary in her suitcase, planning to take it with her as she leaves her parents' house to go off to boarding school and beyond. She has written and imagined herself into freedom from Jim and her parents, away from being degraded by him or idealised as a 'good girl' by them. As she stands poised to leave, she wears the blue shirt that is her schoolgirl uniform, but it is unbuttoned and open in the front, revealing her bra and full breasts. Her head is slightly down, but her mascaraed eyes look up and out defiantly, as the camera holds her in close-up for the film's last image. She is neither a little girl nor a whore. For the moment, she is outside of either role, transcendent.

36 fillette (*Virgin*)

Like Alice, Lili in *36 fillette* is a fourteen-year-old virgin spending summer vacation with her family in France's Landes region. Both girls have petit-bourgeois fathers (Alice's father runs a sawmill, while Lili's owns a café-bar), and their mothers are housewives. Lili is physically mature for her age, bursting out of her child's-size-36 clothing, as were Alice and the young Breillat: 'Je changeais de soutien-gorge toutes les semaines, ça poussait comme dans un dessin animé'[36] (Breillat 2006: 13). Lili, like Alice, is torn between her burgeoning desires and the shame induced in her by her parents and society. Both girls engage in

36 'I was changing bras every week and bulging out as in a cartoon'.

sexual adventures, but while many of Alice's were surrealistic erotic fantasies, all of Lili's experiences are ostensibly real and presented in a very naturalistic manner. To create *36 fillette*, it is as if Breillat had taken the few realistic scenes in *Une vraie jeune fille* – the battles between Alice and Jim in his car over whether to sleep with him – and expanded them into a whole movie of will-she-or-won't-she struggles between Lili and her man, Maurice. In keeping with this move toward realism, there is a somewhat greater objectivity. The voice-over that bound us so closely to Alice's thoughts and feelings is dropped in Lili's case, and the camera does not always adopt her perspective on events. 'My own point of view is undoubtedly a feminine one', Breillat has said, 'but it is above all analytical. I wanted to conduct my analysis like an entomologist; I wanted to plant my camera in one spot and observe what was happening between the two characters [Lili and Maurice]' (Vincendeau 1989: 41).

It should be noted, however, that even this more objective, 'entomologist's' eye-view is still significantly different from the phallocentric perspective of much traditional cinema. As Susan Hayward has said about films made by women directors in the 1970s and 1980s, 'Sexuality and power relationships are often central to these films and are often addressed from the woman's point of view. Alternatively, the point of view is neither male nor female and more that of the camera – that is, the eye of the film-maker (a woman). In either case the male gaze has been displaced which allows for desire to be represented differently' (Hayward 2005: 255). Furthermore, the realistic shooting style of *36 fillette* should not lead us to overlook the film's covert elements of fantasy. When Alice was sitting in the surf in *Une vraie jeune fille*, her imagination transported her to an elegant room where she drinks and dances with an aristocratic gentleman. There is a sense in which this dream comes true for Lili in *36 fillette*, since Maurice is a rich, older man who takes her to his luxurious room at the Hôtel du Palais and offers her a drink and a dance. Thus there is a strong vein of wish-fulfilment fantasy running just below the realism in *36 fillette*.

It is August in the mid-1980s, and Lili's family have left their home in the 'banlieue' (or working-class 'suburbs') of Paris and taken their caravan to a campground on the southwest tip of France, near the ocean and the resort town of Biarritz. Ever since the 'congés payés' ('paid holiday') became law in 1936 – it was two weeks of paid vacation then and five weeks by 1981 – Parisians have shuttered their shops in July or August, escaping the daily grind of 'métro-boulot-dodo' ('subway-work-sleep') to seek solace in the country or by the sea. Unfortunately, many vacationers find that their summer holiday is not all they had hoped it would be: the holiday 'utopia, charged with so many assumptions and yearning daydreams, creates a constant tension between winter anticipation and summer frustration. Often the few vacation weeks fail to live up to the heavy load of those winter expectations. The other side of [caravan] life is claustrophobia, too much pottering about or an overdose of togetherness' (Löfgren 1999: 152). The film begins with Lili's father yelling furiously at her and her brother because their bickering has made it impossible for him to hear the sports broadcast on his radio headphones. Cooped up in their small caravan due to bad weather, the family have started to get on each other's nerves. Lili is desperate to escape her family and the 'good little girl' role in which they have encaged her. She longs to go to the nearby bars and nightclubs to meet men, to have the kinds of adventures that are also sometimes associated with summer vacations, where 'children developed secret territories and experiences of their own, in a wider landscape, not policed by parents, teachers or other adults all the time' (Löfgren 1999: 151). Lili does manage to escape, but when she returns to the caravan late after an unauthorised visit with Maurice, her parents accuse her of being a whore and her father strikes her repeatedly. This scene of family violence and kitchen-sink realism is reminiscent of the ones in Maurice Pialat's *A nos amours* (1983) where fifteen-year-old Suzanne (Sandrine Bonnaire) is verbally and physically abused by her parents for sleeping around. The irony in Lili's case is that, as she defiantly and despairingly tells her parents, she had wanted to sleep with Maurice but could not bring herself to, because of the shame they have instilled in her about losing her virginity to premarital sex.

When Lili is with Maurice, she often says she wants to talk – partly because she is afraid of physical intercourse, but also because she desires a meeting of the minds and not just a brief, bodily connection: 'Je ne coucherai jamais avec un homme qui me parle pas. C'est ça qu'il [Maurice] a pas compris. Parler, c'est la porte du donjon. ... Parce qu'il faut être une personne'[37] (Breillat 1987: 123). The one man

---

37 'I will never sleep with a man who doesn't talk with me. That's what he hasn't understood. Talking is the door to the castle. ... Because one has to be a person'. In Breillat's novel, *36 fillette*, Lili narrates in the first person.

Lili is really able to talk with is a stranger she meets by chance at a hotel bar. Boris Golovine is a renowned concert pianist who had faith in his own abilities from a very young age, and as Lili tells him of her aspiration to become a great writer (she is writing a novel), the attention he pays her and the fact of *his* eventual success lead her to grow in confidence. He seems to understand her ('Vous avez l'air timide, et les gens timides sont les gens orgueilleux') and not to find it ridiculous that she considers herself to be similarly gifted, 'son égale en herbe'[38] (Breillat 1987: 75). This scene has autobiographical roots in that it is based on an encounter in 1977 between Breillat herself, who at that time was just starting out as a director, and Roberto Rossellini, the famous Italian neorealist filmmaker: 'Rossellini ... m'avait très vite demandé: "est-ce que je croyais qu'une fille/femme peut apporter ce quelque chose que les hommes ne peuvent pas apporter au cinéma?" Et j'avais répondu: "Le regard de la honte, il n'y a que moi qui puisse l'apporter"'[39] (Clouzot 2004: 140). With *Une vraie jeune fille*, Breillat had just begun to explore the gaze – external and internalised – that made girls ashamed of their sexuality, and now she is doing so again with *36 fillette* (her novel and her film). Could *36 fillette* be the novel that Lili is writing, much as *Une vraie jeune fille* seemed to be Alice's diary?

This scene in which Lili tells Golovine about her troubles with family, school and the opposite sex also recalls the interview scene in François Truffaut's *Les 400 Coups* (*The 400 Blows*) (1959), where the boy Antoine discusses these same subjects in his own life with the female psychologist at the juvenile detention centre. At age fourteen Jean-Pierre Léaud played Antoine, and now he is in the older role of Golovine, so in speaking to Lili it is as if he is talking with his younger self, a rebel he truly understands from his 'own' youthful experience. Furthermore, *Les 400 Coups* was an autobiographical film for Truffaut, with Antoine/Léaud playing a younger version of himself, just as *36 fillette* contains elements of Breillat's life-story and Lili/Delphine Zentout is Breillat's alter ego. *Les 400 Coups* was Truffaut's debut feature and it went on to become an iconic film of the French

38 'You have a timid manner, and timid people are proud people' ... 'potentially his equal'.
39 'Rossellini was very quick to ask me: "did I believe that a girl/woman can bring this something that men cannot bring to cinema?" And I replied, "The shaming gaze, I'm the only one who can bring that"'.

New Wave. Through this scene with Lili and Golovine, Breillat is in conversation with masters Truffaut and Rossellini, listening timidly to the New Waver and the neorealist, but also proudly declaring her aspiration to equal their greatness.

In telling Golovine about her troubled love life, Lili shares with him a bitter poem she has written about the brevity of the dead-end relationships she has had and confesses that she has thought about slitting her wrists. He attempts to counter her cynicism and fatalism by assuring her that one is never 'coincé' because 'le monde, c'est un grand matelas à ressort. On saute et on retombe ailleurs'.[40] In Golovine's metaphor, the mattress is a vehicle for freedom, and if there is a sexual implication to his message, it is that Lili does not have to feel cornered by sex. Instead, sex could free her from her morbid fear of the body and of losing her virginity; if one relationship ends, she could move on to another. She may even eventually find a relationship in which sex and talk, the body and the head, are harmoniously combined. Lili's conversation with Golovine shows that a meeting of minds is possible. Now, can she combine this sense of mutual understanding with physical intimacy and find both with Maurice? 'J'aimerais bien parler avec toi', Maurice tells her, and when she hesitates to go with him, he adds, 'si je te propose à venir à l'hôtel, ça signifie forcément que je te sauterai dessus?'[41]

However, Lili fears that the mattress will not bounce her to freedom, but will lead instead to her being 'jumped', pinned down, used and degraded. And she has some reason to be afraid. Once they are in his hotel room, Maurice mocks Lili's desire for communication ('et alors, je t'écoute: parle, parle, parle') and he lies on top of her and runs his hands over her body while singing the praises of her gorgeous figure: 'Tu es belle, la plus belle. Tu es faite comme une vraie femme'.[42] Lili is leery of Maurice's romantic blandishments, suspecting that he is merely trying to sweet-talk her into bed: 'C'est toujours la même vieille rengaine, tout ça avec cet air incroyablement sentimental que prennent ... les hommes ... quand ils ont envie de

40 'cornered' ... 'the world is a giant spring mattress. You bounce and come down somewhere else'.

41 'I would really like to talk with you' ... 'if I ask you to go to the hotel, does that necessarily mean that I'll jump you?'

42 'all right then, I'm listening to you: talk, talk, talk' ... 'You're beautiful, the most beautiful. You're built like a real woman'.

vous baiser. ... J'ai horreur qu'on me prenne pour une conne qui gobe les flatteries comme un chien qu'on caresse'[43] (Breillat 1987: 89, 228). Lili realises that behind Maurice's courtly manner and sentimental clichés there lies a cynical contempt for women, a fear and loathing earlier manifested in the barracks-room banter between Maurice and Lili's brother, Gi-Pé (Jean-Pierre). Before going to the hotel with Maurice, Lili was with him and her brother at a nightclub. Seventeen-year-old Gi-Pé, who talks out of the corner of his mouth like a tough guy, wants to be a rich Don Juan like Maurice, and he tries to imitate the older man's macho attitude toward women, speaking of Lili as a pear ripe for the picking. Maurice wonders aloud whether Lili is really still a virgin, saying that if she is not a 'saloperie' ('piece of slutty trash'), she is definitely an 'allumeuse' ('tease'). In a moment of homosocial bonding with homoerotic undertones, Maurice and Gi-Pé lean in close to each other at the club bar and drink in turn from the same glass, while Maurice brags about the time that he and a buddy both had sex with a woman at the same time. Maurice exhibits his devil-may-care attitude by comparing women to cars that he quickly grows tired of and has to exchange for new ones. His fear of being trapped into caring or into marriage is evident when he warns Gi-Pé, 'T'engages ta queue plus de trois fois de suite dans la même bonne femme, t'es cuit! On mieux fait de baiser une chèvre'.[44]

Maurice's misogynistic comments are thus the obverse side of the flattering remarks he makes to Lili. This ambivalent combination of courtly praise for female beauty and ribald denigration of women has a long history in France: 'The coexistence of *l'esprit gaulois* and *la galanterie* is a particularly strong blend, pervasive since the Middle Ages, of obscene humor and exalted idealization in which woman is simultaneously an insatiable cunt and the charming, gracious, virgin mother of God. There is no more constantly vilified object in French than the stupid, inert *con*; there is no more constantly adored object than the elegant, decorative woman' (Marks and Courtivron 1980: 4–5). It is interesting to note that, just as Lili is faced with Maurice's courtly/denigrating comments, so Breillat herself had to deal with this male

43 'It's always the same old tune, all that with this unbelievably sentimental manner which men put on when they want to fuck you. ... I have a horror of being taken for a stupid cunt who swallows flatteries like a dog being stroked'.

44 'Dip your wick more than three times in a row in the same good woman and you're cooked! It's better to screw a goat'.

ambivalence from Etienne Chicot, the actor playing Maurice, during the making of the film. Chicot balked at his character's having to make such derogatory statements about women in the film – statements which he claimed to be uncharacteristic of himself and of men generally – but the actor nevertheless attempted to assert his macho superiority over his female director 'en faisant des plaisanteries de corps de garde'[45] such as calling her '"Latrine" Breillat' instead of Catherine (Puaux 2001: 169). Breillat brought Chicot's self-contradiction to his attention, insisting that he play Maurice as a man who makes degrading jokes about women in the same way that Chicot had just crudely demeaned her. Breillat also has Lili respond to Maurice with a line that seems like a direct rebuttal, in subject and tone, to Chicot's '"Latrine" Breillat' remark: 'La prochaine fois que t'as envie d'éjaculer, j'suis pas une cuvette'.[46]

But Breillat does not side so exclusively with Lili that she is unable to see Maurice's perspective as well. Breillat's 'entomologist's' eye-view allows her to study and understand Maurice's disparaging remarks about women within the context of a male midlife crisis. Forty-something Maurice is still bragging to buddies about his sexual prowess, still picking up girls in his convertible sports car, and still club hopping and having sex all night. In this he resembles the increasingly desperate debauchee in Breillat's first novel, *L'Homme facile*, who 'sait qu'il faut qu'il aille manger puis danser puis boire puis fumer puis baiser, s'il veut non pas vivre mais SURvivre, SURmener le jeu, un train d'enfer: destination enfer certainement quoiqu'il n'ait pas conscience de faire autre chose que de mener une vie facile'[47] (Breillat 1968: 52). With a receding hairline and a growing paunch, Maurice is now struggling to attract the young women he prefers. A confirmed bachelor, he has recently lost his most serious girlfriend Anne-Marie, a woman near his own age, to a younger man, a paratrooper with the courage to marry her. And on the night Maurice meets Lili, he is left at the club bar by a former conquest, Georgia, who though wildly promiscuous doesn't want to go with him anymore.

45 'by making barracks-room jokes'.
46 'The next time you want to ejaculate, I'm not a toilet'.
47 'knows he has to go and eat then dance then drink then smoke then fuck, if he wants not just to live but to OUTlive, to survive[,] to OUTplay the game, a hell of a pace: hellbent without any question though he is not conscious of doing anything but live an easy life' (Breillat 1969: 41–2).

His insulting references to women, including Lili, are thus a kind of revenge on them for abandoning him and a defence against allowing himself to care for anyone new who may also leave: 'La misogynie de mes personnages', Breillat has said, 'vient du fait qu'ils ont peur des femmes, ils sont dépités, ils essuient des échecs'[48] (Sineux 1991: 18).

Yet despite himself Maurice finds that he does start to have feelings for Lili. Granted that he is an ageing playboy trying to confirm his manhood by taking her virginity and granted that he has traded other women in for this newest model, this fresh acquisition to make him feel younger, there is still a sense in which Lili's youth and romantic hopes – carefully guarded as these are under her wisecracking, cynical exterior – rejuvenate him and make him feel tender and protective toward her. One of Breillat's models for the character of Maurice is likely to have been director Maurice Pialat. While making *A nos amours* with young star Sandrine Bonnaire, Pialat 'était complètement tombé amoureux de cette actrice',[49] according to Breillat, who was observing on set. Breillat was struck by the 'nostalgique' and 'tragique' elements of what she saw: 'un être qui a tout l'avenir devant lui [Bonnaire], ... filmé par un maître qui n'a plus tout l'avenir devant lui [Pialat]', a director suffering from 'l'angoisse de vieillir'[50] (Criterion 2006). Pialat cast himself as the father of Bonnaire's character in *A nos amours*, and the scenes between him and her have considerable pathos. Breillat may have been thinking of these two when in *36 fillette* she has Lili respond to a casual remark by Maurice about seeing her 'plus tard' with the poignant reply, 'plus tard, tu seras crevé. Tu t'es pas rendu compte que t'avais la vie derrière toi?'[51]

Another probable prototype for the character of Maurice is Paul (Marlon Brando) in Bernardo Bertolucci's *Last Tango in Paris*. The blond, balding Paul stands about a head taller than dark-haired, buxom Jeanne (Maria Schneider), his younger female companion. Maurice and Lili strongly resemble them in appearance. Jeanne tells Paul he is getting old and fat, much as Lili teases/taunts Maurice. Jeanne is involved with another man, Tom, played by Jean-Pierre Léaud, with

48 'The misogyny of my characters comes from the fact that they are afraid of women, they are resentful, they have suffered defeats'.

49 'fell totally in love with this actress'.

50 'nostalgic' ... 'tragic' ... 'one being who has her whole future ahead of her ... filmed by a master who no longer has his whole future ahead of him' ... 'the anxiety of ageing'.

51 'later' ... 'later, you'll be dead. Haven't you realised that your life is behind you?'

whom she has a very verbal relationship, and we recall Lili's conversation with Golovine (also played by Léaud). Jeanne (like Lili) tries to talk with Paul (Maurice), but it seems that he just wants to have anonymous sex. Paul's wife was unfaithful to him with another man, a fact which seems to have soured his view of marriage and family and to have prompted a vengeful urge to sexually degrade women, as evidenced by the scene in which he buggers Jeanne while delivering a mocking speech about the 'holy family' and its 'children' who are 'tortured until they tell their first lie'. Maurice warns Lili he doesn't believe in marrying or bringing kids into the world because 'la planète est trop pourrie',[52] and when Lili won't put out for him in the hotel room, Maurice, who feels abandoned by other women, gets sexually violent with her.

Paul eventually develops feelings for Jeanne and follows her to a dance hall, where they sit at a table in a vacant and unlit section of the place. Jeanne leans forward in her chair, masturbating him under the table, but her head is down, not looking at him, and his head is lowered as well, not looking at her. They are in almost total darkness. It is a scene where the absence of personal connection between the characters makes for a soulless encounter, a degraded because purely physical experience. Breillat reprises this scene in *36 fillette* when Lili masturbates Maurice in the darkness of a beach grotto. They are seated together, and she has leaned forward to embrace him with her head on his shoulder and her left arm around his back, but her face is turned away from him and from what her right hand is doing. When finished, she pulls away, looking briefly at him and then down, her face covered by her dark hair and by shadow. His head droops onto the sleeve of his black shirt, obscuring his face. The brevity and tenuousness of the connection between Lili and Maurice in this scene are particularly ironic given its location. The beach grotto is a local landmark known as 'la Chambre d'amour', after the legend of two lovers whose passion was so profound they did not notice the rising tide and so were drowned while making love, thus remaining together forever.

A similar irony is present in a scene the next day when Maurice and Lili go to a summer cottage decorated as a love nest with flowery curtains on the windows, heart-shaped pillows on the bed and a bottle

52 'the planet is too rotten'.

of champagne. But Lili remains afraid that Maurice's interest in her is merely physical (is the clichéd romantic setting as hollow as his earlier courtly compliments?) and she cannot overcome her own shame of the body, her own inability to see sex as good. Lying face down on the bed, Lili has only enough daring to peek over her shoulder at Maurice undressing across the room. After he has joined her in bed and removed most of her clothes (because she won't undress herself), she turns aside and hides her face under a pillow, taking only brief glances behind her at his caressing of her body: 'c'est l'harmonie parfaite, il y a ma tête d'un côté, moi, Liliane Barrier qui a toute sa tête et toute sa dignité, et de l'autre il y a mon corps, avec ses deux nichons et surtout ce con ... Et ce corps n'est maintenant plus qu'un objet de prostitution anonyme'[53] (Breillat 1987: 229). Because of the shame that has been inculcated in her, the only way that Lili can think of having sex is if she splits off her head from her body, preserving her 'good little girl' self (note the use of her proper, family name—Liliane Barrier) from 'dirty', carnal knowledge. But by disowning her sexuality in this way, Lili *keeps* it hidden, shameful and unredeemed. It *must* remain an impersonal encounter, like the fleeting, fleshly contact between a prostitute and a client, for she cannot countenance the thought that good girls can have sex – or that a playboy like Maurice might grow to care about her. So, when he removes the pillow and tries to turn their lovemaking into a face-to-face encounter, she turns away and pulls a big strand of dark hair down to cover her eyes. Unable to look at him and have intercourse, Lili tries giving him oral sex while he sits on the bed. The way they are filmed – Maurice with his head back and eyes closed, and Lili unseen below the frame – emphasises the impersonality of the act. And even this fails, for Lili gags and vomits, Maurice leaves the cottage in disgust, and she ends up hiding and weeping under the bedsheets.

It is interesting to take the cottage and grotto scenes and contrast Breillat's filming of them with the way in which director Walerian Borowczyk shot 'La Marée' ('The Tide'), the first part of his omnibus film *Contes immoraux* (*Immoral Tales*) (1974). In Borowczyk's film, virginal Julie performs fellatio on her older cousin André while the

53 'it's the perfect harmony, there's my head on one side, me, Liliane Barrier who has all her head and all her dignity, and on the other side there's my body, with its two tits and above all this cunt ... And this body is now nothing more than an anonymous object of prostitution'.

rising tide conveys a sense of mortal danger to their lovemaking, as in the romantic *Liebestod* legend that backgrounds the grotto scene in *36 fillette*. In 'La Marée', most of the dialogue is spoken by André and consists of his commands, as when he (who remains fully clothed throughout) orders Julie to strip off her bikini so that she will be 'toute nue' under her see-through beach dress, or when he instructs her regarding oral sex, 'tu avaleras docilement and joyeusement'.[54] By contrast, Breillat tends to grant Lili and Maurice equal time for speaking or to give Lili more lines, and while he is certainly the one on the verbal offensive, his tone is cajoling or even commiserating, and her responses are far from being simply obedient: she is timid, proud, yielding, resistant. Visually, Borowczyk repeatedly cuts from André's face to close-ups of Julie's mouth, breasts and pubes, inviting us to look with his male gaze at her as a sexual object. Breillat, on the other hand, favours extended takes with both Lili and Maurice in the frame, or when Breillat wants to convey that the characters are not connecting emotionally, she will show an isolated face (such as Lili's under the pillow, or Maurice's during fellatio) rather than zeroing in salaciously on a female body part. As director Agnès Varda has remarked, 'men seem to cut up women's bodies more frequently and show more often what we might technically call the erogenous zones. They show women's thighs, women's breasts, women's behinds. It seems to me that when women film women, they show their entire bodies' (Gillain 2003: 208).

In sum, everything in the Borowczyk fellatio scene seems to serve a fantasy of male dominance, as when André has Julie drop 'à quatre pattes' and crawl to him, when he forcefully pulls her head to his crotch, and when he orders her to use her mouth (which he has pronounced 'intacta') as if she were a 'putain'.[55] In this sense, the scene is typical of patriarchal pornography, which Susan Hayward has described as being about 'man's profound mistrust, even fear of women's sexuality. Pornography, therefore, is a means whereby men can control it, position women as they want them positioned – particularly as desirous of the phallus' (Hayward 2005: 241). By contrast, the masturbation and fellatio scenes in Breillat are much more nuanced: Maurice may or may not be trying to conquer a virgin and dominate Lili, while she doesn't want to be a prostitute *or* a virgin.

54 'totally nude' ... 'you will swallow docilely and joyously'.
55 'to all fours' ... 'intact' ... 'whore'.

These complexities are given their most significant exploration in the central scene of *36 fillette*: the hotel room encounter between Lili and Maurice. She vacillates between desire and dread throughout the scene. As they approach his hotel room, Lili takes the key from him and opens the door herself, but then lags behind him in the entryway. When they are seated on the sofa, she turns away from him and covers her face with her hand, but then coyly peeks out at him through her fingers. His attempt to pull her close is thwarted when she turns to crouch on the sofa with her back to him, yet she does look over fetchingly at him from behind her shoulder. Maurice sums up these mixed messages by saying (when he is finally lying next to her on the sofa and touching her) that her head doesn't want to, but her sex is dripping with desire. Lili's retort – 'Tu vas pas me couper en deux, non?'[56] – marks her protest against having her mind overruled by her body and against having a man put his finger on one side of this mind/body seesaw to get the body he wants. Most importantly, Lili's remark shows that she does not want to be a divided being, to have sex without feeling or to have feelings without sex. It is interesting to compare Lili's statement with a comment Breillat has made about the 1975 French law that slapped an X rating on any films with explicit sex, thus discouraging serious filmmakers from exploring the physical aspect of relationships in tandem with their emotional side: 'Je suis quelqu'un que la loi sur les films X a beaucoup révolté. ... Couper les choses en deux, en mettant dans certains films des gens qui ont des sentiments mais pas de rapports physiques, dans d'autres, en ne cachant rien mais en présentant les gens d'une manière affreuse, privés d'âme, cela conduit à des extrémités absurdes et intolérables. L'horreur, c'est de couper l'être humain en deux'[57] (Sineux 1991: 16). Lili does not want to become like Julie in the Borowczyk film, a virgin turned into a whore, a soul discarded so that only a body remains. She wants her body and soul to be united in love. But suspicion of Maurice's motives and an inability to acknowledge herself as a desiring body prevent Lili from accepting his advances or approving of her own physical responses.

56 'You're not going to cut me in two, are you?'
57 'I'm someone who was quite outraged by the law on X-rated films. ... To cut things in two, putting people who have feelings but not physical relationships into certain films, while other films hide nothing but present people in a frightful manner, deprived of soul – that leads to absurd and intolerable extremes. The horror is to cut the human being in two'.

Maurice, however, takes her body's wetness as permission enough to move forward, grabbing Lili and pressing her off the sofa onto the floor, where he proceeds to pull down her panties and put her hand on his sex. Either because she wants to or because she feels forced to comply (Maurice has told her that she has no choice), Lili appears to go along with it, masturbating him for a time, but then she suddenly hurts him with her hand. Maurice cries out and hunches over in pain and then, enraged, puts his hands around Lili's neck and begins to strangle her, while she lies there, her arms above her head, not trying to stop him. In order to understand the complexity of Lili's motives in this scene, it is helpful to look at another film, Elia Kazan's *Baby Doll* (1956), especially given that Breillat considers *36 fillette* to be a 'secret remake' of *Baby Doll* (Clouzot 2004: 150). Like Lili, virginal Baby Doll (Carroll Baker) vacillates continually between fending off and surrendering to an older male seducer, Vacarro (Eli Wallach). In a famous scene, Vacarro makes advances to Baby Doll in a swinging chair. Its seesawing serves as a metaphor for her hot-and-cold attitude toward him, as she looks up at him then down, turns her body away from him but her head toward him, and smilingly tells him not to touch her when he puts his hand around her throat. As Breillat has said in speaking of girls like Baby Doll and Lili, 'la jeune fille n'a rien d'exceptionnel, que son état transitoire sur lequel elle se balance, comme Carroll Baker quand elle est précisément sur la balancelle avec Eli Wallach, comme sur la ligne de partage entre la glace et le feu. L'innocence et le meurtre'[58] (Breillat 1994: 13). These words form a complex of related meanings. First, a girl might experience the loss of her virginity as a murder of her innocence, particularly if she has been inculcated by society to value the preservation of her hymen as the safeguarding of her own 'good little girl' character. Second, a girl who has been taught that it is wrong to respond to men or to her own desires may feel that the only way she can have sex is if she provokes an assault, for then she has tried to resist and the man is responsible. Breillat once considered titling her film, '*36 fillette ... Ou comment les jeunes filles réclament leur propre meurtre*'[59] (Breillat 1994: 13) or '*36*

58 'the young girl has nothing exceptional about her except for the transitional stage on which she is balancing, like Carroll Baker when she is precisely on the swinging chair with Eli Wallach, like the dividing line between ice and fire. Innocence and murder'.

59 '*36 fillette ... Or how young girls demand their own murder*'.

fillette, ou comment les jeunes filles appellent à leur propre viol. ... Suivant les mentalités de notre société, il faut en quelque sorte "refiler" la culpabilité du désir à l'homme auquel on n'a pas pu résister'[60] (Breillat 2006: 150). Third, a girl who prizes her 'virtue' above all else may rather be murdered than allow her virginity to be taken. This appears to be the case with Lili when she injures the priapic Maurice and then passively lets him strangle her: 'Tu m'aurais tuée mais pas violée'[61] (Breillat 1987: 131).

Fourth and most importantly, a girl may prefer to remain balanced on the dividing line between ice and fire, innocence and murder, for if her two options are to be a proud but frigid virgin on the one side, or a sexual but guilty whore on the other, then she will avoid either role and try to occupy the impossible middle for as long as she can. In another scene, while Baby Doll alternates between flirting with and fending off her male seducer, she holds onto a beam for dear life because the attic floor – a symbol for her resistance – may give way beneath her at any time: 'Lorsqu'elle est accrochée à la poutre, la peur de la chute est aussi visible que le désir, sinon qu'elle ait lieu, du moins que la mise au supplice se prolonge sans fin'[62] (Breillat 1994: 15). This is what Lili wants too, that her dalliance with and denial of Maurice be extended indefinitely from nightclub to hotel room to grotto to cottage, that she remain an 'enfant-femme' ('child-woman') both innocent and alluring, that the moment when she is finally pinned down to a role be forever postponed. That decisive moment of being pinned down by patriarchy is a kind of murder, and to surrender to it would be suicide: 'La jeune fille n'existe que pour cesser de l'être. C'est un être qui se suicide. Qui passe de l'avenir qu'elle a tout devant elle à la banalité probable de son destin lorsqu'il sera scellé'[63] (Breillat 1994: 13). Breillat notes that even before Baby Doll lets herself be seduced by Vacarro who only wants to use her, she has already calculated the household furniture she would get in return for selling her virginity on the marriage market. Thus,

60 '*36 fillete, or how young girls call for their own rape.* ... Following the mindset of our society, one must in a sense "shift" the guilt for having desire onto the man whom one could not resist'.

61 'You would have killed me but not raped me'.

62 'When she is hanging onto the beam, her fear of falling is as visible as her desire, if not to fall, then at least for the torture to be prolonged without end'.

63 'The young girl exists only in order to cease to be. She is a being who commits suicide. Who passes from a future where she has everything ahead of her to the probable banality of her destiny once it has been sealed'.

whether it's with a seducer or a husband, sex for Baby Doll means that she no longer gets to balance on the virgin/whore dividing line but must fall into the latter role – her banal fate is sealed.

Lili, however, is determined to avoid being cornered and to remain free to bounce somewhere else even after she has been bedded. Rather than allowing herself to be seduced by a 'vieil amant' ('old Romeo') like Maurice, she finds a gangly, freckle-faced boy named Bernard and sweet-talks *him* into believing she likes him. Their relationship is as transient as the camp bed on which they have sex: she tells him to hurry up, pushes him off her as soon as the deed is done, and gets up to dress and leave. When he asks if the fact that she gave him her virginity means that she loves him, she barely pauses long enough to look back and call him an 'espèce de con!' Here it is the man who is the 'idiot' or 'stupid cunt', while Lili seduces and abandons him. It could be said that she is acting rather cruelly, behaving like Maurice or her worst impression of him as a callous rake, and that she has spoiled her own chances of having her first time be emotionally meaningful and not just emptily physical: 'Je me suis fait dépuceler sans désir, sans amour, sans bonheur. Juste parce que ça m'est égal. Juste par méchanceté. J'ai envie de pleurer, pleurer'[64] (Breillat 1987: 245). But Lili has also freed herself from the social prison of being a good little virgin – 'je suis contente d'avoir réduit ça, dont on fait tout un plat, à cinq minutes de saloperie. ... je me suis vengée de tout ce qu'on m'a appris, le respect de moi surtout et le respect des autres!'[65] (Breillat 1987: 245) – even as she refuses to let herself be caged in a new role, the whore who is dominated and then discarded by a man. As Lili leaves Bernard and emerges from the camp tent, there is a birdcage hanging next to her, but the bird has flown. Lili, wearing her denim overalls and a silver crucifix around her neck, has just lost her virginity, but she has not lost her head, her dignity or her soul. She turns to face us directly, proudly raising her chin, then breaks into a seductive smile, lowering her head yet peering coyly up at us with knowing eyes. Breillat freeze-frames her in this position, as if Lili could balance forever on the dividing line between good Catholic girl and seductive slut, never falling into either.

64 'I had myself deflowered without desire, without love, without happiness. Just because it was all the same to me. Just to be wicked. I wanted to cry, to cry'.

65 'I'm satisfied to have reduced "that", which they make such a big deal about, to five minutes of dirty nothing. ... I have taken revenge for all that they have taught me, respect for myself above all and the respect of others!'

References

Breillat, Catherine (1968), *L'Homme facile*, Paris, Christian Bourgois.

Breillat, Catherine (1969), *A Man for the Asking*, trans. Harold J. Salemson, New York, William Morrow.

Breillat, Catherine (1974), *Le Soupirail*, Paris, Guy Authier.

Breillat, Catherine (1987), *36 fillette*, Paris, Carrere.

Breillat, Catherine (1994), 'Un jour j'ai vu *Baby Doll*...', *Positif* 400, 13–15.

Breillat, Catherine (ed.) (1999), *Le Livre du plaisir*, Paris, Editions 1.

Breillat, Catherine (2006), *Corps amoureux: Entretiens avec Claire Vassé*, Paris, Denoël.

Ciment, Michel (1988), 'Entretien avec Catherine Breillat sur *36 fillette*', *Positif* 328, 3–5.

Cixous, Hélène (1975), 'Le Rire de la méduse', *Arc* 61, 39–54.

Cixous, Hélène (1980), 'The Laugh of the Medusa', in Elaine Marks and Isabelle de Courtivron (eds), *New French Feminisms: An Anthology*, Amherst, University of Massachusetts Press, pp. 245–64.

Clouzot, Claire (2004), *Catherine Breillat: Indécence et pureté*, Paris, Cahiers du cinéma.

Criterion (2006), 'Interview with Catherine Breillat', *A nos amours* DVD, Criterion Collection.

Duchen, Claire (1994), *Women's Rights and Women's Lives in France: 1944–1968*, London and New York, Routledge.

Gillain, Anne (2003), 'Profile of a Filmmaker: Catherine Breillat', in Roger Célestin, Eliane DalMolin, and Isabelle de Courtivron (eds), *Beyond French Feminisms: Debates on Women, Politics, and Culture in France, 1981–2001*, New York, Palgrave Macmillan, pp. 201–11.

Guilloux, Michel (1999), 'Rencontre', *Humanité*, 12 April.

Hayward, Susan (2005), *French National Cinema*, 2nd edn, London and New York, Routledge.

Hecquet, Céline (2000), 'Catherine Breillat donne sa langue au Chat', *Inrockuptibles*, 19 May.

Lautréamont (1973), *Œuvres complètes*, Paris, Gallimard.

Lautréamont (1978), *Maldoror and Poems*, trans. Paul Knight, London, Penguin.

Löfgren, Orvar (1999), *On Holiday: A History of Vacationing*, Berkeley and London, University of California Press.

Marks, Elaine and Courtivron, Isabelle de (eds) (1980), *New French Feminisms*, Amherst, University of Massachusetts Press.

Puaux, Françoise (2001), 'Entretien avec Catherine Breillat', *Le Machisme à l'écran*, *CinémAction* 99, 165–72.

Sedgwick, Eve Kosofsky and Frank, Adam (eds) (1995), *Shame and Its Sisters: A Silvan Tomkins Reader*, Durham, NC and London, Duke University Press.

Sineux, Michel (1991), 'Je raconte l'âme et la chair des gens', *Positif* 365/366, 16–18.

Suleiman, Susan Rubin (1990), *Subversive Intent: Gender, Politics, and the Avant-Garde*, Cambridge, MA and London, Harvard University Press.

Vincendeau, Ginette (1989), 'The Closer You Get ...', *Monthly Film Bulletin* 661:56, 41–2.

Weiner, Susan (2001), *Enfants Terribles: Youth and Femininity in the Mass Media in France, 1945–1968*, Baltimore and London, Johns Hopkins University Press.

Wiegand, Chris (2001), 'A Quick Chat with Catherine Breillat', *Kamera.co.uk*, www.kamera.co.uk.

Sisters as one soul in two bodies

A ma sœur! (*Fat Girl*)

The third film in what could be called Breillat's 'virgin trilogy' has two heroines, Anaïs, who is twelve, and her fifteen-year-old sister, Elena. It is as though the singular protagonists of the earlier coming-of-age films, Alice in *Une vraie jeune fille* or Lili in *36 fillette*, had been split or doubled. Indeed, Breillat has said that *Fat Girl* or *A ma sœur!* could have been titled *'Deux vraies jeunes filles'* (Bonnaud 2001: 14). Like Alice or Lili, Anaïs and Elena are both virginal girls on holiday with their families in the Landes region on the southwestern coast of France. It is ostensibly their summer vacation, but the weather is cold and the landscape is ravaged. The film was actually shot in winter, after severe storms had devastated the forests in Saint-Palais in December 1999. (Breillat had originally thought of setting the film in the bleak volcanic landscape of Etna in Sicily, but decided instead to return to the region of her own vacations with her parents when she was young.) The time is the present, but Breillat has said that the film 'n'est pas vraiment situé ni dans le temps … ni dans l'espace'[1] (Goudet and Vassé 2001: 29). It could be any vacation, taking place in 2001, 1987, 1976, or even the early 1960s of Breillat's own youth. One viewer noted that the film has a 'discreetly Sixties look, complete with obsolete, Italian-style bouffant hairdos and subtly retro clothes' (Bonnaud 2001: 14). (Breillat designed the costumes herself and is credited under the pseudonym of Catherine Meillan.) The film's timeless quality points to a general applicability, as if the tale being told could be that of any girl's coming of age. When it comes to the shame that girls are taught to feel about

1 'is not really situated either in time … or in space'.

their bodies and their sexual desires, Breillat strongly implies that not much has changed over the years. In the scene where Anaïs lifts her nightgown up to her eyes and can hardly look at her bared breasts in the mirror without calling herself a 'putain' ('whore'), we have an almost exact echo of the scene where, a quarter century earlier, Alice could only undress bit by bit in front of the mirror without seeing herself as stigmatised by that same word. Another connection between the characters can be found in the fact that, at times of sexual frustration, both Alice and Anaïs sit in the ocean surf (Anaïs also swims in a pool), and that for each of them the water gives rise to erotic musings and reveries.

The darkly romantic songs that Anaïs sings during these watery moments were actually written by Breillat when she was about that age (twelve). They represent early signs of creativity in Anaïs, much as the cynical love poem that Lili shared with Golovine in *36 fillette* was evidence of her budding desire to be a writer. (It is Lili's dialogue with Golovine that Breillat had actresses read when she was auditioning them for the role of Anaïs.) If Anaïs is the one who inherits Lili's critical intelligence, the other sister, Elena, is given more of Lili's flirtatious impatience to become a woman. We recall that Lili was not permitted to leave the family campsite except in the company of her older brother as chaperone. Similarly, Elena's parents will not let her leave their vacation house without her younger sister Anaïs in tow to act as a drag on Elena's desire for boys. Cruising at an outdoor café, Elena displaces Anaïs and takes the seat next to a new love interest, Fernando, and Elena then drives away with him in his convertible sports car, leaving her sister standing by the road. Likewise, Lili and her brother had fought over occupying the seat next to Maurice in his convertible, and later she and Maurice ditched her brother, leaving him to run after their car. Yet the coquettish Lili was also a prude, ashamed of the body and afraid of sex. In bed at the summer cottage, she could only glance over her shoulder at Maurice undressing across the room, much as Elena pulls her nightgown up to her eyes and Anaïs peeks through her fingers at the sight of Fernando undressing in the sisters' shared bedroom. In each of their respective films, both Lili and Elena have occasion to lament, 'Je peux pas! C'est pas de ma faute!'[2] They find it difficult to act on their desires due to a socially induced shame.

2 'I can't! It's not my fault!'

Another sense in which Anaïs and Elena are different facets of what is essentially the same heroine (formerly Alice or Lili) can be gleaned from Breillat's description of the sisters as 'une "âme à deux corps". ... Ce que fait l'une, l'autre le ressent. D'une certain manière, elle le vit tout autant'[3] (Breillat 2001: 7–8). One element in this symbiosis is that, though Anaïs may be obese while Elena is slender, they are both 'enfants-femmes' ('child-women') whose minds are struggling to understand the in-between state of their bodies. 'T'es une petite fille, une petite fille qui ressemble à une femme'[4] is what the seductive Fernando says to the gorgeous but emotionally immature Elena, hoping to overcome her childish timidity by appealing to her eagerness to be seen as a woman. Anaïs, too, is perturbed by pubescence. Breillat had not originally envisioned Anaïs with prominent breasts, but in the time that elapsed between casting and filming, the actress playing Anaïs had developed a large bosom, making hers 'un "corps interdit": un mélange corps de petite fille et en même temps une incroyable opulence sexuelle'[5] (Breillat 2001: 7).

The quasi-corporeal sympathy between Anaïs and Elena is emphasised by having them wear matching yellow shirts in the sisterly bonding scenes where they walk down to the beach together or lean against each other while watching TV. Although Anaïs is frequently seen garbed in the green of youthful innocence and Elena begins to wear red as she becomes more sexually involved with Fernando, there are still these intermediate moments of matching yellow which show both sisters in the transitional stage of adolescence. In another scene while lying side by side in a single bed with their legs entwined, the two sisters reminisce about their shared past, and when one starts to giggle, the laughter proves contagious, with each setting the other off at various intervals throughout the conversation. Similarly, a later shot of Elena crying in the car is soon followed by another shot of Anaïs weeping as well, and Elena's disgust at Fernando's perfidy (the engagement ring he gives her turns out to have been stolen from his mother) seems to be expressed by Anaïs' vomiting. But the two most crucial scenes of sisterly sympathy are the ones where Anaïs feels

3 'one "soul in two bodies". ... What the one does, the other feels. In a certain manner, she lives it just as much'.

4 'You're a little girl, a little girl who looks like a woman'.

5 'a "forbidden body": a body that is a mixture of a little girl and at the same time an incredible sexual opulence'.

the pain of Elena's being taken by Fernando. In the first scene, when Elena is entered anally, her suffering is revealed by a sudden cut to Anaïs' face, which registers her sister's pain. In the second scene, at the moment of Elena's vaginal penetration, another cut to a weeping Anaïs portends how her sister too will soon feel about having given her virginity to a lying Lothario.

Yet concomitant with the sisters' solidarity is an equally intense rivalry. In a sense, this is a primal matter of fusion and differentiation. Where there is love for one's likeness, one's sister, there is also 'de la haine, parce qu'on voudrait exister par soi-même',[6] as Breillat has explained (Goudet and Vassé 2001: 27). In the words of psychoanalyst Juliet Mitchell, 'The sibling is *par excellence* someone who threatens the subject's uniqueness. The ecstasy of loving one who is like oneself is experienced at the same time as the trauma of being annihilated by one who stands in one's place', and this threat from the other can lead one to have 'murderous desires, as a response to the danger of annihilation' (Mitchell 2003: 10, 43). When they are out shopping for clothes and Anaïs chooses the same outfit that her sister had her eye on, Elena lashes out in anger, accusing Anaïs of always copying her, of wanting to be like her and to take her dress and her boyfriend. Because Fernando and Elena have no place to make love except the sisters' shared bedroom, Elena must suffer Anaïs' intrusion upon this most intimate moment, knowing that her sister is looking on with 'une mélange ... de mépris et d'envie'[7] (Breillat 2001: 36) while Elena tries to define herself as a grown woman and an individual without the private physical or mental space in which to do so. For her part, Anaïs feels excluded from and jealous of her sister's relationship with Fernando, and these feelings, exacerbated by her family's negative comments about her own weight, prompt Anaïs to become hyper-critical of her svelte sister, looking askance at virtually everything she does. To Anaïs, Elena's desire to give her virginity to a man she loves is foolish; Elena's flirtation with Fernando at the outdoor café is risible; Elena's actions in bed with Fernando are 'histoires de cul' in which she 'se fait tripoter toute la nuit'.[8]

It is interesting to compare the Elena–Anaïs relationship to the one that existed between Simone de Beauvoir and her younger sister

6 'hatred, because one would like to exist by oneself'.

7 'a mixture ... of scorn and envy'.

8 'sexploits' ... 'lets herself be fingered all night long'.

Poupette (especially given that Beauvoir was such an influential figure for Breillat). Beauvoir notes Poupette's reaction to feeling devalued in relation to Beauvoir herself as the more favoured sister: 'Dans son exaspération, elle se mit à me regarder d'un œil nouveau: elle cherchait mes failles. Je m'irritai qu'elle prétendît, même timidement, rivaliser avec moi, me critiquer, m'échapper'[9] (Beauvoir 1958: 101). Beauvoir's description of how Poupette felt is equally applicable to Anaïs: 'on continuait à considérer Poupette comme un reflet, nécessairement imparfait, de son aînée: elle se sentait souvent humiliée, aussi la disait-on orgueilleuse'[10] (Beauvoir 1958: 101). If Elena is the picture-perfect butterfly, then Anaïs is the unevolved larva, the flesh not yet informed by spirit – 'une gourde', 'une truie', 'une grosse tâche', 'ce bout de viande cru',[11] as she is variously called throughout the film. 'J'en ai marre qu'on me traîne comme un boulet',[12] Anaïs tells Elena, for she is made to feel like a physical weight oppressing her sister's spirit, holding her back from achieving the ideal romance she aspires to with Fernando.

Of the two sisters, Anaïs is of course the 'fat girl'. While some viewers have blamed the international distributors of Breillat's film for giving its title (*A ma sœur!*) such a crude 'translation' (*Fat Girl*), it is important to note that *Fat Girl* was in fact Breillat's original title, before French audiences at test screenings reacted negatively to it due to its foreignness and its harshness on the subject of weight. Interestingly, the foreign sound of '*Fat Girl*' to French ears was essential to the meaning that Breillat had intended: 'the little girl was fat, but the title also expressed an autism, a wall between her and the world that the foreign title reinforced. … It was something completely different from the French of "grosse fille"; it was musical sounding, like a jazz tune' (Criterion 2004). Breillat's complexity of tone here suggests that, as she sees it, Anaïs' obesity has both negative and positive associations.

Most apparent is the isolating effect of Anaïs' weight, which immures her in flesh and causes her to be rejected by a diet-obsessed

9 'In her exasperation, she began to look upon me with a different eye: she picked out all my faults. It vexed me that she should seek, even half-heartedly, to rival, criticize, and do without me' (Beauvoir 1959: 105).

10 'Poupette continued to be regarded as a mere reflection, necessarily imperfect, of her elder sister: she often felt humiliated, so she was said to be haughty' (Beauvoir 1959: 105).

11 'a stupid lump' … 'a sow' … 'a big stain' … 'this hunk of raw meat'.

12 'I'm sick of being dragged around like a ball and chain'.

society that finds only slim women attractive. 'Son propre poids était quelque chose qui l'écrasait et la renvoyait à sa solitude',[13] notes Breillat (Goudet and Vassé 2001: 28), and we get shots of Anaïs belly-up in the pool on the morning after Elena and Fernando have spent the night together, and shots of Anaïs lying like driftwood in the ocean surf while Elena and Fernando make out in the dunes. Society's disgust at Anaïs' size is internalised as self-loathing and self-mortification, as when she imagines crows coming to peck away at the 'bout de viande cru'[14] that is her body. If overeating repels the boys whose attention she secretly craves (Anaïs slathers suntan lotion on her body and poses like a bathing beauty when Fernando has been watching her at the pool), food at least provides her with some sensual satisfaction, transporting her to another world of compensatory comfort. As Lauren Berlant has written about a similar overweight heroine, 'Eating cuts a swath in the anhedonia [lack of pleasure] she experiences in the normal world by liberating her from the time and space of her sociability, which is only inadequate' (Berlant 2002: 84). For Anaïs, food is often a substitute for sex, as when she gorges on a banana split while Elena and Fernando are mouth to mouth across the table from her at the outdoor café, or when Anaïs eats a long piece of bread and later a marshmallow strip after Elena has had oral sex with Fernando. However, just as Fernando turns out to be a cheap Lothario and unfulfilling lover, so the food that Anaïs consumes is really junk, 'la malbouffe' ('unhealthy and unappetising to eat'). Perhaps this is why, near the end of the film, Breillat positions a romantically unsatisfied Elena next to Anaïs, who is consuming fast food at a gas station minimart. (Interestingly, the girl chosen to play Anaïs was first discovered when Breillat saw her eating at a 'McDo' ('McDonald's').)

Granted, Anaïs' weight isolates her from society, but less apparent is the fact that her corpulence also safeguards her, serving as 'une forteresse derrière laquelle elle était invulnérable'[15] (Goudet and Vassé 2001: 28). In using this metaphor, Breillat does not mean physical impregnability, but rather a mental fortitude: Anaïs' obesity 'protects her from becoming a product of society's norms. Since her body makes her unloved, since she isn't looked at and desired, she's more intel-

---

13 'Her own weight was something that crushed her and that drove her back into her solitude'.

14 'hunk of raw meat'.

15 'a fortress behind which she was invulnerable'.

ligent about the world. She can create herself and be herself, with a kind of rebellion. ... She exists to an extreme, as extreme as her physical bulk' (Criterion 2004). More than just a defensive fortress, overeating is for Anaïs an act of rebellion against a society that would have her conform to its bodily norms. It is an expansive assertion of her right to exist on her own terms rather than be passively moulded into the meagre shape to which her mother and sister have already conformed. Their attenuated bodies suggest a life of self-denial and self-sacrifice for others: 'The rules for this construction of femininity ... require that women learn to feed others, not the self, and to construe any desires for self-nurturance and self-feeding as greedy and excessive. Thus, women must develop a totally other-oriented emotional economy' (Bordo 2003: 171). At the lunchtime buffet, Anaïs' mother fills the father's plate with food and brings it over to him at the table, then Anaïs' sister does the exact same thing for Fernando. Elena also criticises Anaïs, who has served herself a heaped plateful of food, for eating like a pig. Physically and ideologically, Elena copies her mother's subservience to men, whereas Anaïs lays claim to the fulfilment of her own desires, as if the entire buffet, the whole world, were hers for the taking. Breillat has described Anaïs' weight as 'une obésité qui est faite pour vaincre le monde': 'Anaïs résiste mieux. Elle absorbe le monde, alors que l'autre [Elena] au contraire est absorbée'[16] (Breillat 2001: 6).

In serving a man food in imitation of her mother, adolescent Elena is already being absorbed by society, already imagining herself as fulfilling her 'destiny' as a woman, which is to become a wife. (In French, 'femme' means both 'woman' and 'wife'.) Whereas independent Anaïs can play-act in the pool that she is kissing a fiancé but then making love with another man, Elena – like the Catholic Church – cannot countenance intercourse outside the context of marriage. She permits anal and oral contact on the grounds that technically these do not count as sex, but Fernando must give her an engagement ring before she will give herself to him. As Anaïs points out in the scene where Elena shows her the ring ('Te "donner" à lui? C'est quoi ces vocabulaires?'),[17] Elena is objectifying herself by viewing her virginity as something exchangeable on the marriage market. Elena's wilful and gullible belief in Fernando as her one true love shows a sentimental

16 'an obesity that is made to conquer the world' ... 'Anaïs resists better. She absorbs the world, while the other [Elena] by contrast is absorbed'.
17 '"Give" yourself to him? What kind of words are these?'

faith which may have been instilled in her by reading 'romans-photos' ('conventional love stories') or 'romans à l'eau de rose' ('romance novels'). (Harlequin-style romances are popular in France, amounting to 15% of all paperback sales (Hughes and Reader 1998: 474).) Elena's Barbie-doll make-up, clingy red dress and slinky posturing around Fernando suggest that she has patterned herself after the young models in the women's magazines that are strewn about her bedroom. Breillat goes so far as to call Elena 'une bimbo de sitcom' (Clouzot 2004: 105), grouping her with other young people today who live life like a stupid reality show, posing and flirting and falling mindlessly into the most gender-clichéd kinds of love situations: 'Les jeunes, je ne sais s'ils ne ressemblent pas plus aux gens de *Loft Story* [or *Big Brother*] qu'à nous ... Très lobotomisés, très enlisés dans des normes, celles de la sitcom, les plus terribles qui soient'[18] (Clément 2002: 277).

It is interesting to see how this contrast between a rebellious Anaïs and a more conformist Elena played itself out in Breillat's own relationship with her sister Marie-Hélène. Breillat has made no secret of the fact that, in creating *A ma sœur!*, 'I drew upon my own life, on the relation between my sister and me when we were young ... the antagonism and complicity' (Rich 2001). To begin with the complicity, for those who wonder about that exclamation point at the end of *A ma sœur!*, Breillat intended the title to have both 'un côté dédicace', as in a toast to her sister ('à ta santé'!), and 'un côté épitaphe ou ex-voto' in memory of the sisters' lost unity: 'elles meurent à leur état de sœurs liguées contre le monde' when 'l'arrivée d'un garçon ... casse leur bulle'[19] (Goudet and Vassé 2001: 28). This is a movie that starts with two sisters walking side by side as they leave their vacation house together, but Elena seems inexorably bound on a trajectory (backed by Italian music on the soundtrack) that will have her splitting off from Anaïs and joining Fernando at the outdoor café – despite the fact that at one point Anaïs has turned, walking backwards, to face Elena and to warn her against falling too easily for a boy. Again and again throughout the film, the sisters will be separated by Fernando as

18 'The young, I don't know if they don't bear a closer resemblance to the people in *Loft Story* [or *Big Brother*] than to us ... So lobotomised, so sucked in by norms, those of the sitcom, the most terrible that there are'.

19 'the sense of a dedication' ... 'to your health!' ... 'the sense of an epitaph or votive offering' ... 'they die away from their state of being sisters in league against the world' ... 'the arrival of a boy ... breaks their bubble'.

Elena is necking with him at the café, petting with him on the dunes, and sharing a bed with him in the sisters' bedroom. Anaïs remembers when she and Elena used to lie together in 'nos lits jumeaux roses'.[20] Now she must watch Elena give up her sisterly solidarity and her female independence in her debilitating desire to please a man, to conform her will and her body to his expectations.

Like Anaïs and Elena, Breillat and her older sister Marie-Hélène were initially inseparable. Born only thirteen months apart (on 13 July 1948 and 2 June 1947, respectively), the sisters were often regarded as twins. As indicated in a 1971 profile on them in the young women's magazine *20 ans*, 'Les deux jumelles Breillat ne se ressemblent pas de façon frappante' (in fact, Catherine was blonde and Marie-Hélène brunette, as Anaïs and Elena were originally scripted to be), but 'Elles ont pourtant adopté le même style vestimentaire'[21] (Godard 1971) – and we recall the matching yellow shirts worn by the sisters in the film. Intriguingly, when Catherine and Marie-Hélène themselves appeared together in a film (*Last Tango in Paris* in 1972), they played assistants at a secondhand clothes shop who were dressed in identical antique outfits. Perhaps Anaïs and Elena's quarrel in the clothing store over wanting the same dress is an autobiographical nod to this earlier sisters' scene. In the magazine profile, Catherine and Marie-Hélène also recalled times when their mother 'nous giflait à tour de bras'[22] (Godard 1971), which brings to mind the scene in *A ma sœur!* when the mother, furious at Elena, slaps Anaïs instead because she is the only one at hand. It is as if both sisters are thought of as one and either will do for punishment. Just as Anaïs and Elena's parents would prefer to keep their girls safeguarded within the walls of the vacation house (in a gated community), so the Breillat sisters were 'cloîtrées dans la maison familiale' by their overprotective parents, and in reaction to this confinement, Marie-Hélène, like Elena, 'eut un amant!'[23] (Godard 1971).

The mention of a lover reminds us that, in addition to the complicity between the Breillat sisters, there was also antagonism – 'Rivalité, jalousie, guérilla',[24] as a 1983 *Elle* profile put it in describing the

20 'our pink twin beds'.
21 'The two Breillat twins don't bear a striking resemblance to each other' ... 'They have nevertheless adopted the same style of clothing'.
22 'would slap us with all her strength'.
23 'Cloistered within the family home' ... 'had a lover!'
24 'Rivalry, jealousy, guerrilla warfare'.

sisters' youth (Anon. 1983). In the film, Anaïs has difficulty accepting the fact that Elena's growing sexual maturity and her interest in boys are splitting the sisters off from one another, meaning that Elena will have experiences apart from Anaïs: 'elle est jalouse', says Elena to Fernando about her sister, 'elle veut pas comprendre que je suis plus grande qu'elle'.[25] We do not know if Catherine was jealous of Marie-Hélène and her lover, but later it was the older sister who felt excluded and covetous regarding Catherine and her boyfriend François: 'Marie-Hélène perd sa complice de toujours [her sister] et se met à dessiner des scènes érotiques où les filles qui sont dans les bras de François ressemblent étrangement à elle'[26] (Godard 1971). Curiously, when the Breillat sisters acted in the 1976 film *Dracula père et fils* (*Dracula and Son*), Marie-Hélène played a woman whom Dracula falls for only because she so closely resembles his first great love – portrayed by Catherine. In this film, then, the younger sister actually preceded her elder in getting there first with a man.

Besides men, another factor in the growing separation between the Breillat sisters was the disparity in their weights and the difference in their attitudes to society related to these body sizes. 'Ma sœur était anorexique,' Catherine has said, 'mais moi, je ne faisais que manger'[27] (Breillat 2006: 17). We recall the defiant overeater Anaïs as contrasted with Elena the compliant beauty, her good looks trapping her into a need to please by conforming her body to Fernando's desires. While Catherine eventually pursued a career as a writer and director whose works often challenge patriarchy and its demeaning views of women, Marie-Hélène remained an actress and model increasingly defined by the male gaze, eventually posing for covers and centrefolds in *Playboy* and *Lui*: 'Ma pauvre sœur a fait la couverture de *Lui* mais moi j'ai refusé … Se tortiller en montrant des morceaux de chair, en relevant légère-ment un bout de robe transparente avec un sourire niais et affriolant … c'est pitoyable!'[28] (Breillat 2006: 198). Like Elena after she has been sweet-talked into anal intercourse by Fernando ('Ça me donne envie de

25 'she's jealous' … 'she doesn't want to recognise that I'm more grown-up than she is'.
26 'Marie-Hélène loses her longtime companion [her sister] and begins to draw erotic scenes where the girls in François' arms bear a strange resemblance to her'.
27 'My sister was anorexic' … 'but me, I did nothing but eat'.
28 'My poor sister did the cover of *Lui*, but me, I refused … To wriggle around while showing off pieces of your flesh, lifting up a little bit of your see-through dress with a silly and seductive smile … that's pathetic!'

pleurer ... j'ai honte'),[29] Marie-Hélène became profoundly depressed that she had let her image be expropriated by the pornography industry: 'J'ai toujours vu dans mon métier un Art mais je m'y suis compromise et désespérée dans des filons vulgaires où je m'abaissais'[30] (Breillat 1986: 67). Ironically, in terms of her own love life, Marie-Hélène held a highly sentimental view of romance, and yet, as with Elena, it is her very idealisation of her lover that makes her so pliable in his hands, so tractable to his will: 'Tout mon être s'en vient à ta demande et je me retrouve dans tes bras, pantelante et ravie ... Tu m'as tout rapporté, toutes les étoiles, et toutes les comètes, tous les Soleils, toutes les Lunes, toutes les galaxies'[31] (Breillat 1986: 108–9). Such starry-eyed idealism in looking upon a lover can make it hard to see if he is being insincere or manipulative, a 'love is blind' trap into which Marie-Hélène has fallen with men in the past, only to discover afterward that 'il ne s'agit plus que d'une séduction. D'une entreprise vulgaire sans noblesse et sans beauté. ... Son "amour" pour moi n'était que la poursuite d'un Objet de Désir et sa possession maladive'[32] (Breillat 1986: 72, 71). Elena is similarly duped by Fernando and by her own overestimation of him on whom her sense of self-worth is all too dependent: 'she cannot understand that she is only an object of desire. And as such she can only be taken. Or had', notes Breillat (Vincendeau 2001: 19).

Exploring the ways in which the Elena–Anaïs relationship maps onto the one between Marie-Hélène and Catherine has enabled us to sharpen the contrast between the sentimental sister open to love and the cynical sister wary of giving herself to some boy who might 'se vanter qu'il m'a eue vierge'.[33] This contrast is highlighted in the scene where Elena and Anaïs examine their side-by-side reflections in a mirror, noting that while the elder has eyes that are 'vagues' ('hazy' or dreamily romantic), the younger's are 'petits et durs' ('small and hard', or suspicious and harshly critical). Yet as each sister continues

29 'It makes me want to cry ... I'm ashamed'.
30 'I always regarded my profession as an Art but I had compromised myself and felt despondent due to this vulgar work in which I was debasing myself'.
31 'All my being comes at your command and I find myself again in your arms, panting and enraptured ... You have brought everything back to me, all the stars, and all the comets, all the Suns, all the Moons, all the galaxies'.
32 'it's about nothing more than a seduction. A vulgar enterprise without beauty or nobility. ... His "love" for me was only the pursuit of an Object of Desire and the feverish possession of it'.
33 'brag that he took my virginity'.

to look into her own and the other's eyes, a peculiar kind of rapprochement occurs. 'Quand je plonge mon regard dans le tien', Elena tells Anaïs, 'ça me fait comme un effet d'appartenance, comme si c'était le mien'.[34] This is more than just a momentary feeling that they are still sisterly soulmates in spite of their growing physical and social separation. It is stranger and more important than that. As Anaïs goes on to tell Elena, 'quand je te déteste, je te regarde et je peux plus, c'est comme si je détestais une partie de moi-même'.[35] The sentimental/cynical contrast *between* the two sisters is also a contrast *within* each one of them. In scorning Elena's romantic naïveté, Anaïs is attacking her own sentimental side in an effort to protect herself from love's disappointments, as when she calls upon 'mon cœur à pourrir' because 'il n'a su que me nourrir d'illusions'[36] (Breillat 2001: 60). But even as Anaïs is purging her heart of sentiment by singing this song in the ocean surf, she knows that Elena is falling for Fernando in the nearby dunes and thus in a sense keeping Anaïs' romantic hopes alive along with her fears of disillusionment, her vulnerability to pain. This is the deeper sense in which the sisters are 'une "âme à deux corps"'[37] (Breillat 2001: 7), one soul split between dreaming and dreading, each sister feeling the other's physical longings and apprehensions because they are also her own. It is as though there were only one girl on the beach, a composite Anaïs-Elena. (In *Sex Is Comedy*, there is in fact only one girl, for in this film about the making of *A ma sœur!*, Roxane Mesquida, who plays Elena, is shown rehearsing scenes with the Fernando-actor in the dunes, but we also see her lying alone in the surf – as if she were Anaïs.)

If there is a sentimental 'Elena' within Anaïs, then there is also a cynical 'Anaïs' inside Elena.[38] (Breillat had originally planned to call

---

34 'When I look deep into your eyes, it makes me feel a sense of belonging, as if they were mine'.

35 'when I hate you, I look at you and I can't anymore, it's like hating a part of myself'.

36 'my heart to rot away' ... 'it has known only how to nourish me with illusions'. The second part of this quotation occurs only in the screenplay.

37 'one "soul in two bodies"'.

38 As the 1971 magazine profile notes about *both* Breillat sisters, 'elles semblent très affranchies, très cyniques, mais en fait elles sont très puritaines, sensibles comme les marguerites et sentimentales à mourir' (Godard 1971) ('they seem very liberated, very cynical, but in fact they are very puritan, as sensitive as daisies and sentimental to their dying breath').

Anaïs 'Maria' and has noted that 'mes deux héroïnes [Anaïs/Maria and Elena] sont ma sœur [Marie-Hélène] divisée en deux'[39] (Goudet and Vassé 2001: 27).) When Elena is trying to make love with Fernando and fears that her sister is spying on her from across their shared bedroom, it is partly the invasion of her privacy and the reinforcement of her sense of shame that disturb Elena. (If Anaïs would just go to sleep, so might Elena's conscience or socially induced sense of guilt that premarital sex is wrong.) But Anaïs' cynical gaze also threatens Elena's sentimental faith, casting doubt on her romance with Fernando: 'même si l'aînée cherche à s'affranchir de sa sœur, elle est toujours tributaire du regard que l'autre porte sur elle'[40] (Breillat 2001: 8). With Anaïs as a sceptical witness (the camera cuts to her doubting eyes just after Fernando tells Elena he will still respect her if she goes all the way with him), Elena's 'grand amour' is shadowed by suspicion, haunted by the pessimistic prospect that it is but a fleeting physical encounter. There is thus a sense in which each sister is ghosted by the other in a kind of double exposure, with Anaïs painfully inhabited by Elena's juvenile romantic hopes and Elena invaded by Anaïs' prematurely jaded view of romance. Among Breillat's inspirations for the Elena–Anaïs relationship was the one between Alma (Bibi Andersson) and Elisabeth (Liv Ullmann) in Ingmar Bergman's *Persona* (1966), particularly the mirror scene in which the two women recognise in their reflections a strange likeness between them despite their differences. (There is also the split-screen shot with the left half of Alma's face on one side and the right half of Elisabeth's face on the other side, as if each were haunted by the internalised presence of the other.) Like Elena, Alma has a fiancé and looks forward to lasting happiness with him, but Elisabeth's critical gaze hollows out Alma's hopes, making her view male–female relationships as empty encounters. Elisabeth listens while Alma tells of a time when another woman watched her having sex on the beach with a boy. For Alma, the experience was ecstatic and meaningful, but the onlookers (the nameless woman and by extension Elisabeth) threaten to make it something other – just 'an orgy with strangers', as Elisabeth calls it, which ended in 'an abortion'. We recall that, after

39 'my two heroines [Anaïs/Maria and Elena] are my sister [Marie-Hélène] split into two'.
40 'even if the older one seeks to break free from her sister, she is still tributary to the gaze that the other directs upon her'.

observing Elena in bed with Fernando, Anaïs subverts her sister's romantic imaginings by referring to their encounters as 'histoires de cul'.[41]

Two further films have scenes of 'sisterly' voyeurism that can be usefully compared to those involving Anaïs and Elena. In David Hamilton's *Bilitis* (1977), which was scripted by Breillat with uncredited assistance from her sister Marie-Hélène (Clouzot 2004: 19), teenage Bilitis watches from outside a bedroom window and then listens from an upstairs window while an older friend Melissa, who seemed to have the perfect marriage, is sexually brutalised by her husband Pierre. First Melissa cries out as he is on her back and taking her anally, then when she is vaginally penetrated in the missionary position, she holds tightly to him as a way of bearing the pain. Anaïs sees and hears Elena undergo these same experiences with Fernando, who may be subtler in his approach but who is basically no less of a brute himself, a fact highlighted by this comparison of him with Pierre. When Melissa is furious at Bilitis for having spied on her, it is because Melissa doesn't want to recognise the full extent of her failed romance as Bilitis sees it: 'Your husband's a brute!' Elena too attempts to block out Anaïs' harshly realistic view and remain blindly in love with Fernando despite the pain he has caused her. *Bilitis* ends on something of a sentimental fantasy: when violent Pierre leaves Melissa to indulge in another of his infidelities, she is provided with ample comfort – first Bilitis herself makes tender love to her, and then Bilitis gives her own gentle boyfriend to Melissa as a superior substitute for Pierre. Alternatively, at the end of *A ma sœur!* Anaïs' cynical perspective prevails: Elena is profoundly disillusioned when Fernando turns out to have taken advantage of her naïve faith in love to seduce and abandon her. In Eric Rohmer's *Pauline à la plage* (*Pauline at the Beach*) (1983),[42] plain-Jane Pauline peers through a window and discovers her gorgeous older cousin Marion in bed with Henri. Marion has tried to hide the affair from Pauline because she knows that her younger cousin regards Henri as a womanising cad, but Marion believes that she can win this playboy's heart with her beauty, so she attempts to ignore Pauline's words of warning which feed the doubts in her own head: 'Tout ce que tu me diras contre Henri, et que je peux me dire

41 'sexploits'.

42 Breillat had actresses read some of Pauline's dialogue from this film when they were being screen-tested for the role of Anaïs.

moi-même d'ailleurs, ne peut me détacher de lui'.[43] In the end, when Henri cheats on her, Marion preserves her romantic idealism by simply refusing to believe that he was unfaithful, and Pauline actually encourages her cousin's self-delusion. By contrast, Anaïs advises her sister Elena to face the fact that Fernando has used and dumped her. Anaïs' words may seem callous ('il t'a déjà oubliée'),[44] but hers is the more meaningful comfort because, unlike Pauline with Marion, Anaïs is trying to instil in her sister a sense of self-worth above and apart from any romantic dependence on men: 'tu mérites beaucoup mieux'.[45]

But Elena is inconsolably broken-hearted, for it is not only that she has been deceived and deserted by a man, but that her adolescent dreams of romance have been devastated: 'c'est beaucoup plus vrai de dire qu'on souffre d'une perte d'illusion que de dire qu'on souffre du départ de l'être aimé'[46] (Breillat 2006: 103). Elena gave her virginity to Fernando in the belief that he would be the love of her life, the knight in shining armour who would rescue her from her parents' confinement and worship her womanly beauty. As Deanna Holtzman and Nancy Kulish have noted, 'many hopes, fantasies, and expectations precede the event [of deflowering] in the minds of young ... women. They expect to be transformed magically, to be swept away by romance and pleasure, to become part of an idealized union or couple, never to feel excluded or left out again' (Holtzman and Kulish 1997: 209). However, the loss of virginity can be 'a painful rite of passage' for these women, 'marked by intense feelings of pain and disappointment in the sexual experience itself and in the men who often leave them' (Holtzman and Kulish 1997: 131). When Fernando pushes into Elena, breaking her hymen, she holds tightly to him, the pain made bearable by the prospect of pleasure in the arms of her future husband (Fernando's engagement ring is prominent on her finger as her hands clasp his back during this scene). But this one night of poignant intercourse is all she will ever get from Fernando, who now abandons her. It is interesting to compare Elena's experience with that of the little

43 'Everything bad that you will tell me about Henri, and that I can tell myself as well, can't separate me from him'.
44 'he's already forgotten you'.
45 'you deserve much better'.
46 'it's much more true to say that one suffers from a loss of illusion than to say that one suffers from the departure of the loved one'.

mermaid in the Hans Christian Andersen tale. After falling in love with a human prince, the fifteen-year-old mermaid parts from her sisters in the sea and splits her fishtail to form two legs in order to be with her beau, who nevertheless forsakes her for another woman. The tail-splitting is depicted as being quite painful – 'every step you take will be like walking on a sharp knife so that your blood flows!' (Andersen 1980: 48) – and it could be viewed as an allegory for the loss of female integrity (and sisterly solidarity) that comes with her loss of virginity to a man. (The mermaid's sisters are described as 'singing mournfully' as they 'looked at her with deep sorrow in their eyes' (Andersen 1980: 51, 53).) The tail-splitting could also be seen as a violation of the little mermaid's virginal hopes, cutting her off from the romantic future she had envisioned with the prince, who betrayed her. Breillat has referred to 'l'innocence, l'idéalisme de la petite sirène dont les jambes indifférenciées symbolisent la virginité', describing her story as 'un conte cruel, solitaire, qui vous fait fondre en larmes, l'histoire d'une illusion, de la première trahison amoureuse'[47] (Argand 2002).

The parallels with Elena's story are strong: she is painfully deflowered, forsaken by her fiancé and bereft of romantic hope, with only her still-virginal sister there to lament the loss of her girlhood innocence. Elena 'est tuée, car disparaît en elle ce désir d'illusions dont on a tellement besoin pour vivre. Et c'est sa sœur qui porte le deuil de cette mort',[48] says Breillat (Goudet and Vassé 2001: 29). Some faith in love is vital to life, but it's important to emphasise that Elena's disillusionment would not be so extreme if she had not idealised romance to such an extent, and that this idealisation is tied to a religious belief that sex must be sanctified by marriage. As Simone de Beauvoir has written about her own Catholic upbringing: 'je me persuadais qu'on peut célébrer au lit des messes blanches: un authentique amour sublime l'étreinte physique, et entre les bras de l'élu, la pure jeune fille se change allégrement en une claire jeune femme. ... J'avais chéri cette hostie immaculée: mon âme; dans ma mémoire traînaient des images d'hermine souillée, de lys profané; s'il n'était pas transfiguré

---

47 'the innocence, the idealism of the little mermaid whose undifferentiated legs symbolise virginity' ... 'a cruel, lonely tale that makes you dissolve into tears, the story of an illusion, of love's first betrayal'.

48 'is killed, because what one needs so much in order to live, the desire for illusions, disappears in her. And it's her sister who wears mourning for this death'.

par le feu de la passion, le plaisir salissait'[49] (Beauvoir 1958: 289–90, 166). With this religious context in mind, we can more readily understand the depth of Elena's disappointment when her sacrament of love with her fiancé turns out to be a black mass of merely degrading sex in which her body's temple is despoiled. It is because Elena so prized her virginity that its loss under these less-than-ideal circumstances makes her feel like a whore. Elena can be compared to Véronika in Jean Eustache's *La Maman et la putain* (*The Mother and the Whore*) (1973). Ever since losing her virginity in a meaningless encounter, Catholic girl Véronika has fought a sickness in her soul, seeking true love with men but feeling degraded by every sexual experience because it doesn't meet her ideal: 'Je me suis fait dépuceler récemment ... Et après, j'ai pris un maximum d'amants. ... On m'a souvent baisée dans le vide. ... On me baisait comme une pute. ... Je pleure toute ma vie passée, ma vie sexuelle passée, qui est si courte'.[50] Like Véronika, Elena cries tears of shame and heartsick disappointment at being turned from a virginal bride-to-be into a whorish object of lust.

There is thus a sense in which, at the end of *A ma sœur!*, Elena is killed by a traumatic loss of romantic illusions; she dies of disillusionment. Having so thoroughly invested in conventional femininity, having conformed her body and soul to pleasing a man, she is not strong enough to survive when that man rejects her. Elena's mother too is 'abandoned' by her man when her husband leaves her behind on vacation to go back to his job, choosing work over his wife despite the fact that she has clearly devoted her life to him. Elena is well on her way to becoming just like her mother, with the same long dark hair and exotically appealing looks, the same sentimental faith in men and the same despair when her hopes are dashed. 'Je voudrais qu'elle

49 'I was sure that the wedding night should be a white mass: true love sublimates the physical embrace, and in the arms of her chosen one the pure young girl is briskly changed into a radiant young woman. ... I had cherished that immaculate host, my soul; my memory was still full of images of mud-stained ermine, of trampled lilies; if physical pleasure was not transmuted by the fires of passionate love, it was a defilement' (Beauvoir 1959: 308, 175).

50 'I had myself deflowered recently ... And after that, I took a maximum of lovers. ... They often fucked me without meaning. ... They would fuck me like a whore. ... I cry over my whole past life, my past sex life, which is so short'. In casting for the part of Elena, Breillat had actresses read from this famous monologue by Véronika.

crève', Elena says about her mother, adding 'je m'en fous de crever avec'.[51] Literally, Elena and her mother are killed at a highway rest stop when they park their car to get some sleep and a madman smashes their windshield with an axe and murders them. They are not responsible for their deaths; the male assailant is. Figuratively, Elena and her mother are two Sleeping Beauties who naïvely trusted that their prince would rouse them with a kiss and who are rudely awakened. Earlier, Elena's mother spoke of having reacted to a terrible storm (presumably the one that ravaged so many trees in the area) by pulling the bedcovers over her head and going back to sleep. The mother slept while her daughter Elena was ravaged by Fernando, and now she and Elena are both asleep when they are felled by the attacker. (Elena is in fact still sleeping when she is struck with the axe, while her mother wakes up but is as if '"sidérée" par ce regard'[52] from her assailant, who strangles her.)

Breillat has said that, in filming the attack, she was trying for a 'Cindy Sherman' effect, 'l'horreur dans la sidération'[53] (Clouzot 2004: 101). After the two women have been struck down, the camera lingers over their supine bodies which seem in their stillness to be the posed subjects of glamour shots. Elena is in her formfitting yellow top and tight red pants with a bare midriff, while her mother wears a chic green scarf, a red dress with white polka dots, and white high-heeled shoes. Cindy Sherman photographed herself in classically feminine poses from 1950s and 1960s films, such as languishing dreamily in bed in her bra and lace panties while holding a hand mirror (*Untitled Film Still* #6) or modelling her face and figure in front of the bathroom mirror and dolling herself up for a date (#81, #2, #56): 'The accoutrements of the feminine struggle to conform to a façade of desirability haunt Sherman's iconography. Make-up, high heels, back-combed hair, respectable but eroticised clothes are all carefully "put on" and "done"' (Mulvey 1996: 68). An earlier scene in *A ma sœur!* has Elena applying red lipstick with the aid of a compact mirror and then lying in bed in her lacy white nightgown to wait for Fernando. It is also for him that Elena buys a clingy red dress which she shows off at the clothing store like a fashion model, while her mother purchases a green scarf after trying it on in the mirror and imagining that it

51 'I wish she'd die' ... 'I don't care if I die with her'.
52 '"thunderstruck" by this look'.
53 'the horror of being thunderstruck'.

will please her husband. Now the mother's dead body displays that same green scarf, as if she were a special kind of fashion victim, killed by conformity to the conventional feminine role which makes her vulnerable to men who are indifferent (her husband) or hostile (the attacker). Sherman's still-photos 'focus exclusively on women, on the roles women play in films, on the nature of those roles as pre-set, congealed, cultural clichés – hence their designation as "stereotype" – and, by implication, on the pall that the real-world pressure to fill these roles casts over the fates of individual women' (Krauss 1993: 41). Breillat dramatises that 'pall', showing the mother's ripped red dress, her torn stockings and the green scarf around her neck after the attacker has strangled her. Elena now has red blood covering her to match her fashionable red pants. In some of Sherman's later photos (*Untitled* #153, #167, #173), she depicts herself as a corpse, the victim of a sexual assault. In this way, she displays the 'wounded body' that lies 'behind the carefully crafted cosmetic façade of her film still beauties' – the 'inner state of emptiness and deadness' (Knafo 1996: 152, 151) that results from so thoroughly conforming herself to male desires.

After the mother and Elena have been killed in the car by their attacker, the madman rapes Anaïs in the woods. Breillat films the assault on Anaïs in a way that calls attention to the similarities between it and the scene in which Elena lost her virginity to Fernando. A frightened Elena had pleaded with him to be gentle, but Fernando silenced her with a no, arguing that one hard push is better. Anaïs' attacker literally gags her (with her yellow panties) and then rapes her. Both Elena and Anaïs cry out and hold tightly to their men – imploringly, desperately, or just to bear the pain? – while Fernando and the madman grunt and thrust away, obscuring the women's faces, heedless of their suffering. The madman's direct assault on Anaïs reveals the truth about the violence latent in Fernando's more subtle abuse of Elena. The smooth-talking law student may have wheedled his way into gaining Elena's grudging consent, but his goal does not seem that different from the rapist's: to render her mute and passive so that she can be taken. What is even more emotionally damaging for Elena is that, because sex outside of marriage is socially prohibited, she has had to talk herself into believing Fernando's romantic lies and his engagement ring in order to sleep with him, so she has been in a sense complicit in her own seduction and abandonment. According to Breillat, Elena 'subit un viol mental. Quoi de plus honteux que de se laisser prendre à des mensonges que l'on sait faux dès le départ?'[54] (Goudet and Vassé 2001: 29). From having first imagined herself as a virginal bride-to-be, Elena is then led by Fernando's deceitful despoiling of her to feel that she has been treated like a whore, and (as noted earlier), 'Elle est tuée, car disparaît en elle ce désir d'illusions dont on a tellement besoin pour vivre'[55] (Goudet and Vassé 2001: 29).

It is on this matter of survival that the similarity between the two sisters becomes a stark contrast. While the sentimental Elena dies of disillusionment, the cynical Anaïs never believed in patriarchy's romantic lies about a perfect Prince Charming or a first time that would last forever. After the madman's sexual assault, Anaïs tells the police that she 'n'a pas été violée',[56] meaning that 'I have never been raped, because nobody can rape my mind', as Breillat has phrased it (Rich 2001). While the rapist may have invaded and degraded her body, Anaïs has preserved the dignity and integrity of her mind, emerging all the stronger for having survived such an attack. Whereas Elena was a Sleeping Beauty dreaming of eternal love only to be rudely awakened by the dashing of all her hopes, Anaïs is wide awake from the start, staring fiercely at us during the opening credits, at her attacker when he smashes in the car's windshield and then breaks her hymen, and finally again at us right before the closing credits, when she asserts that she has not been raped. In this way, Anaïs faces down patriarchal society, defying its attempt to make her overvalue her virginity and feel devastated by its loss. She was never foolish enough to idealise her maidenhood, nor will she be so stupid as to think herself a whore just because a man has abused her. Having watched her sister Elena become 'une proie ... de sa destinée de fille'[57] (Puaux 2001: 172), Anaïs refuses to play either the 'good girl' or the 'bad girl' role and chooses instead to chart her own destiny. Leaving the woods where the madman assaulted her and then turning away from the policemen who would pity and prod her with questions, Anaïs is in independent motion when we last see her. She is facing us down with that fierce look of hers, a 'regard terrible', a freeze-framed stare that 'regarde un

54 'suffers a mental rape. What is more shameful than to let yourself be taken in by lies that you know are false from the beginning?'
55 'She is killed, because what one needs so much in order to live, the desire for illusions, disappears in her'.
56 'was not raped'.
57 'a victim ... of her destiny as a girl'.

monde auquel elle n'appartient pas'[58] (Breillat 2001: 88) – a world which she must transcend in order to be herself.

Anaïs' survival *is* a triumph, but we must wonder how intact her mind can be after her body has been so brutally traumatised. Granted, forewarned is forearmed, and Anaïs has attempted to prevent profound disappointment by saying that 'je ferai jamais ça la première fois avec quelqu'un que j'aime'.[59] Lili in *36 fillette* felt much the same way, but unlike Lili who lost her virginity to a boy from a neighbouring campsite in an act of consensual sex, Anaïs is raped by a madman who has just murdered her mother and sister. Of course, we could switch ontological registers and view the ending of the film not as reality but as a dream. After all, earlier in one of her songs Anaïs had imagined her first time as being with 'un loup-garou / moi je m'en fous / pour rêver'.[60] But even if having her virginity taken by a wild-haired madman in the woods is a kind of wish fulfilment of Anaïs' werewolf fantasy, what kind of fantasy is this? Is she trying to envision the worst possible sexual experience in order to inoculate herself against the harshest reality? Is she attempting to void herself of all romantic hopes so that she will never suffer the pain of disillusionment? But we have already seen Breillat herself refer to 'ce désir d'illusions dont on a tellement besoin pour vivre'[61] (Goudet and Vassé 2001: 29). Anaïs may have no illusions, but does she have any ideals, any faith in the possibility of love, anything to live *for*? Is her fierce look in the end – her terrible face that gazes at a world to which she doesn't belong – a sign of proud independence or an indication that she is angry, alienated and profoundly lost? When Anaïs was staring fiercely into the face of the savage madman, there seemed to be a strange likeness between them, a mirroring or 'fusion de deux êtres qui haïssent le monde et veulent le faire éclater',[62] as Breillat has said (Puaux 2001: 172). We can see why Anaïs would want to distance herself from the femininity represented by her weak and sentimental sister, but what kind of answer has Anaïs really found in her strange kinship with the world-hating masculinity of a rapist and a murderer?

58 'terrible look' ... 'looks at a world to which she doesn't belong'.
59 'I'll never do it for the first time with someone I love'.
60 'a werewolf / me I don't care / just to dream'.
61 'this desire for illusions which one needs so much in order to live'.
62 'fusion of two beings who hate the world and want to make it explode'.

Sex Is Comedy

One year later, Breillat returned to the themes of female adolescence, sexuality and shame in *Sex Is Comedy*, a part-fiction, part-documentary film on the making of *A ma sœur!* Roxane Mesquida again plays the Elena role, but this time there is no Anaïs, or it could be said that the place of the younger sister is now occupied by the director, Jeanne (Anne Parillaud playing a version of Breillat). Like Anaïs, Jeanne is both an intrusive voyeur and a compassionate viewer of Elena/Mesquida, of the character's and the actress's struggle to overcome shame and express her desire. In rehearsing the scene where Fernando (played by Grégoire Colin) kisses Elena/Mesquida in the dunes, Jeanne gives voice to the vehemence of a girl's desire for lasting romance when she tells her, 'Je veux que vous vous embrassiez pendant un temps *in-ter-mi-nable!*'[63] Yet, when Jeanne then watches from behind her video monitor as their kiss is filmed, she has her scarf pulled up to just below her eyes, as if she were embarrassed by the girl's passion, barely able to witness such an indecent display, ashamed for Elena/Mesquida and for herself.

As a director, Jeanne moves the actress's body or positions her own to demonstrate the conflict felt by the girl between desire and disgrace, between inner urges and external embarrassment: 'C'est la contradiction entre le désir – bien sûr qu'elle le désire – et la conception qu'elle se fait de sa propre dignité. Ça correspond à l'image de soi de se faire sauter par un garçon?'[64] While rehearsing the film-within-a-film's sex scene (a conflation of the two bedroom encounters between Fernando and Elena in *A ma sœur!*), Jeanne shows how Elena/Mesquida, supine in bed, strikes a dreamy pose with one arm over her forehead so that she can imagine the perfect suitor ('tu rêves les yeux en l'air')[65] without having to see her actual boyfriend's naked erection. In this way, the girl attempts to preserve her ideal self-image – the image she beholds when she looks at herself through society's eyes and sees a 'vraie jeune fille' (or 'proper young lady') – from the shame that would come if she admitted her own sexual urges and thus had to view herself as a 'bad girl'. Similarly, Breillat herself fought against feeling guilty when she

63 'I want you to kiss each other for a time that is *nev-er end-ing!*'

64 'It's the contradiction between desire – she surely desires him – and the conception she forms of her own dignity. Does it fit her self-image to get herself laid by a boy?'

65 'you're dreaming with your eyes open'.

first came of age, when she felt 'très fort la honte que faisait peser sur moi le regard de la société'[66] (Breillat 2006: 33). Jeanne has Elena/ Mesquida cross her feet but then allow Fernando/Colin to open them and lie between her legs. She wants him, but her token resistance and her passivity require that he be the one responsible for acting on desire, while she maintains plausible deniability if anyone is watching (she is watching herself through the eyes of a judgemental society). She 'forgets' to take her bra off so that he must remove it;[67] she lets him stroke her breasts but then elbows him in the ribs; she twists her body around so that it is turned away from him yet pushes back her bottom until it is tight against his crotch and throws one arm around his neck to grapple him to her.

It is Jeanne who first lies on the bed and uses her own body to demonstrate for Mesquida this torso-twist and arm-grapple, this ambivalent body language expressing the conflict within the girl between dishonour and desire, and then the director stands back to watch as the actress attempts to perform it, to embody it herself. Much as the character Elena fears the disapproving eyes of society if she reveals her sexual desires, so the actress Mesquida struggles with a sense of shame over exposing herself in an intimate scene to viewers of the film. Jeanne, as the director watching this scene on a video monitor, is a stand-in for the public eye, someone whose gaze may make Mesquida feel ashamed. But Jeanne is also a sympathetic witness, a participant-observer who shares the other's embarrassment and encourages her to brazen it out, to seek her pleasure in defiance of social censure. Indeed, to dramatise the conflict between puritanism and pleasure, Jeanne must induce shame in Mesquida and then incite her to push past it to *jouissance*. 'J'ai pas le droit d'être là', Jeanne tells the actress, 'c'est une scène intime. ... Ça doit être indécent que je regarde'.[68] As the scene is being filmed, the camera's eye moves back, showing us that Elena/Mesquida's dress has been pulled up, exposing her sex, while Fernando/Colin moves behind her (as if) to enter her anally. This could be viewed as a scene of humiliation and indecency, of a 'good girl' degraded to a filthy slut. But at the nadir of Elena/

---

66 'very strongly the shame that was placed as a weight upon me by society's gaze'.

67 In *A ma sœur!*

68 'I don't have the right to be there' ... 'it's an intimate scene. ... It must be indecent that I'm watching'.

Mesquida's suffering, as she is gasping in pain, there is a cutaway to Jeanne looking on, her eyes wincing in sympathy, herself struggling for breath. Like the cutaway to Anaïs' symbiotic suffering at this very same moment in *A ma sœur!*, the shot of Jeanne's tormented face inspires us to view Elena/Mesquida's plight with compassion rather than condemnation. 'Ça doit me couper le souffle',[69] Jeanne had told Mesquida about the scene, and we are not only shocked (gasp!) by its indecency but also made to gasp for breath along with the girl, to share her suffering.

To see feelingly is to understand the desire for fulfilment that led the girl to this painfully empty encounter. With Jeanne's compassionate gaze, she approves and encourages the girl to transcend the degrading situations which may seem to be all that life has to offer. 'J'aime la pureté', says Jeanne, 'mais qui sort de la boue. Sinon c'est la niaiserie'.[70] In rehearsing this scene, Jeanne and Mesquida had hugged and embraced cheek to cheek as if they were twin sisters, and then the director had called, with ever louder entreaties, for the actress to 'Crie! Crie plus fort! Crie vraiment!'[71] Thus, after establishing a base of bodily sympathy, Jeanne prompts Mesquida to express herself *in extremis*, to push through her pain in order to affirm the cry of longing within it, a desire strong enough to live through mortifying shame. In directing this film about the making of her movies, Breillat has said:

> J'avais envie de montrer qu'un tournage, c'est le plaisir du supplice. ... quand on va au bout d'une scène intime, les acteurs prennent énormément de plaisir ainsi que tout le monde sur le plateau, même si, après, plus personne ne veut l'admettre. On est dans une société où on ne veut pas avouer son plaisir. Il faut se mortifier, dire c'est pas de ma faute, on m'a poussé à le faire. Bien sûr qu'il faut être poussé à le faire et je suis là pour ça. S'il n'y avait pas le film, je ne le ferais pas non plus, je serais comme eux, je serais mortifiée, je ne voudrais pas céder à mon plaisir, je ne voudrais pas qu'on me regarde faire certaines choses.[72] (Flach Film 2002: 8)

69 'It should make me gasp for breath'.
70 'I like purity' ... 'but the kind that rises from filth. Otherwise, it's a trifling thing'.
71 'Scream! Scream louder! Really scream!'
72 'I had wanted to show that a film shoot is the pleasure of torment. ... when you go to the end of an intimate scene, the actors take an enormous pleasure from it, as does everyone on the set, even if, afterward, no one wants to admit it. We are in a society where you don't want to acknowledge your pleasure. You

By directing Elena/Mesquida to suffer through the torment of shame in order to affirm the strength of her desire, Jeanne/Breillat also pushes herself to acknowledge and approve her own desires. In changing the gaze with which she regards the girl from one of social censure to one of sisterly sympathy, Jeanne/Breillat becomes brave enough to look at her own sexuality through less guilty eyes, to imagine herself giving in to pleasure, to see her own desiring body as 'un corps amoureux dans lequel il n'y a pas d'obscénités parce qu'il n'y a plus de visions obscènes'[73] (Breillat 2006: 35). In speaking about her filming of the female body, Breillat has said, 'La représenter au cinéma – à condition de réussir sa scène – c'est montrer que rien n'est obscène ... Car c'est le regard qui est obscène et non pas ce qui est montré' (Clouzot 2004: 172).[74] As Mesquida comes to the end of her painfully/pleasurably intimate scene, Jeanne tells her, 'c'était magnifique!'[75] Jeanne leaves the video monitor to sit on the bed with the girl, holding her from behind, their arms enfolded, their faces nestled side by side. Both of them are gasping and teary-eyed, and then both of them, for a moment, break into a smile. Twinned in sympathy with her heroine, the director experiences the actress's agonising triumph as her own. In the last we see of Jeanne, her head is slightly down, yet her eyes look up and out. Her gaze is strong and unrepentant, like the freeze-framed look of defiance on the faces of Alice, Lili and Anaïs at the end of their films. Perhaps what the director sees, with and for her girls, is an end to shame, a willingness to watch them – and to see herself – doing 'certain things'.

In this fictionalised 'making of', Breillat not only examines what it means for a female director to look at her lead actress in an intimate scene, she also considers the dynamic of a female director's gaze

---

have to mortify yourself, to say it's not my fault, they pushed me into doing it. Certainly, you have to be pushed into doing it and I am there for that. If there wasn't the film, I wouldn't do it either, I would be like them, I would be mortified, I wouldn't want to give in to my pleasure, I wouldn't want people to watch me doing certain things'.

73 'an amorous body in which there are no obscenities because there are no longer any obscene sights/ways of seeing'.

74 'To represent her on screen – provided that her scene succeeds – is to show that nothing is obscene ... Because it's the gaze that is obscene and not what is shown'.

75 'that was magnificent!'

upon her male star. Given that even today only 3% of directors worldwide are women, this female gaze is still quite a reversal of the norm. More usually – and this is especially visible in metacinematic movies – the auteur is male and the female star is the object of his gaze and often of his desire. As Ginette Vincendeau has noted, 'In most films about film-making the imbalance in male-female power relations is conflated with seduction, a point often echoed in a parallel set of actual seductions, typically between director and female star' (Vincendeau 2003: 22). Sometimes the writer, producer or lead actor is a proxy for the director and his auteurial gaze at and amorous pursuit of the actress. During the shooting of *La Nuit américaine* (*Day for Night*) (1973), director François Truffaut had an affair with the film's star Jacqueline Bisset, while within the diegesis, the lead actor played by Jean-Pierre Léaud – Truffaut's alter ego – sleeps with the actress played by Bisset. In Bernardo Bertolucci's *Last Tango in Paris*, Léaud plays a director who is constantly pointing the camera's eye at Maria Schneider, his star and fiancée. Director Federico Fellini's eye in *8½* (1963) is represented by Marcello Mastroianni as an auteur who seems to covet all his actresses, while it is the characters playing the writer (Michel Piccoli) and the producer (Jack Palance) who desire the character played by Brigitte Bardot in *Le Mépris* (*Contempt*) (1963), a film directed by Jean-Luc Godard, himself married to Anna Karina, the lead actress in many of his films.

However, as Breillat shows in her self-reflexive film, when the roles are reversed and the directorial eye is female, there is often sedition rather than seduction as the male star revolts against being the object of the gaze. This is particularly true in the case of an intimate scene. In many movies by male directors, actresses undress for the camera while actors are allowed to remain clothed, but in Breillat's films the actor is often required to disrobe – even to the point of revealing what customarily remains securely under cover in mainstream cinema: the male sex organ. When the phallus, whose mystique depends on its remaining veiled, is exposed as a mere penis, the result can be a severe blow to an actor's machismo.

Jeanne – the director of Breillat's film-within-a-film, *Scènes intimes* – notes that even though her actor Colin would do nude scenes for male directors, he balks at undressing for her, presumably because he doesn't trust a female director to magnify his masculinity. To fortify him, Jeanne allows Colin to choose a large prosthetic penis to cover and aggrandise his real one, but this attempt at reassurance itself proves problematic. To be fitted with the fake phallus, Colin must endure being touched by the prop man (named Willy) who discovers that, because the actor's penis is bent, the prosthesis tends to droop. Of course, Colin must also reckon with the fact that one reason he is being given an artificial erection is that he cannot be trusted to 'stand up' on cue. For an actor who doesn't even want to take his socks off in front of the camera, showing his sex organ (augmented or not) is way too much exposure, and Colin attempts to remind Jeanne that her script had him wearing undershorts from which his erection protruded but was only visible as a shadow on the wall. When she tells him that these euphemisms were for nervous producers and that in fact his sex will be clearly seen, he begins to waggle his prosthesis in front of the male crew, controlling his exposure by becoming an exhibitionist, covering up his embarrassment by engaging in boastful ribaldry. But being the one to-be-looked-at rather than the one who looks is ultimately terrifying for the actor, who has a nightmare about the loss of humanity that comes from being reduced to a sex object: while his prosthesis has grown huge, he has shrunk to nothing; it is like a vampire sucking his blood or like a stake through him. This fear of being the objectified sex is apparent in the scene where both Jeanne and the actress Mesquida look and laugh at Colin as he sits in his underwear across from them, covering his genitals with one hand and then with crossed legs while defensively smoking a phallic cigarette.

Jeanne's mocking gaze is a turning of the tables against the macho male, a way of exposing his sex to the same scrutiny and ridicule that women have had to endure. But this mockery is more benign than malicious, a comical cutting of a man down to size rather than a castration. In the film's brief coda, for example, Colin, now wearing a sweater and jeans, does a complete 'male model' turn in front of Jeanne. It is a facetious but also aggressive flaunting of his body before her gaze, especially if, as may be the case (the camera does not frame him below the waist), he opens his fly when his back is turned and exposes himself to her when he turns around. But Jeanne, who has just finished eating a banana and is searching for a place to put the skin, smiles and looks down at his front. Jeanne's gaze here is aggressive (devouring), facetious (his penis is but a banana) and possibly desirous (fellatio). As she explained earlier about why she cast Colin, 'Je filme toujours des machos. ... Je crois qu'on ne peut aimer que les hommes qu'on déteste en fait. L'antagonisme, c'est la forme la plus vivifiante du désir. Mais le désir c'est une qualité humaine' – not a matter of mere 'consommation'.[76] The goal of Jeanne's female gaze is not to reduce the macho man to a sex object for her consumption, the way one might devour a banana – even though women have often been eyed by men as fruit for the picking. Rather, Jeanne's ultimate goal is to see beyond male sexual aggression, to break through machismo and reach the human underneath, to playfully antagonise the other until he becomes worthy of her desire.

The role reversal in which a female director looks at a male star is thus much more than a vengeful turning of the tables. It is an attempt to deconstruct the socially inscribed difference between the sexes whereby the man gazes lasciviously and the woman is objec-tified, whereby the man is aggressively active and the woman is mostly passive and compliant. We have seen that Jeanne positions herself in bed to demonstrate how Elena/Mesquida is to lie there while Fernando/Colin makes sexual advances, but Jeanne also has her assistant Léo occupy the girl's supine position ('tu fais la fille') while Jeanne herself acts the part of the lustful male ('moi je fais le garçon').[77] This exchange denaturalises the 'active male' and 'passive female' roles to show that they are indeed roles, with either sex able to play both parts, desiring and desired. When Jeanne, as 'the boy', looks longingly into Léo's eyes and fondles his breast as he plays 'the girl' in bed, he feels the same discomfort as Colin at being the object of the female gaze. 'Faut être une fille pour être un acteur',[78] Jeanne had told Léo earlier (with the camera showing us Léo's – or the actor playing Léo's – nervously smiling face), and now in rehearsing the bedroom scene under Jeanne's amorous gaze, Léo cracks defensive jokes about the size of his erection while holding on to a cigarette. And yet as we look upon Léo's delicate facial features and long blond hair, he seems to have as much 'girl' in him as 'boy', and his smiles may betray a sneaking enjoyment at being 'forced' by Jeanne to play up his feminine side. In Breillat's view, 'L'humanité dans son entier ... devrait être beaucoup plus androgyne. En fait, on ne devrait pas être

---

76 'I always film machos. ... I believe that we can love only the men that we hate, in fact. Antagonism is the most invigorating form of desire. But desire is a human quality' ... 'consumption'.

77 'you be the girl' ... 'me, I'll be the boy'.

78 'You have to be a girl to be an actor'.

beaucoup moins mâle et femelle mais beaucoup moins mammifères, beaucoup moins régis par la loi du plus fort, qui implique que l'on doit aussi se montrer le plus fort dans son désir dans un premier temps. Les femmes peuvent avoir le désir de conquérir ces hommes qui sont plus féminins sans que cela les rende moins forts, sexuellement et intellectuellement'[79] (Breillat 2006: 54). When Léo plays 'the girl', he appears as a kind of masculine/feminine double exposure, and when Jeanne directs Léo to switch roles from 'boy' to 'girl' and back to 'boy' again, he is in a sense between genders, macho and femme by turns. Colin, too, alternates between playing the dominant male in relation to Elena/Mesquida and appearing as the feminised object of Jeanne's directorial gaze, and like Léo, Colin is a composite image of braggadocio and shrinking violet, of his huge (fake) phallus and his (equally ridiculous) fears of emasculation. Thus, by mocking certain gender roles and by revealing that these are indeed performances or role-plays, Jeanne/Breillat shows that sex is comedy. She frees us to exchange, alternate between, or combine roles so that we are no longer bound by the social script.

References

Andersen, Hans Christian (1980), 'The Little Mermaid' [1837], *Tales and Stories*, trans. Patricia L. Conroy and Sven H. Rossel, Seattle and London, University of Washington Press, pp. 34–58.

Anon. (1983), 'Catherine et Marie-Hélène Breillat sont passées du duel au duo', *Elle*, January.

Argand, Catherine (2002), 'Le Livre de leur enfance', *Lire*, July/August.

Beauvoir, Simone de (1958), *Mémoires d'une jeune fille rangée*, Paris, Gallimard.

Beauvoir, Simone de (1959), *Memoirs of a Dutiful Daughter*, trans. James Kirkup, Cleveland and New York, World Publishing.

Berlant, Lauren (2002), 'Two Girls, Fat and Thin', in Stephen M. Barber and David L. Clark (eds), *Regarding Sedgwick: Essays on Queer Culture and Critical Theory*, New York and London, Routledge, pp. 71–108.

Bonnaud, Frédéric (2001), 'First Look: *A ma sœur!*', *Film Comment* 37:2, 14–15.

79 'Humanity as a whole should be a lot more androgynous. In fact, we shouldn't be a lot less male and female but a lot less mammal, a lot less ruled by the law of the strongest, which implies that one must show oneself to be the strongest in one's desire in the first place. Women can have the desire to conquer these men who are more feminine without that making the men less strong, sexually and intellectually'.

Bordo, Susan (2003), *Unbearable Weight: Feminism, Western Culture, and the Body*, Berkeley and London, University of California Press.

Breillat, Catherine (2001), *A ma sœur!: Scénario*, Paris, Cahiers du cinéma.

Breillat, Catherine (2006), *Corps amoureux: Entretiens avec Claire Vassé*, Paris, Denoël.

Breillat, Marie-Hélène (1986), *L'Objet de l'amour*, Paris, Plon.

Clément, Jérôme (2002), 'Catherine Breillat', *Les Femmes et l'amour*, Paris, Stock, pp. 267–300.

Clouzot, Claire (2004), *Catherine Breillat: Indécence et pureté*, Paris, Cahiers du cinéma.

Criterion (2004), Interviews with Breillat on video supplements and in booklet insert, *Fat Girl* DVD, Criterion Collection.

Flach Film (2002), Dossier de presse: *Sex Is Comedy*, Paris, Flach Film.

Godard, Agathe (1971), 'Les Jumelles Breillat', *20 ans* 109, September.

Goudet, Stéphane and Vassé, Claire (2001), 'Une âme à deux corps', *Positif* 481, 26–30.

Holtzman, Deanna and Kulish, Nancy (1997), *Nevermore: The Hymen and the Loss of Virginity*, Northvale and London, Jason Aronson.

Hughes, Alex and Reader, Keith (eds) (1998), *Encyclopedia of Contemporary French Culture*, London, Routledge.

Knafo, Danielle (1996), 'Dressing Up and Other Games of Make-Believe: The Function of Play in the Art of Cindy Sherman', *American Imago* 53:2, 139–64.

Krauss, Rosalind (1993), *Cindy Sherman: 1975–1993*, New York, Rizzoli.

Mitchell, Juliet (2003), *Siblings: Sex and Violence*, Cambridge, Polity Press.

Mulvey, Laura (1996), 'Cosmetics and Abjection: Cindy Sherman 1977–87', *Fetishism and Curiosity*, London, British Film Institute, pp. 65–76.

Puaux, Françoise (2001), 'Entretien avec Catherine Breillat', *Le Machisme à l'écran*, *CinémAction* 99, 165–72.

Rich, B. Ruby (2001), 'End of Innocence', *Filmmaker*, Fall.

Vincendeau, Ginette (2001), 'Sisters, Sex and Sitcom', *Sight and Sound* 11:12, 18–20.

Vincendeau, Ginette (2003), 'What She Wants', *Sight and Sound* 13:5, 20–2.

1 *Une vraie jeune fille* (1976) Charlotte Alexandra (Alice)

2 *Tapage nocturne* (1979) Dominique Laffin (Solange), Daniel Langlet (Bruel)

3 *36 fillette* (1987) Delphine Zentout (Lili)

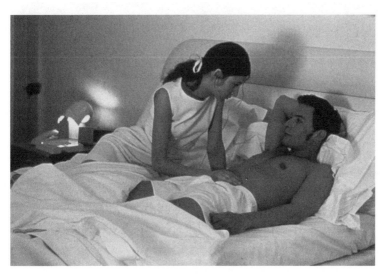

4 *Romance* (1999) Caroline Ducey (Marie), Sagamore Stévenin (Paul)

5 *Romance* (1999) François Berléand (Robert), Caroline Ducey (Marie)

6 *A ma sœur!* (*Fat Girl*) (2001) Anaïs Reboux (Anaïs)

7 *A ma sœur!* (*Fat Girl*) (2001) Anaïs Reboux (Anaïs), Roxane Mesquida (Elena)

8 *Sex Is Comedy* (2002) Grégoire Colin (l'acteur), Roxane Mesquida (l'actrice)

9 *Une vieille maîtresse* (2007) Asia Argento (Vellini)

10 Catherine Breillat

3

Masculine tenderness and macho violence

Sale comme un ange (Dirty Like an Angel)

Colin and Léo in *Sex Is Comedy* are not Breillat's first explorations of male gender identity, and we now turn to a consideration of three earlier films (*Sale comme un ange, Parfait amour!* and *Brève traversée*) in which men's interaction with strong women is less comedic than dire, throwing masculinity into crisis. The story behind the making of *Sale comme un ange* actually begins seven years earlier. Envying the popularity of 'polars' or 'police films' (such crime dramas accounted for 25% of all French films produced in the 1980s), director Maurice Pialat determined to make one himself, which would become *Police* (1985). He first engaged Breillat to write the portion of the script having to do with a drug dealer's girlfriend and her sexual relationship with a police detective, which Breillat wrote based in part on actual letters by a criminal's moll. Then the director asked Breillat to script the cops-and-crooks storyline as well, for which she did research by spending nights with the hardened detectives of the Territorial Brigade and riding with them on stake-outs and drug busts in the criminal underworld of Belleville, Paris. To enter the mindset of her tough-guy police protagonist, Breillat also wrote a first-person novel from his point of view. When Pialat attempted to claim more screenwriting credit than Breillat felt was his due and to block publication of her novel (which would prove the size of her contribution to the screenplay), Breillat had to take back the typescript of her novel from his house (prompting charges that she had 'stolen' it) and then to battle him in court (she won: her novel was published and she received primary screenwriting credit on the film). Despite these tensions, Breillat and Pialat later reconciled, and she has always made a point of acknowledging that, though the original script was largely hers, *Police* is undoubtedly *his* film, represented by numerous changes made to the script during shooting and by the fact that *he* directed it: 'L'auteur du film pour moi est le seul qui compte. ... Maurice a mis dans *Police* quelque chose que je ne sais pas faire. ... toute la partie policière est formidable. ... C'est vrai qu'il y a un côté "film d'homme"'[1] (Breillat 2003: 43–4).

Although the distinction may at first seem overly pat, it can be revealing to consider Pialat's *Police* as predominantly a 'film d'homme' ('man's film') and Breillat's *Sale comme un ange* as more of a 'film de femme' (or 'woman's film'). Breillat herself has sometimes stated this difference rather starkly, asserting that 'Dans *Sale comme un ange*, il y a le désir, alors que lui [Pialat in *Police*] s'intéresse aux dealers, à la drogue, à une pute et à un commissaire qui cogne'[2] (Clouzot 2004: 174). While sexual desire in Breillat's film tends to move the man and woman not only toward each other but toward another way of being that is beyond prescriptive gender roles, the sparks that fly between the violent cop and his shady lady in Pialat's film tend to polarise the genders in stereotypical opposition to each other. One reason for this may be that, underlying its surface style of documentary realism, *Police* is actually a genre film of the most conventional kind – a film noir with a tough guy who falls for a *femme fatale*. In what follows, I give a somewhat detailed analysis of *Police* as a 'film d'homme' to set the stage for my contrasting discussion of *Sale comme un ange* as a 'film de femme'.

All the critics agree that Noria (the drug dealer's girlfriend in *Police*) is 'characterised misogynistically as a *femme fatale*' (Austin 1996: 117). She is 'stereotypically enigmatic' (Powrie 1997: 97) and 'manipulative and unfeeling' (Warehime 2006: 123) – one of those 'belles garces fatalistes qui font tourner la tête des hommes'[3] (Toubiana 1985). Noria lies, steals and seduces one man after another, jeopardising male friendships and lives. When detective Mangin interrogates her about her complicity in drug trafficking, the camera (representing his point

1 'For me, the film's auteur is the only one who counts. ... Maurice put something into *Police* that I don't know how to do. ... the whole part about the police is great. ... It's true that there is a "man's film" aspect to it'.

2 'In *Sale comme un ange*, there is desire, whereas he [Pialat in *Police*] is interested in dealers, drugs, a whore and a chief cop who beats up people'.

3 'beautiful fatalistic bitches who turn men's heads'.

of view) examines her face but it remains an inscrutable mask, except for the tears that may be designed to manipulate him. Later in his apartment when he examines her to find out whether she stole drugs and money, her expression is veiled by the hair partly covering her face and by her turning to offer only a side view of herself. We as viewers actually witnessed Noria commit the theft in an earlier scene, so when she denies it to Mangin, we know that her face masks a lie. 'Elle ment comme on respire',[4] as Mangin's lawyer friend Lambert warns him about Noria. Lambert should know: after Noria and her boyfriend are arrested, she betrays her lover and sleeps with Lambert so that he will get her out of jail, then she jilts Lambert and sleeps with Mangin, whose protection she needs from the drug dealers who (rightly) suspect that she stole from them. Her theft also causes suspicion to fall on her brother, whom they torture with electric wires, and on Lambert whom they threaten to shoot. Noria compromises the cop Mangin who, in protecting her, is harbouring a criminal and who, by eventually returning the stolen booty to the crooks in order to save her from their wrath, ends up embroiled in criminal activities himself. 'Elle partage la mentalité de son milieu', muses Mangin about Noria in the novel, 'Et son milieu est LE MILIEU, voilà!'[5] (Breillat 1985: 207). Coded as dangerously 'other', Noria's femininity is associated with foreignness and illegality: she wears an Islamic charm (the Hand of Fatima) around her neck, and her Arab name 'Noria' is an alias given to her by her boyfriend, who belongs to a Tunisian crime family. No man can tell who or what she really is. Exotic and erotic, she is also inscrutable and inaccessible. 'T'es comme une tour fermée', Mangin tells her, 'y'a rien qui peut t'entamer, rien'.[6]

Interestingly, Pialat himself used the same expression – a 'tour fermée' or 'closed tower' (Pialat 1985: 10) – when referring to Sophie Marceau, the actress playing Noria, a fact that suggests the extent to which the director identified with his male character's point of view toward the woman in the film. Right after Mangin has saved Noria's life by returning what she stole, she tells him (with her face half in shadow) that she is leaving him, and we follow the brokenhearted

4 'For her, lying is like breathing'.
5 'She shares the mentality of her world' ... 'And her world is THE UNDER-WORLD, so there!'
6 'You're like a closed tower' ... 'there's nothing that can break through to you, nothing'.

man as he walks off into the night, accompanied by the immensely sorrowful strains of Górecki's Symphony No. 3. The last shot in the film is of Mangin's face after he has returned alone to his apartment. Sitting on the edge of his bed with his shirt half unbuttoned, he looks up, his eyes vulnerable and pleading, then down as he shakes his head. Finally, he stares out at us in a freeze-framed expression of pain and devastation. We are clearly meant to identify with him as the victim of Noria, the tough guy seduced and abandoned by a *femme fatale*: 'cette fille est faite pour mener tous les hommes en bateau', he thinks in the novel, 'Pas moyen de résister'[7] (Breillat 1985: 47). And yet, as Breillat has pointed out, 'Faire de la femme la tentation, la diabolise. Ainsi le prédateur s'absout-il, se constituant comme victime de sa proie', whereas 'Il est celui qui cède à la tentation'[8] (Breillat 1999: 12) – it is he who gives in *to his own desire and dread* regarding woman. The 'mythe de la *femme fatale*' thus says more about the men who fabricated it than it does about any actual woman; the *femme fatale* 'n'est pas la vérité de la femme, mais elle est la vérité du fantasme. ... Elle n'est que le regard masculin, regard du désir et de la peur d'une incommunicabilité inavouée'[9] (Breillat 1999: 12–13).

In Pialat's film, there is little communication between the sexes in terms of mutual understanding or sharing of gender traits. Just as Noria remains mired in the role of the *femme fatale* regarded with suspicion by the male gaze, so Mangin is stuck in the part of the macho cop whose fear of the feminine taints any potential love with a desire to dominate. As Elisabeth Badinter has noted, 'L'identité masculine est associée au fait de posséder, prendre, pénétrer, dominer et s'affirmer, si nécessaire, par la force. L'identité féminine, au fait d'être possédée, docile, passive, soumise. "Normalité" et identité sexuelles sont inscrites dans le contexte de la domination de la femme par l'homme'[10] (Badinter 1992: 147). When Marie, a police commissioner

7 'this girl was made to take all men for a ride' ... 'No way to resist'.
8 'To make the woman out to be the cause of temptation demonises her. In this way the predator absolves himself, constituting himself as the victim of his prey' ... 'He is the one who surrenders to temptation'.
9 'myth of the *femme fatale*' ... 'is not the truth about woman, but she is the truth about fantasy. ... She is only the masculine gaze, a gaze of desire and fear coming from an unacknowledged inability to communicate'.
10 'Masculine identity is associated with the fact of possessing, taking, penetrating, dominating, and asserting oneself, if necessary, by force. Feminine identity is associated with the fact of being possessed, docile, passive, submissive. Sexual

in training, is assigned to ride with him, Mangin feels threatened by a woman who is about to outrank him. His attempts to reassert phallic dominance include putting his hand between her legs in the car and suggesting she hold his male organ for him while he uses the lavatory. He also tries to cut Marie down to size by belittling other women in her presence (he refers to another policewoman as 'LSD – elle suce debout')[11] and by suggesting to a pimp that Marie would make a good prostitute. Unable to conquer Marie, Mangin does take a prostitute home with him. When this call girl Lydie refers to him as a 'poulet' (slang for 'cop' but a word that policemen don't tend to like; it also means 'chicken' and is uncomfortably close to 'poule', which is slang for 'prostitute'), Mangin begins to strut about like a cock as if in defiant assertion of his masculinity. Then, as Lydie strips and takes a shower (with Mangin and the camera ogling her nakedness), the gun he removes from the holster at his waist while undressing suggests that dominance and desire are connected in his mind.

The scenes between Mangin and Noria show that for him the exertion of power over her is eroticised and that his sexual relations with her are tinged with violence. Mangin's first encounter with Noria is when he goes to arrest her. Coming up behind her as she is standing in a café, he presses his body against hers while whispering in her ear, 'Police. Bouge pas'.[12] Back at the station he orders her strip-searched and then he interrogates her, standing over and circling around her as she is seated in a chair, probing for a response from her, trying to force her to confess a weakness (for him). When she resists, he roughs her up and slaps her face to get her to give in. Mangin's lust is fuelled not only by the exercise of power over her but also by the assertion of dominance over other men. He doesn't just want to *take* her; he wants to take her *from them*. After having grabbed Noria at the café, Mangin forces her to go with him while he arrests her drug dealer boyfriend Simon. As Mangin and Noria stand outside the apartment, a tight shot frames her waist right next to the gun Mangin is holding and the key he is using to open Simon's door. Once inside, Mangin holds his big gun to Simon's head and rousts him out of bed – the bed Simon had shared with Noria. Later in the film, when Mangin suspects her

---

"normality" and identity are inscribed within the context of the domination of a
woman by a man' (Badinter 1995: 97).

11 'LSD – she sucks standing up'.

12 'Police. Don't move'.

of having slept with Simon's brothers as well, he bends her backwards over a desk in the police station at night in order to make her his and his alone. Noria's expression of concern over hurting Simon (with her infidelity to him) serves only to inflame Mangin's jealous desire and to increase the violence of his 'lovemaking'. Similarly, after Mangin grills Noria in the car about whether she has slept with his best friend Lambert, Mangin begins to grope and maul her, demanding that she kiss *him*. Earlier, the homosocial bonding between Mangin and Lambert had included an arrangement whereby Mangin arrested Lydie's pimp so that Lambert could sleep with Lydie, and the friends' rivalry had included Mangin's then sleeping with Lydie as well. Now, with Noria's boyfriend having been arrested and Lambert having slept with Noria, Mangin is laying claim to his 'share' of Noria. In this male bonding/rivalry, Noria sometimes seems to be merely an object of exchange and competition between men.

Although Noria looks to Mangin's love for protection against the men in the crime family who first want to prostitute her (so that she will make money for them) and then to kill her (for having stolen from them), he too treats her like a sex object and is violently possessive of her. In their last scene together in the car, after Mangin has returned what she stole to the crime family and Noria has told him she is leaving him, he says that they still won't let her go, just as earlier he had said they would shoot her for lying. It's not at all clear how different Mangin (the cop) is from these men (the crooks), whether Mangin would love to save her or is threatening to come after her himself. As he muses in the novel, 'si eux veulent la tuer, moi, c'est seulement la sauter. Et … on peut très bien confondre ce genre d'envie avec l'amour. Ou vice versa'[13] (Breillat 1985: 202). It never seems to occur to Mangin that Noria is leaving him *because* he is so possessive, that she eludes his grasp (his understanding, his control, his sexual domination) in order to avoid being manhandled. 'Vous êtes intimidante', he had accused her earlier, 'on sait pas comment vous prendre', to which she replied, 'c'est que j'aime pas qu'on me prenne'.[14] The more domineering Mangin is in his role as macho cop, the more deceptive and elusive Noria becomes in her role as *femme fatale*, for

13 'if they want to kill her, with me, it's only to screw her. And … one can very easily confuse this kind of want with love. Or vice versa'.
14 'You're intimidating' … 'one doesn't know how to handle you' … 'that's because I don't like to be handled'.

the two roles interact in a polarising fashion, pushing the genders apart into diametrically opposed stereotypes.

In Breillat's version of the story, the male and female characters face off according to the same gender stereotypes, but desire tends to deconstruct the opposition between them to a greater extent than is the case in Pialat's film. In this sense, *Sale comme un ange* could be seen as a feminist revision of Pialat's polar, as a 'woman's film' that challenges the stark division between tough guy and *femme fatale* as these roles are usually portrayed in patriarchal film noir. To begin with, there is more 'feminine' vulnerability in Breillat's macho cop Deblache than there is in Mangin. *Police* opens with a point-of-view shot from Mangin's perspective as he makes a male suspect squirm under interrogation, followed by a reverse angle on Mangin that shows him slamming his fist down on a table. By contrast, Breillat's film begins with Deblache being awakened in bed by his alarm clock and clumsily trying to turn it off, then standing shirtless before the bathroom mirror as he brushes his teeth. Deblache is thus as much object as he is subject of the gaze, and he is first shown fumbling about in a domestic environment rather than performing as a man of action in the police station. Mangin is played by Gérard Depardieu with his star power, strapping physique and boyish looks, whereas Claude Brasseur as the fifty-something Deblache has sagging jowls, a balding head and a smaller stature. The aging Deblache now needs to try harder to be a tough guy – and more frequently fails. Mangin is a heavy drinker, but Deblache is clearly an alcoholic rarely seen without a glass of liquor in his hand. In an early scene, he pours himself a pastis and drinks it undiluted by water; we next see him flat on his back on a stretcher being wheeled into a hospital emergency room – whether due to the alcohol, cancer or some other disease, we do not know. Deblache is both more demonstrative and more desperate than Mangin in his macho posturing. With his gun in a holster at his hip, Deblache presses up against a belly dancer, claiming her right in front of the Arab men in their bar. Like Mangin, Deblache takes a prostitute home with him, but we don't get to see him ogle her naked body before sex as Pialat allowed Mangin to do. Rather, Breillat cuts directly to the morning after to show us the prostitute resisting Deblache's attempt to make any further sexual advances.

More than anything else, it is Deblache's amorous interactions with Barbara – the 'Noria' character in Breillat's film – that break through his machismo and enable him to access his 'feminine' vulnerability and tenderness. When Deblache shows Barbara the guns that he keeps in his bedroom, she seems less excited by this display of virility than saddened by it, remarking that gun collections, like collections of women, are a sign of loneliness. Barbara's comment suggests that, if he objectifies her sex by reducing her to just another prostitute for him to possess, then he will also be objectifying his own sex, reducing himself to a 'gun' that 'shoots' and cutting himself off from the rest of his humanity. Deblache has already witnessed this reifying tendency in Théron, a younger cop who is his partner and best friend on the force and who is also Barbara's husband. Early in the film, Deblache rides on the back of Théron's motorbike as the man makes two stops, first to bed a prostitute in a basement brothel and then to meet his wife Barbara, whom he looks up to as she stands on a hotel balcony. Théron has a worshipful attitude toward his new wife, who is a blushing bride and proper young lady from the provinces, while the brazen city women he sees for sex are whores: 'Il y a ma femme et il y a les autres. Ma femme, c'est le sacré. ... Elle était vierge'.[15] Deblache seems troubled by Théron's behaviour. Perhaps he is jealous that this younger man is getting all the women and the best of both worlds (bachelorhood and marriage), but Théron's infidelity also seems to disturb Deblache, which suggests a potential on the part of this older macho cop to sympathise with how Barbara might feel. Deblache may also be starting to sense the inhumanity of Théron's tendency to reify and split women into Madonnas and whores. Later in the film, Théron, who has been performing twenty-four-hour guard duty away from his wife and home, has Barbara brought to him in order to relieve his sexual needs, thus in a way flipping her from Madonna to whore. Afterward, Deblache shares Barbara's outrage at having been treated like a prostitute by her own husband, and when she later cries after consenting to sex with Deblache, feeling that she has in a sense prostituted herself by going with him (a man who is not her husband), Deblache is compassionate, moving quickly to comfort her with the assurance that what they feel for each other is love.

As neither 'the good wife' nor a prostitute, Barbara is *between roles* when she is with Deblache, and he in turn finds that his usual bearings

15 'There's my wife and then there are the others. My wife, that's sacred. ... She was a virgin'.

as a macho man are being disoriented and redefined in relation to this new kind of woman. The cop once known as 'le misogyne le plus maximum de la division'[16] now finds himself wiping away a woman's tears, remarking upon his newfound tenderness for Barbara that 'je sais plus où je suis'.[17] Deblache's feelings for a woman also make him uncharacteristically vulnerable to her, as he discovers to his dismay when Barbara rejects his proposal that she divorce in order to marry him. Sinking down the side of a club chair in which she is sitting, Deblache is too shaken even to take a cigarette from his pack. He says how old he feels, and an angle-down shot reveals his gray hair and bald spot. Opening himself up to her has made him susceptible to the reopening of old wounds, for (what he sees as) Barbara's rejection of him in favour of the younger Théron reminds him that 'Quand j'étais petit, ma mère me trouvait très laid. Elle m'aimait pas. Et il y avait un petit frère qui était très beau'.[18] A boy dependent on his mother, an old man hostage to his failing body – these are 'soft' sides of masculinity normally repressed by machismo, 'sentimental' aspects opened up in the chain-smoking, gun-toting, woman-collecting Deblache by his unexpected love affair with Barbara. And even as he protests these newfound feelings as a wound to his masculine pride – 'Je peux quoi faire devant toi? Je me trouve con. Je m'attendris. Tout ce que je déteste. Je finirai par pleurer sur mon sort'[19] – there is a certain ecstasy of expression in Deblache, a painful joy in being able to admit that he can be touched, even if it's to the quick.

If desire moves Deblache toward a greater departure from the macho cop role than is the case for *Police*'s Mangin, Barbara too finds the amorous inspiration to move between and evolve beyond feminine stereotypes, including that of the *femme fatale*, a role in which Pialat's Noria remains mostly trapped. As Breillat describes Barbara's permutation and passage through a variety of feminine roles, 'Au début elle doit être une petite pimbêche pas très intéressante qui, quand elle rencontre le regard de Brasseur [Deblache], devient une espèce de femme-enfant, à la fois complètement perverse et innocente,

16 'the absolute biggest misogynist on the force'.
17 'I no longer know where I am'.
18 'When I was little, my mother found me very ugly. She didn't love me. And there was a little brother who was very handsome'.
19 'What can I do when I'm in front of you? I find myself stupid, weak. I grow tender. Everything that I hate. I will end up crying over my fate'.

pour devenir une femme magnifique quand elle connaît le désir'[20] (Katsahnias 1991: 75). Théron married Barbara as a virgin from the provinces and then cloistered her in a gated house near an observatory, like a princess in a tower. He seems to worship her as the perfect wife while turning his sexual attentions to prostitutes. In the beginning, Barbara draws her sense of identity and value from her husband's view of her as a proper young wife, and she resists Deblache's advances as an affront to her dignity. When he comes to see her at her house, she acts like a 'petite pimbêche' around Deblache, exaggeratedly prim and proper, not wanting him to see her casually dressed or without make-up, 'négligée' or 'affreuse'.[21] And yet her very protests indicate that she feels his eyes upon her, eyes more desiring than worshipful like her husband's. When she declines to take a walk in the rain with Deblache, saying weakly 'c'est gênant',[22] she seems to sense that more is involved than getting a bit dishevelled or a little wet (we recall that water is often a sexual symbol for Breillat). Gradually, almost imperceptibly, the proudly defiant 'bonne petite ménagère' (as Deblache calls her) becomes seductive in her very propriety, asking him, 'Vous avez vu mon canapé? Comment vous le trouvez?'[23] Barbara's question is consciously meant to distract Deblache from making advances on her person, but unconsciously it invites him to make love to her. (She showed a similar ambivalence in an earlier scene when, after first balking at his attempts to kiss her in the car, she then leaned over – in meaningful close-up – to kiss him, while demurely insisting that it was just a kiss between friends.) Deblache thus has reason to believe that Barbara is running hot beneath her cold exterior, so when she serves him a drink on the sofa and then asks him (politely? suggestively?), 'vous voulez des glaçons?' he replies, 'c'est vous que je veux'.[24] Soon after, as Deblache and Barbara are standing in her foyer with its pebbled-glass doors and blue walls, his eyes and hands are all over her in an attempt to melt this ice princess, who is wearing a red dress under her blue raincoat. Later as he is leaving her house, he shows the

20 'In the beginning she has to be a stuck-up little madame, not very interesting, who, when she meets Brasseur's [Deblache's] gaze, becomes a kind of woman-child, at once completely perverse and innocent, in order to become a magnificent woman when she knows desire'.

21 'stuck-up little madame' ... 'unkempt' ... 'frightful'.

22 'it's annoying'.

23 'good little housewife' ... 'Have you seen my sofa? How do you like it?'

24 'do you want ice?' ... 'it's you that I want'.

strength of his desire by moving her up against a wall, with his black leather jacket pressed against her fluffy pink bathrobe. Deblache's aggressive advances may be stereotypically macho, but he succeeds in breaking through Barbara's ladylike hauteur and in bringing out the woman inside the virginal bride. The pink-clad Barbara now seems more coy than innocent when, even as she is pushing Deblache out the door, she calls him 'tu' instead of 'vous', seductively inviting the intimacy she appears to be refusing.

Barbara has moved from 'good little housewife' toward naughty seductress, her child-bride innocence 'perverted' to sexual pleasure. Having once regarded herself as a proper young lady in accord with her husband's view of her, she now sees herself at least in part through Deblache's eyes as the object of his desire. As he tells her, from the moment he first saw her he knew she was 'une Anglaise' – his word for a woman who may appear closed or indifferent but who has 'le cul dans les yeux'.[25] To some extent, Barbara has become the male sexual fantasies he beholds when he looks at her – the frigid woman who melts for him, the erotic child-bride, the seductively adulterous wife. When she goes to his apartment, Barbara engages in a flamboyant tease as tango music plays on the soundtrack. She backs away from Deblache but as a way of leading him to the bedroom. Her head is demurely lowered while her eyes gaze brazenly up at his. She is properly attired, even wearing gloves, but has one hand held up to her mouth as if she were going to strip the glove off with her teeth. Barbara's act recalls the 'glove striptease' performed by Gilda, the *femme fatale* in the 1946 film noir that bears her name. Has Barbara simply gone from virginal bride to *femme fatale*? Has she been freed from her husband's view of her as a Madonna only to be trapped as the sex object of Deblache's gaze? Breillat's comment about Gilda is telling: 'Quand on regarde Rita Hayworth dans *Gilda*, il y a un orgueil et une douleur d'être un objet, de se prêter au mythe et au fantasme érotique. Elle en est à la fois la victime et la souveraine'[26] (Rouyer and Vassé 2004: 36). While Barbara is objectified in the male-defined and hypersexualised role of the *femme fatale*, she also uses the part to escape the frigid role her husband had assigned her, to express

25 'an Englishwoman' ... 'sex in her eyes'.
26 'When one watches Rita Hayworth in *Gilda*, there's a pride and a pain in being an object, in lending herself to myth and to erotic fantasy. She is at once its victim and its conqueror'.

some of her own desires and to exert some power over the macho Deblache by seducing him. Breillat describes Barbara and Deblache as 'la femme et le pantin. Quand elle séduit, la femme est sincère, elle pose un peu, elle se voit faire sa scène de séduction'[27] (Sineux 1991: 18). While seriously invested in her seductive wiles, Barbara at the same time remains aware that she is performing a role. As a subject, she is greater than the part she plays, embodying but exceeding the *femme fatale* stereotype, expressing herself through and beyond this limited male fantasy. In this, she is like 'toutes les actrices qui interprètent des putes, des patronnes de cabaret, des strip-teaseuses; donc qui font la codification érotique parfaite, mais qui sont en même temps convoquées comme être humain. Elles ne sont plus l'image, elles sont quelque chose d'autre. Et ça, c'est magnifique'[28] (Breillat in Rouyer and Vassé 2004: 38). It is interesting to note in this regard that Lio, the actress who plays Barbara, was at the time best known as a pop singer and a Lolita-like sex symbol: 'on ne voyait que son côté petite idole s'amusant à être une femme objet'[29] (Breillat 2006: 185). In her performance as Barbara, Lio both re-enacts her stereotypical role and surpasses it.

In Barbara's sex scenes with Deblache on her sofa and in her and his bedrooms, she can be seen performing certain male-defined 'feminine' roles as a way of permutating beyond them. She is the guilty adulterous wife who turns away from the wedding photo of herself and Théron ('c'est horrible par rapport à lui!')[30] when Deblache wants to take her on her marriage bed. She is the innocent virgin ('vous serez responsable')[31] who has him undress her and then lies back in bed with her arms above her head, denying any involvement in what he is doing to her. And she is the shamefaced bad girl who cries and buries her head in the sofa after betraying when she orgasms that she too has desires: 'Je me sens comme une prostituée'; 'J'aime pas jouir!

27 'the woman and the puppet. When she seduces, the woman is sincere, she poses a little, she sees herself creating her scene of seduction'.

28 'all the actresses who perform as whores, cabaret owners, strip-teasers; so, all those who perfectly fit the erotic codes, but who are at the same time represented as a human being. They are no longer the image, they are something else. And *that* is magnificent'.

29 'people saw only the side of her that was a little pop idol playing at being a sex object'.

30 'it's horrible, when you think of him!'

31 'you will be responsible'.

J'ai horreur de moi quand je suis comme ça!'[32] Finally, she is also the 'femme-enfant' and *femme fatale* ('tu es une Anglaise'),[33] the perverted innocent and haughty bitch that Deblache finds so seductive. The words spoken by the characters in the film ('vierge', 'prostituée', 'Anglaise')[34] tend to be social labels which are pinned on Barbara but which she is trying to act herself out from under in her moments of silent lovemaking with Deblache. (Interestingly, Breillat has noted that at first the editor who worked on her film was cutting the silences in favour of the dialogue, which might have turned it into something closer to the conventionally talky *Police*, whereas Breillat's tendency was the exact opposite, to move away from social language toward the individuality of Barbara's physical expression (Sineux 1991: 17).)

Like the sexist terminology, Deblache's macho advances can be seen as his attempt to pin Barbara down, to define and possess her as his 'Anglaise', but Barbara embodies her role in a way that exceeds his grasp. In the scene where he is fingering her on the sofa, where he thinks of himself as demonstrating complete sexual mastery over her ('Je te veux toute entière'),[35] her orgasm acts not as proof of his mastery but as evidence of her ability to escape his categories and control. 'Contrairement au vocabulaire que les hommes nous ont imprimé dans la tête, c'est-à-dire qu'ils "prennent" et qu'ils "possèdent" les femmes', says Breillat, 'Ils ne les possèdent absolument pas, elles leur échappent. C'est un mystère absolu une femme qui jouit'[36] (Breillat 2006: 75). An over-the-shoulder shot from behind Deblache shows him searching Barbara's face as she orgasms, looking to find his dominance reflected in her submission, his gender identity confirmed by her feminine role play, but her eyes are closed as she comes (she is not 'coming to him') and the camera follows her leftward as she arches her body and throws her head back in actively owned pleasure, a *jouissance* beyond him who is momentarily excluded from the frame. In this scene, Barbara is a desiring subject in her own right and not just a reflection of his objectifying gaze; she is a 'femme qui est

32 'I feel like a prostitute' ... 'I don't like to come! I abhor myself when I'm like that!'
33 'woman-child' ... 'you are an Englishwoman'.
34 'virgin', 'prostitute', 'Englishwoman'.
35 'I want all of you'.
36 'Contrary to the vocabulary that men have imprinted in our head, namely, that they "take" or that they "possess" women' ... 'They absolutely do not possess them, women escape them. A woman having an orgasm is an absolute mystery'.

regardée en train de jouir par un homme qui ne fait rien d'autre que la regarder'[37] (Breillat in Jousse and Strauss 1991: 77). He cannot 'take' or 'possess' her as a 'virgin' or a 'whore' because in her ecstasy she has exceeded these simplistic sexist categories along with the shame and guilt that go with them. She is 'sale comme un ange'[38] – both good girl and bad while being neither. 'Perdre les repères du bien et du mal' is what Breillat wanted to show by filming a woman's face during *jouissance*, 'montrer ce qui ne serait ni le bien ni le mal, mais peut-être la confrontation des deux, leur implication dans une même spirale qui forme une *moire*'[39] (Breillat 1999: 14).

Ultimately, Barbara is more able than Deblache to sustain a desire-inspired freedom from stereotypical gender roles. The tenderness and vulnerability he shared in amorous interactions with her give way to a frustrated machismo brought on by his inability to possess her physically or matrimonially. Now he is either making cave-man demands for sex (or 'ça!'[40] as he gruntingly calls it, putting her hand on his fly) or giving patriarchal commands that she 'divorce!' and marry him, but she eludes his efforts to pigeonhole her as either *his* mistress or *his* wife. In the end, when Barbara's husband Théron is killed in a botched police raid, Deblache follows her as she is leaving the cemetery after the funeral. Addressing her as 'Madame Théron', he expects to see a properly grieving widow, but when she turns around and is revealed to be smiling, he slaps her face, calling her a 'salope!'[41] Even though Deblache knows that Théron overidealised and neglected his wife, Deblache is outraged on behalf of his male friend at Barbara's apparent lack of grief. Male bonding and patriarchal values override any attempt to understand how she might really be feeling. The slap is to punish her for not being a good wife, loyal in belonging to her man – Théron or Deblache. From Deblache's patriarchal perspective, a woman is either a 'madame' or a 'salope', a wife or a whore, and a little violence may be necessary to reprimand her bad-girl behaviour. Interestingly, Breillat has noted that a movie critic once said he'd

37 'woman who is watched while she is coming by a man who does nothing else but watch her'.
38 'dirty like an angel'.
39 'To lose one's bearings regarding good and evil' ... 'to show what would be neither good nor evil, but perhaps the confrontation of the two, their implication in the same spiral which forms a moiré'.
40 'that'.
41 'Mrs Théron' ... 'bitch!'

like to slap her for having made *Tapage nocturne*, her film about a sexually adventurous woman, and that another critic once wrote that the only good part of Breillat's *36 fillette* was when the girl's father in the film slapped her for disobeying him with her sexual impudence (Jousse and Strauss 1991: 78). Thus, when Deblache slaps Barbara, he represents all the patriarchal attempts to punish and 'reform' Breillat's heroines and herself. And yet, while Deblache may have reverted to type with his macho violence, Barbara evades his effort to fix her in any male-imposed 'feminine' role. In a reprise of the earlier orgasm scene, the camera is not centred on Deblache (as it is on Mangin at the end of *Police*) but instead situated behind Deblache's shoulder, and he can do nothing but watch her elude him as he tries but fails to assert phallic mastery over her. After he has slapped her, she briefly registers the pain by touching her face, but then she looks straight at him, smiles again triumphantly and turns away from him and his impotent gaze. Breillat freeze-frames Barbara as she is turning and defining herself as a being in motion, between and beyond feminine types, neither a wife nor a whore but coming into her own.

Parfait amour! (Perfect Love)

The slap that ends *Sale comme un ange* has escalated to fatal violence in *Parfait amour!*, another film about masculinity in crisis and the attempt to assert male gender identity by putting woman in her place. Based on a 'fait divers' ('news account') of an actual crime, *Parfait amour!* ends with a man sodomising a woman with a broom handle and stabbing her over forty times with a knife. This scene was booed when the film screened at Cannes, and Breillat theorises that it was not just the misogynistic violence but the fact that it was committed by a young, good-looking guy that so disturbed audiences: 'c'est ... qu'il a un visage de James Dean, qu'il est adorable et qu'on le plaint ... on voit bien que la société refuse de se reconnaître dans une histoire comme celle-là et, pour préserver ses tabous, veut des monstres'[42] (Strauss 1996: 29). By making the murderer 'ordinary' and appealing rather than monstrously repellent, Breillat forces society to confront

---

42 'it's ... that he has the face of a James Dean, that he's adorable and that one feels sorry for him ... it's clear that society refuses to recognise itself in a story like *that* and, in order to preserve its taboos, wants monsters'.

the common and quotidian nature of male violence (it could be and often is 'the boy next door') while also encouraging an empathetic understanding of how social forces can turn a potentially gentle man into a macho brute. In his study *Les Hommes violents*, Daniel Welzer-Lang points to the 'constructions sociales du masculin' that often contribute to misogynistic acts, arguing that '*on ne naît pas homme, ni homme violent, on le devient*, pourrait-on dire en paraphrasant Simone de Beauvoir'[43] (Welzer-Lang 1991: 9).

For Christophe in *Parfait amour!* as for most men, the impact of socially gendered roles is first conveyed through parental influence. His highly sexed father clashed with his more conventionally senti-mental and possibly prudish mother, who refused to participate with her husband in orgies and who came to loathe his constant sexual demands. She tells Christophe that he was only conceived through rape and that she had not wanted any more children, presumably because of the loveless marriage. As a result of this strongly gendered clash between father and mother, between sex and sentiment, Chris-tophe struggles with a dichotomous gender identity, torn between identifying with his father's Don Juanism and sympathising with his mother's feelings. When his father takes him to dinner on his eight-eenth birthday, Christophe is disturbed by the presence of the father's younger mistress, feeling displaced by her in his father's affections much as his mother would, and when his father then takes him to an orgy afterward, he refuses to have sex with a series of women along-side his father, as if the son were more in sympathy with his mother's monogamous view of relationships. Christophe has spent many nights with his mother in the hospital, caring for her after suicide attempts, trying to convince her of his own fidelity in contrast to his father's callous promiscuity.

When Christophe at age twenty-eight begins an affair with thirty-seven-year-old Frédérique, he has already had one prior sexual relation-ship with another older woman. The latest relationship seems part of a pattern of making amends for the father's infidelity, of trying to win a mother's love, of demonstrating that he can be a different kind of man. If middle age, a balding head and a failing body had tempered some of Deblache's machismo in *Sale comme un ange*, revealing his tenderness and vulnerability, it is youth, blond hair and a boyish body

43 'social constructions of masculinity' … '*one isn't born a man, or a violent man, one becomes one*, we could say, paraphrasing Simone de Beauvoir'.

that signify Christophe's androgynous potential, a 'feminine' gentleness not yet driven out by macho gynephobia. When Christophe and
Frédérique meet at a wedding reception and later spend the night at a
country inn, it is as if they were getting married and going on a honeymoon, as if he were indicating his intention to be faithful in a senti-
mentally 'feminine' way. When they first make love, he looks directly
into her eyes as if their souls were in sync, avowing afterward that 'Je
t'aime. J'ai tout de suite su que tu étais la femme de ma vie'.[44] And
Christophe comforts her when she cries over the sexually degrading
things she has allowed men to do to her in the past, when she was
lonely and desperate and when her first husband, a homosexual,
would leave her behind to go with other men.

And yet, even though he knows that it pains Frédérique in the
same way his mother was hurt, Christophe begins to leave 'the love of
his life' at home in order to go out womanising with Philippe, an older
and more macho friend whose amorous exploits are reminiscent of
his father's. At one of their debauches, Christophe has sex with a
woman while Philippe watches and then Christophe offers her to his
friend. Having refused his macho initiation at the earlier orgy with his
father, Christophe is now trying to confirm his masculinity in the eyes
of a father-figure, a confirmation which in patriarchal culture can only
be given by another man: 'La femme ne peut pas rendre un homme
viril – elle n'est que la récompense ultime de la virilité. Les hommes
sont les arbitres de la virilité'[45] (Löwy 2006: 56). Christophe's need
to prove his potency extends to a 'dragueur' ('cruising') competition
with his friend over women. While on a double date, Christophe
leaves Frédérique behind at the bar and takes off on his motorbike
with Philippe's 'meuf' ('chick'). Locked in combat over who is the
bigger man and the bigger spender, who possesses more women and
more money (Christophe likes to be the one who pays because 'il
se dit, c'est moi qui paie, c'est moi qui baise'),[46] Christophe increasingly rejects Frédérique and his own 'feminine' side in an effort to
become 'all man'. 'La virilité', notes Pierre Bourdieu, 'est une notion
éminemment *relationnelle*, construite devant et pour autres hommes
et contre la féminité, dans une sorte de *peur* du féminin, et d'abord

---

44 'I love you. I knew right away that you were the love of my life'.

45 'Woman cannot make a man virile – she is only the final reward for his virility.
Men are the arbiters of virility'.

46 'he tells himself, if I'm the one paying, then I'm the one doing the fucking'.

en soi-même'[47] (Bourdieu 2002: 78). But even when Christophe is supposedly at his most dominant, proving his sexual prowess by conquering women at the debauch, he remains strangely inactive. One woman he is with removes a bottle of whiskey like a baby bottle from his mouth, undresses him and climbs on top to ride him while he just lies there in the passive 'feminine' position, failing to achieve 'masculine' supremacy. Swinging wildly between macho poseur and mama's boy, Christophe is still suffering from a split identification, unable to mediate the gender conflict within him. He is unable to become 'l'homme réconcilié', an androgynous ideal that Elisabeth Badinter has described as resulting from 'la remise en question d'une virilité ancestrale, l'acceptation d'une féminité redoutée et l'invention d'une autre masculinité compatible avec elle'[48] (Badinter 1992: 239, 272).

Rather than finding a way to combine sex and sentiment when he is with Frédérique and thus to heal the divide between 'corps' and 'cœur'[49] that existed between his parents, Christophe re-enacts the antagonism. This conflict is then exacerbated by the Oedipal complications that derive from his dating an older woman. When Christophe and Frédérique are about to make love at her place, he is disturbed by the fact that he is not the first to have shared her bed: she has had other lovers and two husbands prior to him. Like a son who is always already secondary to his father in his mother's affections, Christophe feels belated and inferior, as if he can't measure up to other men. This sense of inadequacy is highlighted when Christophe strips naked as Frédérique watches him from the bed. Breillat had Francis Renaud, the actor playing Christophe, revealed in full-frontal nude scenes where his flaccid penis is exposed, and what the older female director said to her younger male actor was designed to make him extremely uncomfortable for the benefit of his performance: she told him 'que je l'avais engagé comme j'aurais engagé Brigitte Bardot et qu'il n'était qu'un objet sexuel. Humilié, il est devenu ... formidable!'[50] (Puaux

47 'Manliness' ... 'is an eminently *relational* notion, constructed in front of and for other men and against femininity, in a kind of *fear* of the female, firstly in oneself' (Bourdieu 2001: 53).

48 'the "reconciled man"' ... 'first, questioning an ancestral virility, then accepting a feared femininity, and last, inventing a different masculinity compatible with that femininity' (Badinter 1995: 161, 184).

49 'body' ... 'heart'.

50 'that I'd hired him as I would have hired Brigitte Bardot and that he was only a sex object. Humiliated, he became ... sensational!'

2001: 169). In a later scene, after Christophe has urinated outside Frédérique's apartment building like one of those 'chiens quand ils pissaient ... pour marquer leur territoire',[51] his virile display is undercut when he stands before her in wet undershorts like a little boy who has wet himself. Christophe tends to feel diminished as the object of Frédérique's gaze, for she is older, more sexually experienced, and even makes more money in her job (this woman with the active gaze is in fact an ophthalmologist).

Despite his macho posing (the cigarettes, the leather jacket, the red motorbike between his legs), Christophe often finds himself impotent with her, perhaps because he associates desire with degradation and does not want to hurt her the way his father hurt his mother, but also because he fears he is not man enough to conquer her the way his father could. While Christophe can bed anonymous women, he balks at having sex with Frédérique, a woman he cares about as he does about his mother. For him, the more his relationship with Frédérique is about sentiment, the less it can be about sex, and when the woman he loves tries to stop him from having sex with other women, he feels that she is trying to castrate him ('vous essayez de lui couper les couilles',[52] as Philippe warns Frédérique). Fidelity would be emasculation; either Christophe is a womaniser or he feels unmanned. Ultimately, Frédérique is right when she tells Christophe that 'tu n'aimes pas les femmes'[53] because his is a desire to conquer, to prove himself superior to women, to dominate them as a way of differentiating himself from their 'passive' femininity. To get too close to women would be a mortal threat to his manhood; it would mean to feel what it's like to be used as a sex object by an aggressive male, to feel what his mother felt when his father raped her. This is why Christophe fears that forming a lasting sentimental bond with Frédérique would be like suffering a kind of death: 'Après trois fois' of doing it, when sex might turn to love, 'même la plus belle fille du monde, c'est un morceau de chair qui pue'[54] is what he tells her.

For her part, Frédérique insists on both body and soul, on a relationship that is both passionate and lasting. In one scene where Christophe takes her brutally from behind like an anonymous woman

51 'dogs when they piss ... to mark their territory'.
52 'you try to cut off his balls'.
53 'you don't like women'.
54 'After three times' ... 'even the most beautiful girl in the world is a hunk of stinking meat'.

to be conquered, she laments that they did not 'faire l'amour'; instead, 'on a baisé'.[55] Then, in their final scene together when Christophe cannot get sexually excited while they are face to face (the prospect of true intimacy renders him impotent), she refuses to accept his lame excuse that love is more important than sex; she counters that 'c'est pas l'amour que j'aime, c'est le cul'.[56] In each case, Frédérique pushes him to integrate the opposite, to combine the physical with feeling, to become an 'homme réconcilié', but Christophe is unable to overcome the social conditioning that defines his manhood as *opposed to* femininity: 'le féminin, c'est du passif, du maso et surtout c'est du châtré qui ... déclenche terreur de la castration et sidération de l'appareil psychique. Et ajoutons que c'est ainsi que s'explique la peur que les hommes ont des femmes: elles évoquent la castration, car elles sont castrées and castratrices!'[57] (Cournut 2001: 77). Trying to conquer his fear of weakness and passivity by being the dominant one, Christophe pushes Frédérique face down onto the kitchen table and sodomises her with a broom handle, ordering her not to turn around, but she *looks back* at him, sees his continuing impotence and laughs. He then grabs a knife and stabs her repeatedly until she has been rendered entirely passive, literally dead meat, and no longer a threat to his masculine identity. By using violence, Christophe has attempted to root out the femininity within himself, to cut himself off from his mother and from the sentimental feelings he associates with weakness. As Jessica Benjamin writes:

> The danger that violation is meant to oppose ... is easily equated with the return to oneness with the mother, and can now be evoked by any profound experience of dependency or communion (emotional or physical), such as erotic love. The only defense against losing difference lies in reversing the power relationship so that the master now controls the other, while still proclaiming his boundaries intact. Erotic domination represents an intensification of male anxiety and defense in relation to the mother. The repudiated maternal body persists as the object to be done to and violated, to be separated from, to have power over, to denigrate. (Benjamin 1988: 77–8)

55 'make love' ... 'we fucked'.
56 'it's not love that I like, it's sex'.
57 'reconciled man' ... 'to be feminine is to be passive, masochistic and above all castrated which ... triggers a terror of castration and an overwhelming of the psychic apparatus. And let's add that this is what explains the fear that men have of women: women evoke castration, for they are castrated and castrating!'

Having repudiated his mother and all 'feminine' softness by fatally penetrating Frédérique, Christophe hopes to have attained the definitive hardness of his macho father. As the film ends, woman has been reduced to nothingness (Frédérique is literally out of frame) and Christophe has become pure he-man action, stabbing and stabbing as the image cuts to black. But the endlessly repeated stabbing suggests desperation more than confidence, and the knife, like the broom handle, is a phallic substitute, an overcompensation for his continuing lack of potency. When Christophe re-enacts the crime as part of a police inquiry (shown at the beginning of the film), we see him bringing his right arm down in a stabbing motion while he is crouched on the floor with his left hand on his head. If Christophe has finally become 'all male', it is in the sense of having devolved to the condition of a primitive ape-man. And in going through these motions, Christophe is passively following the orders of an older female magistrate who is directing the inquiry. Ultimately, he is still caught between being a macho man and being a mama's boy, unable to free himself from the prison of gender.

Brève traversée (Brief Crossing)

The formation of male gender identity and the way in which stereotypical gender roles are contested or confirmed by the interaction between the partners in a relationship are subjects taken up again by Breillat in *Brève traversée*, a movie commissioned by the French TV channel Arte as one in a series of ten films grouped around the theme of 'Masculin/Féminin'. As in *Parfait amour!* Breillat chooses to focus on a younger man/older woman romance, in this case the fleeting love affair between sixteen-year-old Thomas and thirty-something Alice that occurs on board an overnight cruise ship crossing the English Channel. Two factors make it possible for Thomas and Alice to have somewhat more success than Christophe and Frédérique in departing from rigid gender roles. First is the fact that the lovers' shipboard romance isolates them from some of the usual pressure to conform to gender norms and other social prescriptions. As Thomas tells Alice, 'Nous sommes sur l'océan. Nous sommes au-dessus des lois'.[58] For a brief passage of time, the Channel crossing enables the

---

58 'We're out on the ocean. We're above any laws'.

lovers' desire to enact a crossing of social boundaries that would normally keep these two apart, boundaries related to gender, age, language and nationality (he is French; she is English). This crossing is emblematised by the framing of an early shot in the ship's cafeteria as Thomas is looking for a place to sit and Alice is already seated at a table. Shooting through an X-shaped partition in the foreground, Breillat frames Thomas in the left portion of the X and Alice in the right portion just as he is about to cross the masculine/feminine, youth/age, French/English divide and join her.

The second factor in the lovers' favour is that Thomas is considerably younger than the twenty-eight-year-old Christophe and has not yet been wounded by women in the way that has led Christophe to erect a macho defence and to mount a wounding counterattack. If we note that Christophe and Thomas are linked by their love of Coca-Cola and that Christophe had his first affair with an older woman at the same age Thomas is now when he will lose his virginity to Alice, then Thomas could be seen as a younger and more innocent Christophe, before he became so hardened and aggressive. Similarly, Alice could be seen as an older version of the Alice from *Une vraie jeune fille*, after she has lost her virginity and become disillusioned by men. The contrast between jaded, bitter Alice and Thomas with his youthful vitality is apparent when he sits across from her at her cafeteria table and she, with her sallow face above a pale yellow turtleneck sweater, looks at his ruddy complexion and dark red sweater while watching him eat a crème brûlée with great appetite. (This contrast between their skin colours was important enough to Breillat that she decided to shoot using 16mm film rather than the digital video normally used for the TV series: 'j'aime la carnation et le blanc de la peau qu'on obtient avec la pellicule'[59] (Arte 2001).)

We have seen with Christophe how young men are expected to prove their manhood by actively and often aggressively differentiating themselves from women and mama's boys:

'Prouve que tu es un homme,' tel est le défi permanent auquel est confronté un être masculin. ... Beaucoup de garçons définissent simplement la masculinité: ce qui n'est pas féminin. Le propos est si vrai que l'on pourrait dire que dès la conception, l'embryon masculin 'lutte' pour ne pas être féminin. Né d'une femme, bercé dans un ventre

59 'I like the flesh-tint and the whiteness of the skin that you can get on film stock'.

féminin, l'enfant mâle ... est condamné à la différenciation pendant une grande partie de sa vie. Lui ne peut exister qu'en s'opposant à sa mère, à sa féminité, à sa condition de bébé passif.[60] (Badinter 1992: 14, 57–8)

However, even as they are struggling to assert their masculinity, young men today, especially after the advent of feminism, are expected to temper their aggressive tendencies, to moderate the macho behaviour they thought they were supposed to demonstrate: 'De quoi avoir le vertige pour tous ces jeunes hommes qui naviguent à vue pour éviter deux écueils: ne pas être assez mâle ou l'être trop. ... A l'interdiction traditionnelle de montrer sa féminité s'ajoute celle d'exprimer une virilité contestée. La nouvelle équation mâle = mal a engendré une perte d'identité pour toute une génération d'hommes'[61] (Badinter 1992: 18, 186).

Thomas too struggles to find a middle ground between effeminacy and machismo in which to define himself, but unlike Christophe, Thomas is less panicky about inhabiting the interstices between gender boundaries which for him, in his young and unformed state, are still fluid and permeable. After finishing his crème brûlée, Thomas smokes a cigarette and rubs his lip with his thumb like would-be tough guy Michel (Jean-Paul Belmondo) imitating Humphrey Bogart in *A bout de souffle* (*Breathless*) (Jean-Luc Godard, 1960). Thomas explains to Alice that he started smoking in order to show off in front of his male friends, but he also tells her that his mother is a smoker, that she's 'très cool' and that 'elle m'adore'.[62] Smoking is thus linked to phallic display and masculine toughness but also to a boy's continuing identification with his mother and a desire for her love, a desire here

60 '"Prove you're a man" is the constant challenge confronting a male person. ... Many boys define masculinity simply as what is not feminine. The observation is so true that one could say that, starting from conception, the male embryo "struggles" not to be female. Born of a woman, cradled in a female belly, the male child ... is condemned to differentiation during a large part of his life. He cannot exist except by opposing himself to his mother, to her femininity, to his condition as passive baby' (Badinter 1995: 2, 32).

61 'Cause for bewilderment on the part of all those young men who are trying to navigate a safe passage between two dangers: not being masculine enough and being too masculine. ... Traditionally forbidden to display his femininity, a man is now also forbidden to express a manliness that is being challenged. The new equation, male = bad, has given rise to a loss of identity for a whole generation of men' (Badinter 1995: 4, 124–5).

62 'very cool' ... 'she adores me'.

being transferred rather seamlessly onto Alice, an older woman who Thomas hopes will similarly adore him. Later in the ship's nightclub, the two watch a performance in which a magician puts a woman in a box, sticks swords through her body and then makes her disappear. Alice interprets this act as a parable for the way men subject women to phallic penetration and then afterward ignore them, and she warns Thomas not to continue this patriarchal pattern of mutilating lust and emotional distance: 'ce qu'il faut, c'est d'échapper absolument à la condition d'hommes, à toutes leurs contorsions et leur arrogance'.[63] When Alice says this, Thomas hangs his head as if chastened then glances up rather shyly and obediently at her, yet there is also a potentially impudent look in his eye, just as later on the dance floor after she has further harangued men as a group, he protests, using her native English to get through to – and back at – her: 'I could take that badly. I'm a man, you know'. It gradually becomes clear to Thomas that one of Alice's motives for attacking men is actually to get a rise out of him, to prompt him to 'be a man' and make a move on her, as when she says that she usually prefers brawny men or 'bêtes'[64] and Thomas obligingly bears down fiercely on her on the dance floor, kissing her hungrily. But Alice, having been hurt by a man, has in fact become something of a sexual masochist who really wants Thomas to make her suffer, and yet he balks at becoming that kind of man, saying instead that he prefers 'la tendresse' and 'des câlins' – not just devouring kisses or the act of penetration but a kind of sexuality connected with emotional empathy and the whole body: 'Auparavant réduit dans l'érotique à un axe tête-queue avec une cravate pour relier les deux, le corps de l'homme, simultanément à l'évolution des rapports avec les femmes, s'ouvre à d'autres imaginaires et à d'autres territoires'[65] (Welzer-Lang 2004: 247).

Another (loving and non-masochistic) part of Alice is trying, with her diatribes against men, to prevent Thomas from becoming a brute, to encourage his gentleness and sensitivity. Even as he is forcefully advancing upon her on the dance floor, she tells him that there may

63 'what's needed is to make a total escape from men's condition, from all their macho antics and their arrogance'.

64 'beasts'.

65 'tenderness' ... 'hugs' ... 'Having been previously reduced in his erotic life to an axis running from his head to his cock with a tie to link the two, man's body, concurrent with the evolution in relations with women, is opening up to other imaginaries and to other territories'.

still be some good men, 'peut-être ceux qui sont très jeunes, qui ont encore de la poésie un peu comme les filles, des lèvres comme les fruits mûrs', and when they later make love together in her cabin, she caresses him, saying 'j'aime ta peau. Elle est douce. Tu est doux comme un enfant'.[66] While a certain kind of man would consider his masculinity to have been slighted by these comparisons of him to a girl and to a child, Thomas is able to occupy the space *between* manhood and boyhood and *between* masculinity and femininity without feeling infantilised or emasculated. Whereas *Parfait amour!*'s Christophe in his gender panic was driven to extremes of violence to separate himself from a sexualised mother-figure, Thomas is able to live his relationship with Alice as a continuity between mother and lover, esteem and desire. Christophe could lust after women for whom he had no regard but was impotent with his soulmate Frédérique, much as Alexandre (another Coca-Cola drinker) in Jean Eustache's *La Maman et la putain* suffered from a Madonna/whore complex: 'Vous aimez une femme et vous en baisez une autre'.[67] By contrast, in Thomas' love scene with Alice he can suck tenderly on her nipple ('j'adore les seins', he says, using the same word he had used before to describe his mother's love for him – 'elle m'adore')[68] while also thrusting vigorously into her. On the ship's deck prior to this love scene, Thomas can kiss and pursue Alice passionately, forcing her to walk backwards (in a reverse tracking shot), but then he can walk side by side with her and even let himself be led by her to her cabin – though it is he who opens the door. Inside, the virginal Thomas is initially shy: he undresses with his back to Alice and shuffles toward her in his underwear while biting his thumb as if sucking it like a little boy. However, after they have made love and showered, he towels off in full view, unafraid to be seen by her when he is not in a 'manly' state of erection. In his ability to be both subject and object of the gaze, active and passive, man and boy, lover and son, Thomas is reminiscent of Laurent in Louis Malle's *Le Souffle au cœur* (*Murmur of the Heart*) (1971), a young teenager whose love for his mother and whose desire to comfort her for wrongs she has suffered from other men eventually lead to a brief sexual encounter with her whereby he is tenderly initiated into manhood.

66 'perhaps those who are very young, who still have some poetry a bit like girls, with lips like ripe fruits' ... 'I love your skin. It's soft. You're soft as a baby'.

67 'You love one woman and you fuck another'.

68 'I adore breasts' ... 'she adores me'.

These two films, however, come to very different conclusions. Laurent's mother gently disengages from him ('Je ne veux pas que tu sois malheureux, ni que tu aies honte, ni même que tu regrettes. Nous nous en souviendrons comme d'un moment très beau, très grave, qui ne se reproduira jamais plus'),[69] a loving parting which enables Laurent to retain both his sensitivity and his self-confidence when he goes on to see other women. Thomas is callously abandoned by Alice when the ship docks at Portsmouth. Though she swore she would wait, Alice has disappeared from the deck by the time he returns with his bag, and when Thomas finally catches up with her outside the terminal, he finds that she has lied to him about other things as well: she is not childless and she has not left her marriage, since Thomas sees her getting into a car with her husband and son. Alice also sees Thomas but her face betrays absolutely no recognition; instead, she maintains a mask of indifference toward him, like the loveless look on the face of her husband that she had earlier described as having hurt her so much, 'cette opacité terrifiante, dure et laide afin de vous ignorer'.[70] Whether consciously or not, Alice ends up abusing Thomas in the same way that she has been mistreated by men, seducing and then ignoring him. Alice may be taking vicarious revenge on Thomas for what other men have done to her, or it could be that she has real feelings for him but is simply trying to do 'the right thing' by returning to her husband and child (as Laura (Celia Johnson) does at the end of *Brief Encounter* (David Lean, 1945)). Whatever her intentions, the effect on Thomas is devastating, leaving him feeling seduced and abandoned by a woman to whom he had opened himself up, allowing himself to be physically and emotionally vulnerable in his first sexual experience. When Thomas sees Alice's hard face ignoring him, he closes his eyes as if receiving the impact of a blow. Pouring rain runs down his face along with what appear to be tears as well. This is a far cry from the souvenir photo they had taken together on board the ship, where Thomas had his arms around Alice, his head on her shoulder, and his eyes closed as if dreaming of romance. Even back then, though, Alice in the photo had been staring straight ahead, her face a frozen mask. Now, outside the terminal, Thomas sees Alice's

69 'I don't want you to be unhappy, or for you to feel ashamed, or even for you to have regrets. We'll remember it as a very beautiful and very solemn moment that will never happen again'.
70 'this terrifying opacity, hard and ugly in order to ignore you'.

cold look and his own face seems to stiffen from the blow, to age and harden. It seems unlikely that Thomas will ever show the same tender regard for a woman again. The boy has become a man.

References

Arte (2001), Dossier de presse: *Brève traversée*, Paris, Arte.

Austin, Guy (1996), *Contemporary French Cinema*, Manchester, Manchester University Press.

Badinter, Elisabeth (1992), *XY: De l'identité masculine*, Paris, Odile Jacob.

Badinter, Elisabeth (1995), *XY: On Masculine Identity*, trans. Lydia David, New York, Columbia University Press.

Benjamin, Jessica (1988), *The Bonds of Love: Psychoanalysis, Feminism, and the Problem of Domination*, New York, Pantheon.

Bourdieu, Pierre (2001), *Masculine Domination*, trans. Richard Nice, Stanford, Stanford University Press.

Bourdieu, Pierre (2002), *La Domination masculine*, revised edition, Paris, Seuil.

Breillat, Catherine (1985), *Police*, Paris, Albin Michel.

Breillat, Catherine (1999), *Romance: Scénario*, Paris, Cahiers du cinéma.

Breillat, Catherine (2003), 'Témoignages', *Cahiers du cinéma* 576, 42–4.

Breillat, Catherine (2006), *Corps amoureux: Entretiens avec Claire Vassé*, Paris, Denoël.

Clouzot, Claire (2004), *Catherine Breillat: Indécence et pureté*, Paris, Cahiers du cinéma.

Cournut, Jean (2001), *Pourquoi les hommes ont peur des femmes*, Paris, Presses Universitaires de France.

Jousse, Thierry and Strauss, Frédéric (1991), 'Entretien avec Catherine Breillat', *Cahiers du cinéma* 445, 76–8.

Katsahnias, Iannis (1991), 'Catherine Breillat tourne *Sale comme un ange*', *Cahiers du cinéma* 440, 71–5.

Löwy, Ilana (2006), *L'Emprise du genre: Masculinité, féminité, inégalité*, Paris, La Dispute.

Pialat, Maurice (1985), 'Entretien avec Maurice Pialat', *Positif* 296, 5–11.

Powrie, Phil (1997), *French Cinema in the 1980s: Nostalgia and the Crisis of Masculinity*, Oxford, Oxford University Press.

Puaux, Françoise (2001), 'Entretien avec Catherine Breillat', *Le Machisme à l'écran, CinémAction* 99, 165–72.

Rouyer, Philippe and Vassé, Claire (2004), 'De l'évanescent qui n'est plus de l'ordre du charnel', *Positif* 521/522, 36–40.

Sineux, Michel (1991), 'Je raconte l'âme et la chair des gens', *Positif* 365/366, 16–18.

Strauss, Frédéric (1996), 'Entretien avec Catherine Breillat', *Cahiers du cinéma* 507, 23–9.

Toubiana, Serge (1985), 'L'Epreuve de vérité', *Cahiers du cinéma* 375, 10–13.
Warehime, Marja (2006), *Maurice Pialat*, Manchester, Manchester University Press.
Welzer-Lang, Daniel (1991), *Les Hommes violents*, Paris, Lierre & Coudrier.
Welzer-Lang, Daniel (2004), *Les Hommes aussi changent*, Paris, Payot.

4

Staging masochism, facing shame

Tapage nocturne (Nocturnal Uproar)

Having considered three female coming-of-age films (*Une vraie jeune fille, 36 fillette, A ma sœur!*) and three movies about masculinity in crisis (*Sale comme un ange, Parfait amour!, Brève traversée*), we now turn to the three films Breillat has made about the sexual odysseys of adult women (*Tapage nocturne, Romance* and *Anatomie de l'enfer*). Equipped with more agency and experience than their virginal girl counterparts in the earlier films, these women actively seek to move beyond the notion that sex must be associated with sin and suffering, with a masochistic submission to men. Each film charts a woman's journey toward fulfilment of her desire, which is ultimately not for degradation of the flesh but for integration of body and soul. To achieve this goal, each woman goes in search of the ideal male partner who values both sex and sentiment.

The pressbook for *Tapage nocturne* describes the film as 'une histoire d'Amours vécue comme aujourd'hui et racontée comme aujourd'hui. Avec impudence'[1] (Axe Films). The movie's twenty-something heroine, Solange, tells the tale of her serial love affairs in saucy voice-over and provocative dialogue: 'Je ne suis pas vieux jeu. Je couche avec tout le monde'.[2] Solange (a film director) sleeps with her husband Bruel (a producer), but she also sleeps with Jim (an actor), Bruno (a director), Frédéric (a rock musician) and others. It is Paris in the 1970s and Solange appears to be living the life of a sexually liberated woman, a freedom made possible by the gains of

1 'a story of Loves, lived like today and told like today. With impudence'.

2 'I'm not old-fashioned. I sleep with everyone'.

the Mouvement de libération des femmes (MLF) (Women's Liberation Movement). Given renewed energy by the revolutionary spirit that swept the country in May 1968, the MLF championed a woman's right to sexual pleasure without fear of unwanted pregnancy (as in the slogan 'jouir sans entraves').[3] In 1971, 343 prominent women signed a manifesto declaring that they had had illegal abortions and calling for free access to abortion and contraception. A law granting abortion rights was passed in 1975 and made permanent in 1979, and the 1967 law making contraception legally available was further liberalised in 1974. A survey by the Institut national d'études démographiques (INED) (National Institute of Demographic Studies) revealed that, by 1978, nearly 95% of French women between the ages of twenty and forty were using contraceptives. Along with these new laws enabling the sexual freedom of women like Solange, women also claimed the right to expect sexual fulfilment from men and to leave a relationship if this desire was not being met ('plutôt pas de rapport que pas de plaisir').[4] Solange refuses to settle for a husband or lover who does not satisfy her, exchanging one for another as need be. As David Vasse has noted, it sometimes seems as though the film director Solange 'change d'amants comme de plans'[5] (Vasse 2004: 33), and when she is supervising the editing of her latest film, it is 'de vérifier que le montage des scènes est conforme à mes désirs'[6] (Breillat 1979: 34).

Solange's willingness to go from one man to another in order to get what she wants is reminiscent of Angela (Anna Karina) in *Une femme est une femme* (*A Woman Is a Woman*). (Breillat has described *Tapage nocturne* as a 'secret remake' of this 1961 Jean-Luc Godard film (Clouzot 2004: 150).) Angela's boyfriend Emile (Jean-Claude Brialy) loves her and especially desires her when they are apart, but he won't make love to her when they're together, even though Angela wants a baby: 'C'est injuste. C'est toujours quand on est ensemble qu'on n'est pas ensemble. Et réciproquement'.[7] So Angela pretends to go with another man, Alfred (Jean-Paul Belmondo), in order to incite Emile's jealousy and to excite his sexual interest (along with his interest in having the

3 '(orgasmic) enjoyment without hindrances'.
4 'better to have no relationship than no pleasure'.
5 'changes lovers like film shots'.
6 'to verify that the editing of the scenes conforms to my desires'.
7 'It's unfair. It's always when we're together that we're not together. And vice versa'.

baby be his), a devious stratagem that prompts Emile, after he has made love to her, to accuse Angela of wickedness ('tu es infâme'), to which she replies that no, 'je suis une femme'.[8] Angela's flirtation with promiscuity is thus actually an effort to find both sex and sentiment combined in one man. She is unafraid to flout social convention and behave like a 'bad girl' in the active pursuit of her desires. Solange too finds that Bruel grows excited again when she goes with Jim and that Jim's sexual interest in her is reignited when she sleeps with Bruno, but she is frustrated by the fact that passion and fidelity do not seem to coincide for any one of these men: 'les mecs, c'est complètement insupportable. D'abord si on est fidèle, ils ne vous baisent pas, et si on n'est pas fidèle, ils vous baisent tout le temps'.[9] Using the same kinds of witty Godardian turns of phrase as in *Une femme est une femme*, Solange explains that when she sees other men, she is really thinking of instilling jealousy in the men (the man at the time) she actually loves, whereas the other men she's seeing aren't really thinking of her even when they're with her: 'je pense beaucoup plus à eux quand je pense à plein d'autres, qu'eux à moi quand ils ne pensent qu'à moi. ... Moi, quand j'aime, c'est complètement, c'est pour toujours, c'est pour la vie'.[10] Solange remains a romantic in hot pursuit of true love, one that would combine both passion and constancy, even though the men she meets seem fragmented and incomplete.

As she 'cuts' from a scene with Jim to one with Bruel or another with Bruno, it is as though Solange is trying to piece together one whole man from the fragments of body, heart and head that each presents to her. Jim, the actor, has an impressive physique, and during the editing of her film Solange admires him in his muscle-revealing tank top and tight blue jeans in a scene where he is lifting lumber at a sawmill. (Solange's film looks a lot like Breillat's *Une vraie jeune fille*, and Joe Dallessandro, who plays Jim, bears a strong resemblance to Hiram Keller, who played a character named Jim in Breillat's film.) Unfortunately, Jim tends to be more interested in himself and his acting career than in Solange. Temptingly clad in nothing but his

8 'you're infamous' ... 'I'm a woman'.

9 'guys are totally unbearable. First, if you're faithful, they don't fuck you, and if you're not faithful, they fuck you all the time'.

10 'I think a lot more about them when I'm thinking about tons of others than they do about me when they're thinking about me. ... When *I* love, it's totally, it's forever, it's for life'.

underwear briefs, he will sit on the bed next to her but be entirely absorbed in the scrapbook he keeps of his film roles. Jim also spends whole nights discussing career prospects with Emmanuelle, a fashion model and would-be actress who plays Echo to his Narcissus (and who is played by Breillat's sister, Marie-Hélène, a fashion model and actress). Emmanuelle, with her extravagant hair and her red lips, nails and shoes, has photos of herself all over the wall, and she encourages Jim in his self-involvement. Because Jim is American and speaks virtually no French, his communication with Solange tends to be limited to the physical, in the times when he does direct those energies toward her and not toward himself or the male prostitutes he frequents. In the end, even the sexiest man proves insufficient if he is just a body, and Solange 'commence à le trouver bête'[11] (Breillat 1979: 90).

Bruel, an older man who is her husband and a film producer, is all heart: he offers her bourgeois sentiment and comfort along with financial support. When she needs money, he writes her a cheque, but it is mostly to show how magnanimous he can be. Bruel has a big marital bed with silk sheets and a fur blanket into which Solange can slip easily – too easily. In one scene, the camera pans from the paintings of female nudes that cover Bruel's walls, to a mirror reflection of Solange in bed with Bruel, and finally to her actual person in bed with him. It is as though she is one of his possessions, part of his collection, displayed mostly for the sake of his vanity. In this scene Bruel is using a vibrator on her, an artificial substitute for physical contact, a mere stand-in for desire. As Solange realises, Bruel doesn't actually desire her as much as he needs to think of himself as the kind of man who does – a virile, passionate man: 'il a besoin de s'imaginer qu'il me désire'[12] (Breillat 1979: 20). Unlike Jim, Bruel is too disembodied to be truly passionate, which is perhaps why Solange tells him that 'je suis amoureuse de Jim. Toi je t'aime'.[13] Bruel does seem to feel some real tenderness for Solange, as when he worries about the scratches that her other lover Bruno has given her in the heat of passion. Bruel also cannot bring himself to masturbate her as hard as Bruno did because he is concerned about her getting hurt: 'trop, c'est trop',[14] he warns her. But Bruel's solicitude and moderation seem to

11 'begins to find him stupid'.
12 'he needs to imagine himself as desiring me'.
13 'I'm in love with Jim. You, I love'.
14 'too much, it's too much'.

be more about bourgeois paternalism and timidity than they are about love for Solange. The fact is that Bruel wishes he could have rough sex with Solange (and so does she), but he is incapable of breaking certain taboos. He is trapped in the role of the kindly and overprotective husband ('Tu dois être un mari avec toutes les femmes. C'est un vice')[15] and unable to become a passionate lover.

Bruno is a heady intellectual whose caustic wit and wicked iconoclasm appeal to the anti-bourgeois rebel in Solange, the side of her character that prompts her to wear a death's-head T-shirt in public. Himself a film director like Solange, Bruno is more her mental equal than Bruel or Jim, the kind of verbal sparring partner that her handsome hunk of an actor could never be, as she tells Jim: 'avec lui [Bruno] je peux parler, et pas avec toi'[16] (Breillat 1979: 66). Unlike Bruel's lavish abode with its antique furniture, erotic paintings and other prize possessions, Bruno's apartment consists of books, a bed and bare walls. A 'séminariste transi'[17] is how Solange describes Bruno, and when he does overcome his inhibitions to sleep with her, he always keeps his clothes on, making contact with his teeth and his nails more than with his flesh, 'punishing' her for 'making' him cede to her sexual demands. For Bruno, sex is a kind of sadistic game – hard, cold and highly cerebral. Solange grows to miss the warm flesh of her actor lover, realising that Bruno is in a sense a 'pâle dérivatif'[18] of Jim, and when Bruno is contemptuous of the tears she cries after he has been cruel to her, Solange could use a little of her husband Bruel's sentimental concern. If only Solange could splice together her lovers and her husband so that passion and compassion would be united in one man. Intriguingly, Breillat uses a disguised cut to link a shot of Bruno about to ravage Solange with a shot of Bruel trying to do likewise but being concerned about the pain caused to her by 'love' scratches. Later, another nearly invisible cut links a shot of Bruel's tender but too tentative masturbation of Solange with a shot of Bruno's exciting but painful approach. The editing seems to convey Solange's wish for a composite Bruno-Bruel, as if superimposing the two could lead to a harmonious whole.

15 'You have to be a husband with all women. It's a vice'.
16 'I can talk with him [Bruno], and not with you'.
17 'scared-stiff seminary student'.
18 'pale derivative'.

Of all the incomplete men Solange sees, Bruno with his sadistic tendencies is the most problematic. Why does she keep returning to him for more abuse? According to Françoise Audé, it is because Solange is a masochist: 'Dans *Tapage nocturne*, l'amour se réduit à l'alternative domination/soumission. Quand Solange, du statut de subjugante passe à celui de subjuguée, c'est l'extase'[19] (Audé 1979: 79). As a film director in her public life, as a woman who gives orders in what is predominantly a male profession, Solange may find pleasure in taking direction (from another film director) in her private life, in submitting to his commands: 'Those who are most attracted to masochism may be the women whom feminism has served best, whose self-assertion has mostly been achieved. The women who have made it, who are successful in their own eyes, turn to masochism to live out the humiliation, the submission that they no longer have to endure anywhere else' (Phillips 1998: 55). Such masochistic desires may be disturbing if they indicate that a woman has internalised patriarchal values and feels the need to be chastised for her success ('la volonté inconsciente d'être punie pour sa transgression du rôle féminin traditionnel'), but these very desires may paradoxically enable her continued success if they serve as a '"soupape de sécurité" lui permettant de s'affirmer ou d'être même dominante dans ses relations avec les hommes'[20] (Löwy 2006: 65).

Private masochism may well function to support Solange's public authority in this way. There is certainly a stark contrast between her commanding presence in public and her private self-abasement, and cutting back and forth between the two suggests their interdependence. However, the particular masochistic scenarios that Solange enacts with Bruno would seem to indicate other factors at work. Certainly, part of what Solange finds exciting about her trysts with Bruno is that they are the opposite of a comfortable marriage: they are furtive, adulterous and scarifyingly intense. Whether Solange and Bruno's assignation is at her place or his, there is the constant threat – and thrilling possibility – that they will be caught *in flagrante*

19 'In *Tapage nocturne*, love is reduced to the alternative of dominance/submission. When Solange moves from the position of the subjugator to that of the subjugated, it's ecstasy'.

20 'the unconscious wish to be punished for her transgression of the traditional feminine role' ... '"safety valve" permitting her to assert herself or even to be dominant in her relations with men'.

delicto by her husband Bruel, by her other lover Jim, by Catherine (the woman Bruno lives with), by Dorothée (Bruno's press agent) or by other 'shocked' bourgeois citizens. Of course Bruel is Solange's husband in name only, but Bruno has only to mention her husband's possible arrival for the lovers' illicit passion to be ignited: 'On avait besoin de ce mensonge, le mot "mari", pour se faire croire que j'étais coupable et que rien ne pouvait exister entre nous, que des lambeaux provisoires'[21] (Breillat 1979: 151). When the couple begins to meet for sex in a tiny rented apartment, Solange's cries of pleasure and pain bring the neighbours pounding on the door in outrage at the lovers' passion. Solange is like Jeanne (Maria Schneider) in *Last Tango in Paris* who regularly leaves her fiancé and her impending marriage to have rough, anonymous sex in a virtually bare apartment with Paul (Marlon Brando), a man she hardly knows. Solange describes herself and Bruno as 'des inconnus qui ont rendez-vous tous les soirs dans la même chambre'[22] (Breillat 1979: 108).

But Solange's guilt over being a 'naughty girl' is not just some outrageous game she plays in order to spice up her sex life. Although she may seem to be a liberated woman, Solange is deeply ashamed of her desires. She may be a young woman living in the swinging 1970s, but she was a child in the repressive 1950s and early 1960s when a Catholic upbringing instilled in her a sense of guilt regarding female sexuality. Her transgressive behaviour now is a desperate attempt to break the taboos of her past, which means that she is still tied to those taboos and not really free. As Breillat has said, 'Entre l'aliénation religieuse et la soi-disant liberté sexuelle, c'est terrifiant. Ce sont de drôles de liberté que nous enseigne la société'[23] (Breillat 2006a: 123). Solange may be compared to Véronika in *La Maman et la putain*, another young woman in the 1970s desperately trying for sexual liberation from shame ('Pour moi il n'y a pas de putes. Tu peux sucer n'importe qui, tu peux te faire baiser par n'importe qui, tu n'es pas une pute') but often falling back into self-mortifying religious guilt ('c'est une merde, c'est une poussière, les super-couples

21 'We needed this lie, the word "husband", to make ourselves believe that I was guilty and that nothing could exist between us that wasn't tattered or temporary'.

22 'strangers who have a rendezvous every night in the same room'.

23 'Between religious alienation and so-called "sexual freedom", it's terrifying. These are some funny kinds of freedom that society teaches us'.

libres').[24] The more brazenly 'liberated' Solange is in expressing her desires, the more she feels she needs to be punished for them, in an increasingly vicious cycle of sexual expression and violent repression, leading to ever greater degrees of humiliation, scarification and degradation. Solange can don black leather pants in order to seduce Bruno, but it is he who must remove them while she lies passively in bed, barely able to look at her own 'shameful' sex. The kind of lovemaking they then engage in, here and in later scenes, involves Bruno's punishing her for her desires, giving her bites instead of kisses, scratches in place of caresses, and hard thrusting with his sex and his hand rather than empathetic contact. As Solange descends the stairs after one of these sessions with Bruno, she appears to sink below him, her face at the level of his crotch, as she muses, 'je suis *tombée* amoureuse'.[25]

Solange's self-abasement and degradation continue in that tiny rented apartment (she rented it) which has but a single mattress (she had it brought there) laid out on the floor. In this way, Solange has set the scene for herself to be shamefully debauched by Bruno: 'une chambre où il n'y a qu'un matelas pour baiser, ce qui est sinistre. J'ai honte'[26] (Breillat 1979: 107). When the neighbours pound on the apartment door, the fact that they have overheard her orgasmic cries only deepens Solange's shame and humiliation – feelings which she deliberately compounds when, after she and Bruno have been hounded from the apartment, she has sex with him in the stairwell where she is exposed to public view and even to potential assault by the male neighbours. Indeed, a part of Solange seems to be soliciting such an assault: 'je vais me faire attaquer dans la rue',[27] she tells Bruno, as if longing to be abused not just by one 'stranger' but by hordes of strange men. Because Solange associates female desire with being a 'bad girl', she thinks of herself as a dirty whore who deserves to be used and humiliated for the sexual feelings she has. In one scene, Solange tries to get Bruno to take her inside a 'hôtel de passe' where she can express her 'côté "Pigalle"',[28] and later, having

24 'For me there are no whores. You can suck anyone, you can get yourself fucked by anyone, you're not a whore' ... 'it's shit, it's dust, the great liberated couples'.
25 'I *fell* in love'.
26 'a room where there is only a mattress for fucking, which is sinister. I'm ashamed'.
27 'I'm going to get myself attacked in the street'.
28 'hooker hotel' ... '"red-light district" side'.

sunk as low with Bruno as he is willing to go and seeking to expose herself to the maximum possible degradation, she goes with a total stranger to such a hotel and lets herself be taken from behind, bitten on the neck and almost killed.

In returning again and again for more and increasingly severe abuse, Solange would seem to be a masochist ruled by the death drive, compelled to repeat the same shameful scenario in which she confuses pain with pleasure, in which she abases herself before sadistic men who punish her for her desires. However, there is also reason to believe that Solange's self-willed suffering may be an attempt to work through shame rather than simply acting it out, an effort to become conscious of the vicious cycle of brazen sexual expression and violent repression in which she is caught so that she may eventually escape it. To see the extent to which her scenario both does and does not fit that of a pathological masochist, it is helpful to compare Solange to O, the heroine of *Histoire d'O* (*Story of O*), the 1954 novel by Pauline Réage (pseudonym of Anne Declos). Like O who is given by René to Sir Stephen, Solange is in a sense prostituted when Bruel steers Bruno toward her. In each case, the first man feels that he can continue to enjoy her through the second – 'c'était lui qui la possédait et jouissait d'elle à travers ceux aux mains de qui elle était remise',[29] thinks René (Réage 1975: 55), while Bruel says, 'j'aime bien téléguider les amants de mes femmes'[30] – and in each case, the second man is crueller than the first, increasing the pain and humiliation. Both O (a successful fashion photographer) and Solange (a film director) are strong professional women who are deprived of their power as gazing subjects and ordered to expose themselves to the male gaze. O is told that 'vous avez perdu le droit de vous dérober' and that in front of the men 'vous ne fermerez jamais tout à fait les lèvres, ni ne croiserez les jambes, ni ne serrerez les genoux ... vous aurez seulement la peine, si l'on vous en requiert, d'ouvrir vos vêtements'[31] (Réage 1975: 35, 36). Bruno requires Solange to walk around the room with her top raised and her pants pulled down so that her sex is exposed to view, even

29 'it was he who possessed and enjoyed her through those into whose hands she had been given' (Réage 1973: 31).
30 'I like to guide the lovers of my women by remote control'.
31 'you have lost all right to privacy or concealment' ... 'you will never close your lips completely, or cross your legs, or press your knees together ... you need only take the trouble, if we require you to do it, of opening your clothes' (Réage 1973: 15, 16; translation modified).

though she tries to bury her head in his shoulder because she is dying of embarrassment.

However, once Solange has successfully completed her 'walk of shame', Bruno reaches out a hand to her as if pulling her to safety and asks her if she is happy, to which she says yes. Bruno's gesture and question may be ironic (a sadistic mocking of sentiment), but whatever his intentions, the effect on Solange is to help her overcome her shame by staging a controlled exposure to it, a humiliating exhibition which she can survive: 'Sans lui, je n'aurais pas pu faire un pas'[32] (Breillat 1979: 160). By contrast, O is ordered to expose herself so that the men can overcome *her*, invading her with their eyes and then their sex. Similarly, when Sir Stephen thrusts his hand between O's legs, her submission is in the service of his phallic power: 'La certitude où elle était que lorsqu'il la touchait, que ce fût pour la caresser ou la battre, que lorsqu'il ordonnait d'elle quelque chose c'était uniquement parce qu'il en avait envie, la certitude qu'il ne tenait compte que de son propre désir, comblait O'[33] (Réage 1975: 236). But when Bruno roughly masturbates Solange, it is her own desire she is put in touch with, her own shame she is feeling and struggling to overcome: 'Il n'y a que moi qui compte. Il y a quelque chose de moi qui m'échappe et que je sens que je vais saisir'.[34] O compulsively repeats her masochistic encounters until she is degraded unto death. In the end, men 'la possédèrent tour à tour' and, when Sir Stephen declares his intention to abandon her, O tells him that 'elle préféra mourir. Il y consentit'[35] (Réage 1975: 250–1). Whereas O is ultimately reduced to an orifice, an object, a nought, Solange recovers from her abuse by Bruno and by the violent stranger at the 'hôtel de passe';[36] she takes steps toward affirming her own desires and articulating them to Bruno; and when he is about to reject her, it is she who abandons him and moves on.

32 'Without him, I would not have been able to take a single step'.
33 'Her absolute certainty that when he touched her, whether it was to fondle or flog her, when he ordered her to do something it was solely because he wanted to, her certainty that all he cared about was his own desire, so overwhelmed and gratified O' (Réage 1973: 187).
34 'I'm the only one who counts. There's something of me that escapes me and that I feel I'm going to grasp'.
35 'possessed her one after the other' ... 'she would prefer to die. He gave his consent' (Réage 1973: 198–9; translation modified).
36 'hooker hotel'.

Solange's scenario thus departs considerably from the death-driven masochism of *Histoire d'O*, and we can get a better understanding of Solange by comparing her story to that of a 'closer relative', Camille, in Christine Pascal's *Zanzibar* (1989), a film co-scripted by Breillat. Actress Camille is self-destructively hooked on drugs much as director Solange is hooked on degrading sex with men: 'je suis "accrochée"', Solange realises about Bruno, 'Je le veux. Je le veux. Je le veux. ... C'est une drogue. Je ne peux plus survivre. Plus respirer sans ça. Je suis capable des pires bassesses'[37] (Breillat 1979: 65–6, 126–7). Vito, a producer like Bruel, offers Camille financial and emotional support, writing cheques to her and trying to help her kick the habit, but Maréchal, a director like Bruno, orders Camille to enact masochistic scenarios that require her to keep injecting drugs in order to plumb the depths of degradation and find out about herself. 'L'histoire du film', says Maréchal, 'c'est pourquoi il faut s'enfiler les choses à l'intérieur de son corps pour pouvoir vivre, pour pouvoir survivre'[38] – things like needles or, in Solange's case, violent men. During a 'rehearsal', Maréchal instructs Camille to confront her embarrassment by walking naked around a hotel room, and then on set (which consists of nothing but a mattress on the floor) he watches the pain and pleasure on her face while she shoots up. Camille uses Maréchal's (the camera's, the public's) gaze to intensify the shame she feels to the point where she must *face* it or die. Once her shame is brought to consciousness, fixed in an image (her face on film), she may be able to gain some critical distance from it, understand its cause, and stop repeating the same masochistic acts. As Maréchal says, 'Cinéma, c'est pour guérir. ... Maintenant qu'on a filmé le désespoir des personnages, on va pouvoir filmer son espoir'.[39]

What the film image is for Camille, language is for Solange – a means by which she tries to represent her desire, exercise and exorcise its shame, and free herself from the cycle of brazen sexual expression and violent repression. And once again Bruno is her guide: not only does he get her to expose herself, to burn with and (potentially)

37 'I'm hooked' ... 'I want him. I want him. I want him. ... It's a drug. I can no longer survive. No longer breathe without that. I am capable of the worst base acts'.

38 'The film's story' ... 'is about why one needs to have things pushed inside one's body so that one can live, so that one can survive'.

39 'Cinema is for healing. ... Now that we have filmed the characters' despair, we're going to be able to film their hope'.

through shame, but he is constantly goading her to confess her desire, interrogating her about what she wants, whether she is in love with him, and why she cries out as much in pain as in pleasure during lovemaking. Being forced to formulate some answers may help Solange to give a verbal structure to her confused feelings so that she can 'read' and 'rewrite' the masochistic scenario in which she is caught. For example, when Bruno and Solange are out walking in the street and he challenges her about her going barefoot, her response – 'je vous suivrais jusqu'au bout du monde'[40] – is both sexually brazen and masochistically servile, both wildly romantic and flippantly cynical. It does not suggest a woman at ease with her own desire, but in saying it Solange has perhaps found out something about herself. In a later scene, she tries to tell Bruno that she wants to sleep with him, but the repressive censor in her head causes her to substitute 'dormir' for 'coucher' and then she is unable to push past this mental block, managing only to say that she doesn't really want 'de dormir' with him but rather 'de faire autre chose'.[41] Solange begins to make more progress when she sends Bruno three separate telegrams – *JE, T'* and *AIME*[42] – which at least convey her feelings, albeit in a distanced and fragmented fashion allowing her to continue to disown them.

Finally, Solange's greatest moment of self-realisation occurs in the letter she composes to Bruno while she is being degraded almost to death by the violent stranger in the 'hôtel de passe': 'Je n'ai envie que d'un au-delà des limites, quelque chose qui me bouleverse complètement et qu'en moi-même je ne sais pas articuler: désir'.[43] What Solange reaches toward saying here, what she struggles to know and articulate about herself, is that her true longing is not for masochistic pleasure in pain but for *jouissance*. She does not really want to suffer at the hands of Bruno or other sadistic men, to find her joy in patriarchal punishment of her 'shameful' sexuality. What she wants is a *jouissance* or ecstasy that will take her beyond the limits of patriarchal law, beyond brazen defiance and servile obedience, to an

40 'I would follow you to the ends of the earth'.

41 'to go to sleep' … 'to sleep' … 'to go to sleep' … 'to do another thing'.

42 '*I … LOVE … YOU*'. Near the end of *Une femme est une femme*, Angela makes a similarly indirect communication of her love when she shows Emile a book with the words '*JE T'AIME*' in one part of its title.

43 'hooker hotel' … 'I want only what is beyond the limits, something that overwhelms me completely and that is in myself and that I don't know how to articulate: desire'.

affirmation of her own desire for something more, something better, something other than what the incomplete and fragmented men she meets have had to offer her. Solange's masochistic scenarios – her staged humiliations and her verbal reflection on the meaning of these in her dialogue, her telegrams and her letter – are thus actually an attempt to *see* and *understand* the cycle of shame and punishment in which she is caught so that she can free herself from it. When some critics attacked *Tapage nocturne* for its degrading depictions of a woman, Breillat defended her film by saying that, 'si l'on ne prend pas en compte le masochisme des femmes, si on ne le raconte pas dans la fiction pour s'en délivrer', women may not be able to see or free themselves: 'La fiction est toujours un acte où l'on se retrouve ou alors où l'on se délivre des choses. C'est elle qui nous donne la vision. C'est elle qui nous permet de voir que c'est finalement la timidité, la pudeur, l'inhibition que l'on a par rapport à son propre corps qui font que l'on va se retrouver coincée dans des attitudes extraordinairement masochistes'[44] (Breillat 2006a: 94–5). As we consider how Solange uses such fictions as the writing of her letter to free herself from masochistic attitudes brought on by sexual shame, it is interesting to compare her situation to that of Brigitte in *L'Intérimaire* (*The Temp*), a 1982 novel by Brigitte Lozerec'h which Breillat and Maurice Pialat worked on adapting for the screen but which was never filmed. Like Solange, Brigitte suffers from the belief that her own desires are dirty ('C'était mal de jouir, c'était grossier, c'était honteux') and also like Solange, Brigitte goes from man to man, unable to remain in any relationship for long ('j'étais sûre d'être intérimaire. ... En amour aussi, je n'ai fait que des remplacements'[45] (Lozerec'h 1995: 151, 260)). But, much as Bruno's interrogations compel Solange to examine her psyche and to face her sexual fears by writing a letter, so Brigitte has a stern publisher whose probing questions prompt her to

44 'if we don't take into account women's masochism, if we don't recount it in fiction in order to liberate ourselves from it' ... 'Fiction is always an act where we recognise ourselves or rather where we liberate ourselves from things. It's fiction that gives us vision. It's fiction that allows us to see that it's finally the timidity, the modesty, the inhibition we have regarding our own bodies which ensures that we're going to find ourselves trapped in extraordinarily masochistic attitudes'.

45 'It was wrong to have an orgasm, it was base, shameful' ... 'I was sure of one thing, of being a temp. ... My love affairs too have just been temporary' (Lozerec'h 1984: 100, 189).

write a memoir ('*Mémoires d'une jeune fille dérangée*'[46] (Lozerec'h 1995: 181)) and then a novel (which becomes *L'Intérimaire* itself) in which she moves beyond unconsciously repeating the past by deliberately restaging scenes of shame so that she can now gain some control over and distance from them.

Solange's writing has enabled her to understand that her true desire is to move beyond masochism, but when she has Bruno read her letter he seems to misunderstand its meaning, for he continues his sadistic behaviour toward her. When it becomes clear that she no longer enjoys playing the submissive partner, he just sits and reads the newspaper, revealing that he is really indifferent to her if she won't conform to her assigned role, and when she orders him to leave, he slinks away without being able to look her in the face, as if afraid of her newfound strength. With Bruno gone, Solange dissolves into tears, less because she misses *him* than due to the fact that she has failed once again to find a man who can fulfil her ideal of body, heart and head combined. We recall that Elena at the end of *A ma sœur!* could not stop crying and in a sense died of disillusionment when her lover failed her. In Solange's last scene, she is crying on a bench next to an old woman who is feeding the pigeons in a park square – a woman who may represent Solange's fear of a future of lonely spinsterhood. In the film's first scene, Solange was sitting in a café waiting for a man and she is still waiting at the end – waiting or almost giving up in despair. But just as writing that letter had helped Solange to overcome her masochistic dependency, so now she thinks of some words to contain her tears and to move her beyond despondency over this latest failed love: 'pleurer est d'habitude une affaire de vingt-quatre heures'.[47] As Solange stops crying, rises to her feet and begins to walk away, birds fly into the air in front of her, and the camera freeze-frames her in motion as she is freeing herself from dependency and dejection in order to actively seek her ideal.

---

46 '*Memoirs of a Disturbed Daughter*' (Lozerec'h 1984: 127) – inspired, of course, by Simone de Beauvoir's *Mémoires d'une jeune fille rangée* (*Memoirs of a Dutiful Daughter*) (1958).

47 'crying is usually a twenty-four-hour affair'.

Romance

Twenty years after *Tapage nocturne*, Breillat returned to the theme of
a woman's sexual odyssey in *Romance*, a movie she considered to be
a kind of 'fantasy remake' of the earlier film (Murphy 1999: 20), one
more mythic and symbolic, less rooted in a particular time and place.
Yet it is important to understand that she first conceived of the idea for
Romance and even wrote a synopsis of the film in the late 1970s, and
like *Tapage nocturne* it is centrally concerned with the conflict between
sexual liberation (post-May 1968) and religious inhibition (due to
Breillat's Catholic upbringing in the 1950s and 1960s). Like Solange,
Marie (the heroine of *Romance*) is seeking fulfilment of her female
desire for sex *and* sentiment in a man who can help to integrate her
body and soul, but the men she meets tend, like Solange's partners,
to be fragmented and incomplete – sentimental, physical or intellectual but not all three combined. If Marie's steady boyfriend Paul is
heart, then her lover Paolo is body and her schoolmaster Robert is
head, which roughly correspond to Solange's Bruel, Jim and Bruno.
Like Solange, Marie is unwilling to settle for sex without romance or
for romance without sex: 'Elle n'en est pas aimée comme elle estime
qu'elle devrait l'être', Breillat has explained, 'D'où la souffrance d'aller
d'homme en homme dont aucun n'est à la hauteur de cette espèce
d'idéal flamboyant que chaque femme porte en elle. ... parce qu'ils
ne s'y intègrent pas. ... Parce qu'ils sont trop rationnels. Ils sont
cartésiens, les hommes'[48] (Clément 2002: 274). Marie's boyfriend
Paul exhibits a mind/body dualism that manifests itself as a Madonna/
whore complex. As with Christophe and Frédérique in *Parfait amour!*
Paul was hot for Marie at first when she was a strange body to be
conquered, but now that they have been together for some months
he can only think of her as a future wife and mother, a spiritual being
who must not be degraded by sex. Paul's bifurcated view of Marie only
exacerbates the split within her between flesh and spirit, reinforcing
the religious guilt she feels that a 'good girl' like her could have 'dirty'
desires.

On one night when Paul has left Marie alone in his bed, the
camera slowly moves up her naked body – from her crossed legs to

---

48 'she is not loved in the way that she believes she should be' ... 'And because of
this she suffers by going from man to man, none of whom lives up to this sort
of shining ideal that every woman carries within her. ... because men are not
integrated in this way. ... Because they are too rational. Men are Cartesian'.

her sex and up to her face – as she lies there masturbating. She is not filmed in integrated long shot but in piecemeal close-up, emphasising the disconnect between her 'spiritual' love for Paul (the only kind of love he now accepts from her) and her physical urges, as she muses in voice-over that 'dans ma tête, y'a Paul. Il aurait pu me réconcilier avec mon corps. Mais c'est pas ça qu'il voulait'.[49] It is interesting to contrast this scene with another from one of Breillat's favourite films, Jean-Luc Godard's *Le Mépris*, in which the camera pans over the naked body of Camille (Brigitte Bardot) as she asks her husband Paul (Michel Piccoli) whether he loves each part of her body, erogenous zones and face. When Paul affirms that he does, Camille (in a wide shot) remarks that 'Donc tu m'aimes totalement'.[50] Marie's Paul is 'present' only as the disapproving censor in her head, the one who prompts her to close her legs against pagan pleasures even as her hand fights to fulfil her body's needs: 'Je me branle toujours les jambes serrées. ... Je suis pas capable de m'offrir. Je me viole'.[51] Because Marie is ashamed of her own desires, pleasure is not something she can admit to wanting or accept without resistance, and she can only reach orgasm by violating her own sanctity. As Kay Chadwick notes, while 80% of French people identify themselves as Catholics, two-thirds of these reject the Church's declarations on sexuality (Hughes and Reader 1998: 92–3). Yet despite a conscious sense of having been liberated from dogma, 'une réticence spécifique et souterraine à l'égard de la masturbation persiste chez les femmes attachées à la religion, en particulier chez les catholiques. La condamnation répétée jusqu'à nos jours de cette pratique par l'Eglise, que seules les femmes ont intériorisée, est une survivance du refus augustinien du plaisir, considéré comme d'autant plus condamnable ici qu'il serait obtenu en-dehors d'une union'[52] (Bozon 2002: 79). In reference to this scene

49 'in my head, there's Paul. He could have reconciled me with my body. But that's not what he wanted'.

50 'So you love me completely.' This scene in which a woman is affirmed in her totality was Godard's sardonic response to the producers who had insisted that there be some salacious nude shots of Bardot in the film.

51 'I always masturbate with my legs closed tight. ... I'm not capable of offering myself. I rape myself'.

52 'a specific and deeply ingrained reluctance with regard to masturbation persists among women with religious ties, particularly among Catholics. The repeated condemnation even today of this practice by the Church, which only women have internalised, is a survival of the Augustinian rejection of pleasure, considered as all the more condemnable here since it is obtained outside of a union'.

where Marie guiltily masturbates, the French film poster for *Romance* shows a red X over a close-up of a woman's hand between her naked legs, with the X representing 'la honte sexuelle, l'inconnue des mathématiques, le chromosome féminin'[53] (Breillat 2006a: 130). Masturbation is Marie's attempt to get beyond self-censorship and shame to discover an unknown part of herself, the female desires that have been forbidden to her as unacceptable in a 'proper' woman.

Breillat was inspired to film this scene of Marie's struggle to get in touch with her own sexuality by a similar moment in Christine Pascal's *Félicité* (1979) where the title character, bravely played by Pascal herself, masturbates despite her legs being crossed and her body being tensed against the pleasure she feels it is wrong to receive. *Félicité* and *Tapage nocturne* were released in the same year, and Pascal and Breillat grew as close as sisters ('une âme à deux corps')[54] after they were both heavily criticised for having given such bold cinematic expression to women's sexual desires. 'Si ces films avaient été faits par des hommes', Breillat has said, 'il n'y aurait pas eu tant de scandale. A l'époque il était encore interdit à une femme de parler de son sexe. C'était une chose répugnante'[55] (Milon and Renouard 1999). The opprobrium heaped upon Pascal by disapproving critics made her something of a pariah in the film industry, hurting her chances of getting work as an actress and contributing to her manic depression. When Pascal took on the subject of female desire again in *Adultère (mode d'emploi)* (*Adultery: A User's Manual*) (1995), Breillat believes that Pascal censored herself and did not make the movie she had wanted to make for fear of inciting the same kind of condemnation as had greeted *Félicité*. This self-stifling led to further hospitalisation and Pascal committed suicide by jumping out the window of a psychiatric clinic in 1996. In Breillat's view, Pascal 'en est morte, de ce scandale. Elle est morte de *Félicité*'[56] (Milon and Renouard 1999), but before her death Pascal fought to obtain the 'avance sur recettes' ('subsidy funding') so that Breillat could make *Romance*, a film which

53 'sexual shame, the unknown in math, the female chromosome'.

54 This expression – 'one soul in two bodies' (Breillat 2006a: 235, 242) – is the same one that Breillat used to describe *A ma sœur!*'s Anaïs and Elena, who as we have seen were modelled in part on Breillat and her sister Marie-Hélène.

55 'If these films had been made by men' ... 'there would not have been such a scandal. At the time it was still forbidden for a woman to speak of her sex. It was a repugnant thing'.

56 'died from it, from this scandal. She died from *Félicité*'.

Breillat dedicated to Pascal and which features this uncensored scene of female self-pleasuring in affirmation of the one in *Félicité*.

Although Marie can express and seek fulfilment of her desires by herself, she is barred from doing so in the company of the man she loves, for sex and sentiment are two separate things for Paul and he cannot imagine sullying his future spouse by getting down and dirty with her. Freud argued that there are many men like Paul: 'Where they love they do not desire and where they desire they cannot love. ... There are only a very few educated people in whom the two currents of affection and sensuality have become properly fused; the man almost always feels his respect for the woman acting as a restriction on his sexual activity, and only develops full potency when he is with a debased sexual object' (Freud 1989: 397, 399). No longer just dating but not yet married, Paul and Marie are now essentially living together in a 'union libre' ('cohabitation'), and Marie is confused by Paul's sudden lack of libidinal interest in her, as if the prospect of her as a marital partner meant the end of her as a sexual partner. Paul's apartment, which she basically shares with him now, is as white and pristine as his sacred ideal of marriage, and Marie always wears white around Paul as if she had to live up to his expectations regarding her virginal purity. In the scenes where Paul and Marie lie side by side without touching and virtually motionless in their white bed, Breillat shoots them in long take/long shot to emphasise their frozen isolation. Paul may think that he is showing respect for his lady by not debasing her with his beastly desires, but for Marie true love and respect must include the physical along with the spiritual: 'On dit d'un homme qui baise une femme qu'il l'honore. ... Paul me déshonore'.[57] In bed, Paul wears his white T-shirt and his white undershorts as a kind of *cordon sanitaire* against fleshly contact with Marie. When she insists on stroking and sucking him, he can barely even watch what she is doing, as if his head wanted nothing to do with his sex, and when she remarks that she likes the smell of it, he is disgusted. It seems clear that Paul has as much trouble accepting his own body as he does Marie's.

Paul will allow Marie to stroke him but never to climax or detumescence, which suggests that another reason for Paul's unyielding nature is a need to remain hard and dominant. Paul is a male model,

57 'One says of a man who fucks a woman that he honours her. ... Paul dishonours me'.

and in his first scene he is posing as a matador for a commercial photo shoot where he is instructed to stand on tiptoe in order to grow in size so that he can tower over the female model by his side, who is ordered to incline her head back toward him in a femininely submissive manner. As Michèle Pagès has pointed out, 'les travaux menés sur la présentation corporelle des sexes dans la publicité montrent de manière irréfutable à quel point la hiérarchisation des sexes marque les représentations: ainsi la femme est souvent représentée dans une attitude corporelle indiquant sa position subalterne ou soumise, alors que l'image masculine réfère à une position protectrice'[58] (Pagès 2001: 228). Literally shaped by this patriarchal world of advertising images, Paul no doubt expects Marie in real life to submit to him as the dominant one. But Paul must also realise that he is only impersonating a macho man and even having to fake it (by standing on his tiptoes, by wearing a matador costume, by being fixed in a photo image of hardness). Moreover, modelling is often considered a feminine profession, and in the film's opening shots Breillat not only constructs Paul as the object of the camera's (and Marie's) gaze, but he is also seen having his face covered in white powder like a geisha by a make-up woman wearing an Asian-print shirt. So some of Paul's hardness toward Marie can be understood as a defence against femininity, which he fears might undermine his precarious gender identity. In this sense, Paul is less like the androgynous Thomas in *Brève traversée* who was able to integrate both hard and soft traits, and more like Christophe in *Parfait amour!* whose macho behaviour was the sign of a gender panic. Paul leaves his 'virginal' Marie behind in the white apartment to go to red-lit bars where he dances seductively with 'loose' women and shows that he can 'conquer' them before the admiring eyes of his male friend Ashley. Paul finds pleasure in proving his virility by making women submit to 'degrading' sexual advances, whereas the only sex he can contemplate having with Marie is the painful but necessary chore ('il faut aller au charbon')[59] of impregnating her to make her a mother. Paul is briefly excited by Marie when

58 'the studies conducted on the bodily representation of the sexes in advertising show in an irrefutable manner to what extent the hierarchisation of the sexes marks these representations: thus the woman is often represented in a bodily stance indicating her subaltern or submissive position, whereas the image of the man puts him in a protective position'.
59 'one has to head off to the coal mines'.

he thinks she might be cheating on him ('whorish' behaviour that makes him want to 'conquer' her again), but when she wears a red dress and positions herself on top of him, he cannot stand the active expression of her desires, which puts him in the passive 'feminine' position, and he throws her off him and onto the floor. In this way, he remains hard and dominant, managing also to impregnate her without coming (to her), losing only a drop of manly fluid and reproducing himself as if spiritually in the form of a son while essentially avoiding any physical contact.

Paul's idealisation of his 'virgin' Marie and his denigration of her sex only make her further ashamed of her desires, which her Catholic upbringing already tells her are improper in a good wife and mother. Paul's Madonna/whore complex does psychic violence to Marie, as depicted in a nightmare fantasy where she imagines her head cut off from her sex by a guillotine-like contraption. On one side of the divide, the upper half of a white-clad Marie lies in a white maternity ward as her husband-to-be Paul bends tenderly over her bed to give her loving comfort. But protruding through the other side is Marie's lower half, garbed in garters and a flouncy red skirt like a whore, her sex a hole which anonymous, apelike men use to demonstrate their phallic dominance in a scene with red lighting. As cinematographer Yorgos Arvanitis has said, 'je me suis inspiré des vases grecs où des hommes nus en plein priapisme dansent une ronde infernale, se poursuivant, le pénis en érection. Ici, la dominante rouge est essentielle. Elle est comme l'enfer où ces hommes cherchent des sexes de femmes qui sont comme des trous'[60] (Clouzot 2004: 87). This nightmare is the metaphorical truth of Marie's relationship with Paul, a scene which is then acted out in a more realistic register when the two of them go to a nightclub and, after solicitously patting Marie's pregnant belly (she is wearing a white jumper), Paul leaves her behind at the bar in order to go 'hunting' for women to 'conquer' on the red-lit dance floor. Women are either sacred mothers or disgraced whores, and there seems to be no way of reconciling maternity and sexuality. (Interestingly, Keith Reader has pointed out that the only pornographic films that are still being prosecuted as against the law in France appear to be 'those

---

60 'I was inspired by the Greek vases where nude and fully priapic men dance an infernal round, pursuing one another, with penises erect. Here, the dominant red is essential. It's like Hell where these men are hunting for the sexes of women which are like holes'.

showing pregnant women engaged in sexual activity, which has been judged to fall under the prohibition on images depicting the "degradation of the human person"' (Hughes and Reader 1998: 435).)

In the weeks before she becomes pregnant, with Paul's coldness blocking her desires, Marie goes in search of physical fulfilment and finds it in Paolo, an Italian-stallion variant of Paul, a lover as sensual as her future husband is repressed. (Sagamore Stévenin, who plays Paul, was originally considered for the role of Paolo – another indication of the extent to which the two men are alter egos.) Paolo kisses her hungrily when she lets him pick her up in a bar, and outside in the car he paws her breasts (as Jim does to Alice in *Une vraie jeune fille*) and tries to sweet-talk her into giving him oral sex (like the Italian Lothario Fernando with Elena in *A ma sœur!*). Unlike Paul's icy white apartment, Paolo's artist's studio has warm woods and golden bed linen, and he is eager to press his naked flesh against hers, even wanting to do it without a condom. Paolo is played by legendary 'hardeur' ('hardcore porn actor') Rocco Siffredi whose impressive endowment and staying power have made him a megastar of the X-rated film industry ('L'homme qui a fait jouir près de 3000 femmes'[61] (Zimmer 2002: 371)). Breillat kept her hiring of Siffredi a secret from the cast and crew until the day before shooting for fear that if they knew any earlier they would desert the film, and when she shot the scene where Siffredi's erection is visible and he appears to penetrate Caroline Ducey (Marie) from behind, the sound engineer protested by shouting out that this is not cinema. There is certainly a sense in which Paolo is an icon of sex, the anti-Paul whose ready responsiveness makes her feel desired and desirable, the man whose body brings her to orgasm. However, his is not the face she loves and so she has not yet been reconciled, body and soul.

But it's important to see that Breillat has also cast Siffredi *against* type as a man of feeling who *could* help Marie integrate sex and sentiment and that it is she who ultimately resists this reconciliation. Although Paolo's desire for her is strong, he is vulnerable and insecure around Marie for she is the first woman he has been with since the death of his former love some months ago. (Paolo's vulnerability is like that of Paul (Marlon Brando) in *Last Tango in Paris*, a man who also recently lost his wife and who is trying to renew his

61 'The man who has made close to 3000 women come'.

sensual life through a kind of adulterous sex with another woman.) When Paolo and Marie first have intercourse, he hides his sex from her and she, ashamed of all things physical, doesn't dare to look, but the next time as he is putting on a condom she encourages him to show himself while she peeks through the strands of hair she has pulled down over her eyes. In a moment of bodily self-loathing, Paolo says that he finds used condoms repellent and Marie agrees, significantly comparing them to used tampons that women hide from men, each gender fearing the other's disgust and here helping each other to overcome it. As Paolo begins to take Marie from behind, the camera holds them in a wide shot including their heads and their lower bodies. Then, in the same continuous film-take, the camera slides back and forth between his hips thrusting into hers (on the right) and their faces, especially hers, contorted in pleasure (on the left). In this way, the camera movement itself works to connect flesh and feeling rather than isolating body parts from personalities by cutting to the fragmented shots of sex organs usually seen in patriarchal porn. As Sara Diamond notes, 'pornography concentrates on fragments of the female form: a breast, foot, mouth. This allows the viewer to distance himself from the real person to whom the fragment belongs, avoiding the demands of relating to the whole, intelligent, emotional and active woman' (Diamond 1985: 43). In her pornographic nightmare fantasy, Marie was cut in two, her body deprived of its head and reduced to a hole for soulless use by anonymous men, but in this intimate scene with Paolo, he engages with her sexually and emotionally, and their love's potential as an integrated whole is dramatised by the unbroken take, the wide framing and the connective camera movement.

These techniques mark a complex and innovative departure by Breillat from the facile conventions typically used to film sex scenes in porn: 'toucher au sexe n'est pas si simple dès qu'on ne l'aborde pas sous l'angle classique du porno sans âme et qu'on tente de le réintégrer dans l'identité humaine'[62] (Milon and Renouard 1999). Not only does the expression of pleasure on Marie's face show that she is more than just a passive receptacle (there is no isolated 'beaver shot'), but Paolo is also depicted as something more than the ever-rampant stud that Siffredi usually plays in porn films. Unlike Paul who withholds himself from Marie in order to remain hard and dominant, Paolo

62 'approaching the subject of sex isn't so simple as soon as you stop tackling it from the classic angle of soulless porn and try to reintegrate it into human identity'.

gives himself freely to her, and unlike the priapic satyr (played by a porn actor) in Marie's nightmare fantasy whose ejaculating organ is shown in close-up, Paolo gets no 'money shot' to prove that he is a big spender. Instead, the camera shows us Paolo's face as he climaxes, after which his head droops onto her back and then his penis is visible going soft. It took some courage for porn star Rocco Siffredi to show his feelings and his flaccidity along with his hard body, but these are crucial to Breillat's representation of an integrated man as having evolved past mere machismo to incorporate both hard and soft traits: 'Quand un homme est extrêmement viril, comme l'est Rocco, il peut se permettre d'être le plus faible, ce qui est la réalité de l'acte physique entre un homme et une femme. ... l'homme qui jouit est en train de cesser d'être un homme au sens où il se représente lui-même en tant qu'homme, c'est-à-dire comme un sexe en érection. Et ça, ça se voit sur le visage de Rocco'[63] (Flach Film 1999).

But when Paolo displays weakness and makes himself vulnerable to rejection by needing her kisses after sex, Marie rebuffs him by refusing mouth-to-mouth contact, maintaining the distance between them that she had first established by insisting he wear a condom and by having him take her from behind. While one reason for this could be that she is saving her kisses, cuddling and fecundity for Paul (the man she truly wants to reconcile her sexual and spiritual selves), the more disturbing explanation may be that, in her current unintegrated state, Marie associates sex with shame and suffering and that she can find excitement only with macho strangers who degrade her as the punishment she 'deserves' for her 'sinful' desires. It is impersonal, animalistic, 'dirty' sex that she craves, so when Paolo looks to her for tenderness, she turns her head away, saying that she doesn't want to see the men who take her and that she wants to be an obscenely gaping hole. By dissociating sex from sentiment in this way, Marie *reduces herself* to a pornographic body (like the one in her nightmare fantasy). Earlier she had told Paolo she was married, but was this to remain faithful in her mind to Paul or to excite her body with the prospect of 'dirty' adultery? Similarly, when she told Paolo that she

63 'When a man is extremely virile, as Rocco is, he can allow himself to be the weaker one, which is the reality of the physical act between a man and a woman. ... the man who comes is in the act of ceasing to be a man in the sense in which he represents himself as a man, that is, as a sex in erection. And that, that is what is seen on Rocco's face'.

quite likes repellent things like used condoms and men's penises, was this to help him overcome his disgust or to wallow in her own? Marie tries to understand her 'envie d'être un trou' as something 'métaphysique: je disparais à proportion de la bite qui prétend me prendre. Je m'évide. C'est ça ma pureté'.[64] Marie wants to believe that she isn't just being taken but instead is working toward gaining control, that her physical degradation is something she can turn into metaphysical transcendence, and that shameful sex can be re-imagined as holy and pure. But her insistence on casting Paolo as nothing but a 'cock' to root out her 'hole' suggests that, rather than moving toward integration and transcendence, Marie may be stuck in a masochistic cycle of 'sinful' sex and self-punishment.

In a later scene, Marie lets a strange man paw her in her white dress ('sans faux-semblant sentimental, juste du désir cru') and then kneel to perform cunnilingus on her ('le déshonneur, c'est une jouissance de fille')[65] while her legs are splayed on the stairs inside Paul's apartment building. On the one hand, Marie could be seen as looking for a sexual complement to Paul's sentiment, as wanting her sex to be worthy of worship, not just her spirit. On the other hand, Marie's thoughts seem potentially nihilistic and self-mortifying, as when she imagines 'se vautrer pour le plaisir de se vautrer' with this 'cloche', for whom she is 'juste une chatte qu'il a envie de bourrer'.[66] When this stranger then forces her face down and anally rapes her (like the violent man who assaults Solange from behind in *Tapage nocturne*), Marie is right to wonder whether her odyssey is driven by a desire not to discover her sex but to punish it, not to integrate herself but to cut off the offending lower half: 'A la limite, mon désir c'est de rencontrer Jack l'éventreur. C'est certain qu'il ouvrirait en deux une femme comme moi' and reveal that the sacred 'mystère' of womanhood 'n'est qu'un amas de tripes'.[67] These dark thoughts suggest that Marie may end up knifed to death like Theresa (Diane Keaton) in *Looking for Mr Goodbar* (Richard Brooks, 1977), an influential film at

64 'desire to be a hole' ... 'metaphysical: I disappear in proportion to the cock that pretends to take me. I hollow myself out. That's my purity'.
65 'without the pretext of sentiment, just raw desire' ... 'dishonour is what makes a girl come'.
66 'wallowing for the pleasure of wallowing' ... 'lowlife' ... 'just a pussy he wants to stuff'.
67 'At the limit, what I desire is to meet Jack the Ripper. He would certainly cut in two a woman like me' ... 'mystery' ... 'is only a load of tripe'.

the time when Breillat first conceived of *Romance*. Theresa is another young Catholic woman struggling with self-disgust over her body and its 'filthy' desires. Like Marie, Theresa is dissatisfied with a boyfriend who idealises her as a future wife and mother ('Don't love me. Just make love') and so she goes to bars to pick up strange men for sex ('Saint Theresa by day and swingin' Terry by night'). As she engages in ever more risky encounters, it becomes increasingly clear that, behind Theresa's search for acceptance of sensual pleasure as an integral part of her spirit, there lies a darker desire for pain and punishment driven by a loathing of her body and an urge to have it expunged. In the end, Theresa is raped and stabbed to death by one of her anonymous pick-ups – a fate that almost befalls Marie.[68]

As was Theresa, Marie is a teacher of young children, which emphasises the conflict within her between the good Catholic girl and the promiscuous sinner ('virgin schoolteacher, bar-hopping slut' is what one character called Theresa). When her previous night's bar adventure with Paolo makes Marie late for school one morning, she runs under an archway with a statue of Christ on the Cross looming over her and arrives at her classroom to face her disapproving headmaster. In a later classroom scene, the white-clad Marie makes spelling errors on the blackboard (writing 'Les moi d'hiver' instead of 'Les mois',[69] an unconscious comment on the frigid purity Paul has enforced on her) while her headmaster, wearing an angry red shirt, watches with a severe look on his face. After taking her back to his apartment, the headmaster Robert reprimands her for the 'trou'[70] in her teaching and then thrusts his fingers into her sex, using her as and reducing her to a hole. Marie feels that she deserves to be punished in this way for her errant sexuality, her inability to live up to Paul's ideal of her purity. Simone de Beauvoir's comments on female masochism seem relevant here: 'L'amante qui se retrouve devant l'amant dans la situation de l'enfant devant ses parents retrouve aussi ce sentiment de culpabilité qu'elle connaissait auprès d'eux; elle ne choisit pas de se révolter contre lui tant qu'elle l'aime: elle se révolte contre soi. S'il l'aime moins qu'elle ne le souhaite, si elle échoue à l'absorber, à le rendre heureux, à lui suffire, tout son narcissisme se convertit

68 This man stabs Theresa in a panicky attempt to affirm his masculine identity much as Christophe knifes Frédérique at the end of *Parfait amour!*
69 'The wintry me' ... 'months'.
70 'hole'.

en dégoût, en humiliation, en haine de soi qui l'incite à des auto-punitions'[71] (Beauvoir 1949: 488).

Marie's masochism also serves as a compromise formation: her desire to indulge in sensual enjoyment is fulfilled but she simultaneously defends against this wish by making sure that she suffers for it, punishing herself for her infidelity to Paul's ideal. Wearing a white dress and standing in front of a white windowshade, Marie lets herself be bound and gagged by Robert, who is in his red shirt near a red curtain. In this way, her purity is 'forced' to submit to being sullied by his passion for she cannot speak or act to prevent it. Later, having been deliciously and dirtily eroticised by Robert, Marie wears a red dress which he has pulled down to reveal her black bra and panties. With her mouth gagged, her arms tied behind her back, and her legs spread open by a steel rod, Marie is finally 'free' to express her sexuality (as evidenced by the wetness Robert finds between her legs) *because* she is also being severely censured for it, punished for her pleasure. One of Breillat's models for Marie was Séverine (Catherine Deneuve) in *Belle de jour*, directed by Luis Buñuel. A proper housewife whose relationship with her bourgeois husband Pierre is without passion, Séverine finds that she can only free her sexuality by prostituting herself to anonymous men in a brothel. Desire is thus associated with sordid self-abasement, and Séverine imagines further dirty delight and chastisement in a fantasy of her being bound to a post and having mud thrown on her white dress while Pierre watches. In other tied-to-a-tree fantasies, Séverine is wearing red while being whipped and raped by a man from the lower classes, and Pierre ends up shooting her in the head. Like Séverine's, Marie's pleasure-seeking is severely compromised by guilt and self-condemnation. Her every attempt at sexual expression is met by increasingly harsh repression in a masochistic cycle in which her life instincts now seem ruled by the death drive. When Robert lays her body on his red bed after their first masochistic session, Marie describes the experience as having been 'comme de la mort. ... Tu te transformes en charogne petit à

71 'The woman in love who before her lover is in the position of the child before its parents is also liable to that sense of guilt she felt with them; she chooses not to revolt against him as long as she loves him, but she revolts against herself. If he loves her less than she wants him to, if she fails to engross him, to make him happy, to satisfy him, all her narcissism is transformed into self-disgust, into humiliation, into hatred of herself, which drive her to self-punishment' (Beauvoir 1978: 651–2).

petit'[72] and, at the end of their second session, we see Marie's twisted form lying roped and gagged on the floor with her legs spread and her red dress in disarray like the corpse of a rape/murder victim.

But it is possible to understand Marie's masochism as controlled rather than compulsive, as a staged and scripted scenario in which she gains life-affirming consciousness and empowerment rather than becoming increasingly mute, immobilised and mortified. We might begin by noting that Robert, despite his fashionably furnished playboy pad and his macho bragging (he claims to have possessed over 10,000 women), seems less interested in phallic penetration or domination than he is in prompting Marie to exercise and exorcise her own sexual demons. Breillat had originally wanted Jean-Luc Godard or Roman Polanski for the part of Robert, and like the film director Bruno in *Tapage nocturne*, Robert is essentially a 'metteur en scène' whose apartment, as he tells Marie, is 'un théâtre' where 'je fais des répétitions'.[73] Much as Bruno had Solange walk around a room with her sex exposed to view, so Robert directs Marie to walk down a corridor with her white dress hiked up and her white panties pulled down and then to gaze at herself like that in a mirror, even though she can barely look for shame. In this way, Robert humiliates her, but he also frames Marie's shame in an image that she can confront, potentially helping her to face and conquer her sexual embarrassment, to brazen it out, and the next time he leads her to a mirror she is able to stare boldly at herself in a flaming red dress. In the scene where Robert stages a sacrilegious tableau with Marie's sex exposed and her arms tied above her head like Christ on the Cross, he intensifies the suffering she feels she deserves for her disgraceful desires, but he also represents sex and spirit together in the same frame, potentially enabling her to imagine their integration. 'Masochism is one way of bringing together a Christian contempt for the flesh with a pagan delight in it', writes Anita Phillips, 'Religious self-mortification involves a wide array of practices ... all designed to humble the flesh. Sexual mortification, on the other hand, has its rewards in this world and in erotic satisfactions that are out of bounds for religious devotees' (Phillips 1998: 36, 140). But neither body nor soul is 'out of bounds' for Marie who enacts a possible coming together of the two in this sublimely sordid tableau.

Just as Robert stages scenes so that Marie may be able to *see*

72 'like death. ... Little by little you're transformed into dead meat'.
73 'director' ... 'a theatre' ... 'I conduct rehearsals'.

and *understand* her desire to be humiliated, so he prompts her with questions (do you want to be dominated? gagged? tied up?) which lead her to formulate words that could help her to gain consciousness of and control over her masochistic impulses. Often Marie is unable to speak these words aloud, but she thinks them in voice-over interior monologue, gradually realising that she has been unconsciously and compulsively masochistic in her relationship with Paul, allowing him to project his loathing for the body onto her – she whose religious upbringing has already made her ashamed of her sexuality: 'parce que j'aimais pas mon corps, j'étais une proie facile. Je veux dire une victime. De toute façon, les femmes sont les victimes expiatoires des hommes. ... Je me fais attacher. C'est de sa faute'.[74] Words enable Marie to recognise that it is Paul's (and patriarchal religion's) disgust with her female flesh which has led her to seek self-mortifying punishment from Robert, that bondage with ropes and manacles is the physical symbol of her psychological enslavement to Paul's shaming attitude toward her sex. Words could help Marie to think differently about the body, to understand her suffering (she has internalised the patriarchal split between sex and spirit) and to move beyond it toward re-integration. According to Breillat, 'Marie sait les choses, mais elle ne les sait que sous l'emprise d'une émotion, elle ne se les formule qu'à ce moment-là et c'est comme ça qu'elle va avancer sur son chemin vers elle-même. ... La voix-off fait le passage entre les deux parties de ce corps coupé en deux'[75] (Flach Film 1999). Breillat even had Caroline Ducey (Marie) record her voice-overs immediately after acting each masochistic scene in order to dramatise the passage of emotion into words, of suffering into self-knowledge.

Marie's suffering with Robert is thus a repetition of her suffering with Paul – but with a potentially saving difference in that with Robert the headmaster she is learning to visualise and vocalise her pain, to comprehend and contain it as a self-conscious performance. Lying bound and gagged in her red dress on the floor of Robert's apartment, Marie may look like dead meat, but she approved the costume and

74 'because I didn't like my body, I was easy prey. I mean, a victim. Anyway, women are men's sacrificial victims. ... I go and let myself be tied up. It's his fault'.

75 'Marie knows things, but she knows them only under the influence of an emotion, she formulates them only at that moment and this is how she's going to make progress on the road toward herself. ... The voice-over creates a passage between the two parts of this body that was cut in two'.

props and she is now consciously acting the part of a rape/murder victim, of the soulless flesh or hole to which men have reduced her. She is increasingly aware of this as a role which they have wanted her to play on the stage of their domineering fantasies (she lies on a raised platform, flanked by two folding screens like curtains) and if this is a role, then this shame is not natural to her sex, this passivity is not part of the eternal feminine, but something that can be spoken and staged differently. As Anne McClintock has said about consensual sadomasochism, 'On the one hand, it seems to parade a servile obedience to conventions of power. ... Yet, on the contrary, with its exaggerated emphasis on costume and scene S/M performs social power as *scripted*, and hence as permanently subject to change. ... S/M manipulates the *signs* of power in order to refuse their legitimacy as *nature*' (McClintock 2004: 237, 239).

But is Marie (or Breillat) fooling herself to think that letting herself be bound and gagged is the way to freedom of sexual expression? As Emma Wilson notes, 'The film seems to suggest that acting out her masochistic fantasies releases her from her psychological bondage to Paul and lets her discover her own autonomy as female desiring subject ... Some may dispute the film's investment in masochism as therapy in a process of personal self-renewal' (Wilson 2001: 155). Marie seems to derive a great deal of pleasure from the pain inflicted upon her, and Breillat dwells on these scenes of masochism for an exquisitely extended period of time, which suggests that there may be a continuing erotic investment in shame and humiliation. Has Marie played this role (that of the girl who gets her excitement from being degraded by men) for so long that she has become 'typecast' in the part? Why in her scenes with Robert does Marie conform her body to male fantasies of woman as passive victim rather than breaking out of this mould to shape some more empowering fantasies of her own? As Ginette Vincendeau sees the film, 'some of its erotic tropes are rather too close to old-fashioned, oppressive male fantasies. ... Is the price Breillat pays for auteur recognition that of endorsing male-pleasing fantasies of what "masochistic" women supposedly want?' (Vincendeau 1999: 52).

Whether Marie's bondage sessions with Robert are compulsive repetitions or controlled 'répétitions',[76] whether they entangle her further in masochism or enable her to extricate herself from it,

76 'rehearsals'.

must remain open questions and among the film's most interesting subjects for debate. Certainly, the film works hard to make the case that in the end Marie has freed herself from self-degradation and dependency on men like Paul. When her boyfriend is passed out in bed after drinking and dancing with other girls on the night that pregnant Marie goes into labour, it is Robert who drives her to the hospital and who serves as her birthing partner. As she lies there with her legs spread and her face contorted in pain and pleasure, the scene is similar to a masochistic session with Robert, and in both cases he assists her in giving birth to herself as an integrated being of body and soul who is ultimately unashamed of her sex. Unlike the Virgin Mary of patriarchal religion, this Marie has desired to be sexually active as well as spiritually dignified, and the miracle of birth has rarely been filmed with such unabashed attention to physical detail, including the dilated cervix, the baby's head crowning and the actual delivery from the vagina. Marie as a mother is neither virgin nor whore but a corporeal-spiritual being who defies patriarchal categorisation by men like Paul who would revile or revere her.

Unwilling to settle any longer for Paul's worshipful/degrading treatment, for a man whose incomplete and fragmented self has made her suffer, Marie gives up on her boyfriend but not on her ideal of the integrated man, who may now be incarnated in the baby boy whom she has also named Paul. In a scene accompanied by electric guitar sounds which suggest that it is a fantasy and not a murderous reality, we have seen Marie rig the gas in the apartment before leaving her boyfriend behind to go to the hospital, and just when the new Paul emerges from her womb, the old Paul dies in an explosion and then has his body buried in the earth. It is finally Marie who, rather than being reduced to a hole, asserts the whole of her female power to create and destroy. Her 'sexe' is a 'trou noir d'où le monde est sorti, et dans lequel on doit inévitablement disparaître', says Breillat (Brouste 1999: 23), describing Marie as an Earth Mother or 'vierge primordiale ... qui donne naissance au principe masculin. ... Le principe féminin, c'est le principe fondamental'[77] (Milon and Renouard 1999). At the (fantasy) funeral for Paul, Marie is dressed in black and walks barefoot on sharp stones for she truly grieves the loss of the man she loved in

---

77 'sex' ... 'a black hole from which the world emerges, and into which one must inevitably disappear' ... 'primordial virgin ... who gives birth to the masculine principle. The feminine principle is the fundamental principle'.

spite of his failings, but Marie also cradles the baby Paul in her arms, smiling down at him and then directing her gaze up and out at the camera, giving us a powerful look. Rather than conforming herself to dominant male desires, she is literally remaking patriarchy in the image of her own ideal.

Anatomie de l'enfer (Anatomy of Hell)

Upon completion of *Romance*, Breillat has said that 'j'ai immédiate-ment ressenti le besoin de refaire le même film, mais sur un mode inverse, plus sensuel, plus agressif. En fait, je devais m'attaquer frontalement et réellement à la pornographie'[78] (Goumarre 2001: 58). Whereas *Romance* had shown brief shots of the vagina in close-up (as Marie masturbates but with legs crossed, or as she glances guiltily at her sex in a hand mirror, or as she gives birth), *Anatomie de l'enfer* would offer Breillat's most sustained confrontation with that part of the female body often demonised by patriarchy as if it were a burning shame, a gaping obscenity, a den of iniquity. In many pornographic films, women are reduced to lewd holes and sinful whores for the lascivious male gaze, whose excitement comes from degrading the female sex. It is this humiliating view of the female body that Breil-lat's film is designed to counter: 'Je suis contre la confiscation de la représentation du sexe par l'industrie du porno. Pour moi, l'industrie du X ... désigne l'indignité du sexe féminin. Or j'estime que je garde ma dignité même quand j'écarte les jambes'.[79] In *Anatomie de l'enfer*, a woman (Amira Casar) spends much of the film with her legs spread before the gaze of a man (Rocco Siffredi)[80] as she attempts to challenge patriarchy's denigrating view of her sex, which has led

78 'I immediately felt the need to remake the same film, but in an opposite mode, more sensual, more aggressive. In fact, I had to conduct a real frontal attack on pornography'.

79 'I'm opposed to the porn industry's confiscation of the representation of sex. For me, the X-rated film industry ... signifies the indignity of the female sex. Well, I believe that I keep my dignity even when I spread my legs'. Breillat made this comment in a 3 May 2001 appearance at the Beaubourg with author Catherine Millet.

80 The man and woman in the film are unnamed (for in a sense they represent all men and all women under patriarchy). For ease of reference, I will refer to the male character as 'Rocco' and to the female character as 'Amira'.

her to look upon herself with shame. By posing this challenge in an effort to remake the male-dominated socio-symbolic order, Breillat has much in common with the women's liberation group known as Psychanalyse et politique (or Psych et po), whose members have included Hélène Cixous and Julia Kristeva. These psychoanalytic feminists have argued that 'Masculinity controls even at the level of the unconscious, and women operate within the confines of masculine unconscious structures and have been turned into misogynists, despising their own womanhood. To free themselves from this internalised oppression, each woman must, according to *Psych et Po*, work to "chase the phallus from her head"' (Duchen 1986: 20).

The need to be seen through other than patriarchal eyes guides Amira in her selection of the man she hires to watch her, for Rocco is a homosexual she encounters at a gay nightclub. The idea here is that, unlike heterosexual men who profess to love women but who deep down fear and loathe them (think of Paul in *Romance*), a gay man's indifference to the female sex could enable him to look at her with fresh eyes: 'Parce que vous qui n'aimez pas les femmes, vous pouvez justement me regarder – je veux dire, avec impartialité'.[81] Also operative here may be the idea of homosexuality as linked to androgyny: if Rocco has a feminine side, he might be able to accept Amira's femininity without feeling threatened by it. Amira is used to seeing herself negatively through hetero male eyes, but in Rocco she hopes to find a man with a positive view of femininity, to gain a respectful regard for *her*self through *him*. It's important to note that as Rocco looks at Amira, his thoughts are expressed in voice-over by Breillat herself as if he/she were struggling toward an androgynous acceptance of him/herself. As Breillat has said, 'je suis l'homme qui découvre la femme qui est moi. C'est sans doute la raison pour laquelle le personnage est un homosexuel'[82] (Flach Film 2003). While some may object to these associations of gayness with impartiality or androgyny (Are homosexuals sexually indifferent to women? Are gays more 'feminine' than heterosexual men? Is homosexuality an identity or a variable orientation along a 'queer' spectrum of affects and acts?), it is at least possible to construe these associations as

81 'Because you who don't love women, you can simply look at me – I mean, with impartiality'.

82 'I am the man who discovers the woman who is me. That's doubtless the reason that the character is a homosexual'.

neutral or positive stereotypes. However, matters become much more problematic when Rocco's eventual failure to appreciate Amira, when his increasingly violent dread and disgust regarding her womanhood, are linked to his homosexuality, as in the scenes where he wonders whether the 'obscénité' of her female sex is 'ce qui m'avait détourné des femmes' and where he compares it unfavourably to 'l'anus des garçons', telling her that 'je bénis le jour qui m'a fait naître à l'écart de vous et toutes celles de votre espèce'.[83] These scenes represent a gay man as exhibiting the worst of patriarchy's disregard for women. Such scenes perpetuate a pernicious stereotype of homosexuality which ignores the extent to which a gay man is himself often the victim of patriarchal misogyny displaced as homophobia (a fear of effeminate men).

Amira is actually taken to the gay nightclub by her ostensibly hetero boyfriend, who has gone there to flirt, dance and have oral sex with other men. Here again the film tends to conflate homosexuality with homosociality, implying that men prefer the company of other males to that of the 'female species'. Amira is left all alone by her boyfriend and she is shown in a belittling angle-down shot as she walks like a ghost across the dance floor, completely ignored by the men who only have eyes for each other. The men's disregard confirms her in her disgust for her own sex and she cuts her wrist with a razorblade, exhibiting the 'bloody slit' that they and she see her as being: 'elle est rongée par sa blessure interne comme à tout ce qui est répugnant en elle .... Elle a – elle est un sexe de femme'[84] (Breillat 2001: 15, 16). It is Rocco who saves Amira's life. Having accidentally brushed past her on the stairs and having noticed something in her face as she was on her way to the toilet to commit suicide, Rocco goes to check on her, finds her bleeding and takes her to a pharmacy for help. Unlike the other men, he proves himself capable of *looking at* and *feeling for* her ('vous m'avez touché', he says), so it makes sense that Amira would ask him to try to help her see herself with something other than self-loathing: 'me regarder par là où je ne suis pas regardable'.[85] Amira seeks Rocco's approval as a kind of substitute for that of her boyfriend,

83 'obscenity' ... 'what turned me off women' ... 'the anus of boys' ... 'I bless the day that I was born apart from you and all those of your species'.

84 'she is eaten by her inner wound as with everything that is repulsive in her ... She has – she is the female sex' (Breillat 2006b: 10).

85 'you touched me' ... 'to watch me where I am unwatchable'.

much as Marie in *Romance* had turned to Paolo as a stand-in for Paul. After accusing Rocco of having gone to the lavatory for gay oral sex (like the kind her boyfriend was having), Amira sinks to her knees and fellates Rocco herself, but her hope is that he will view her not as having debased herself, but as being exalted through sexual desire, as reaching for spirit through the flesh. The close-up we see of Amira with semen dribbling from her mouth would be 'obscene' in a pornographic film in which the viewer is excited by female degradation, but Amira's glowing face and defiant look show her struggle to transcend feeling sullied or shamed: 'c'était le visage immaculé de sperme d'actrice, qu'elle ait l'air dans un trouble et presque mise au-dessus d'elle-même par ce qu'elle a fait et non pas au-dessous. ... c'est le visage d'une madone. ... C'est rejoindre le trivial and le sacré, donc c'est très beau',[86] as Breillat has said (Devanne 2004). In fact, Breillat modelled this shot on a similar close-up in Nagisa Oshima's *L'Empire des sens* (*In the Realm of the Senses*) (1976) where the heroine Sada is fulfilled rather than humiliated by fellating the man Kichi, who has helped her to liberate herself from repressive taboos ('Are you ashamed of your desire? ... I want to feel your pleasure. ... I want you to feel free'). In 'Theory of Experimental Pornographic Film', Oshima argued that taboos are actually created by censorship and that sexual acts are only 'obscene' because they are repressed or hidden away in dark places such as in X-rated or pornographic films. When these same acts are viewed in the light of day, when they are represented as part of mainstream cinema, they will no longer be seen as sinful: 'internalized taboos make for the experience of "obscenity". ... The concept of "obscenity" is tested when one dares to look at something that he has an unbearable desire to see, but has forbidden himself to look at. When one feels that everything that one had wanted to see has been revealed, "obscenity" disappears, the taboo disappears as well, and there is a certain liberation' (Oshima 1992: 261).

On the first night that Amira pays Rocco to watch her where she is 'unwatchable', the conflict within her between a desire to reveal her sexuality and a shameful need to conceal it is apparent. She has invited Rocco to view her naked in the bedroom of her house by the sea, but

---

86 'it was the actress's face immaculate with sperm, for she appeared to be agitated and was almost raised above herself by what she had done and not put down. ... it's the face of a Madonna. ... It's a reuniting of the lowly and the sacred, so it's very beautifu'.

as she feels his eyes upon her, she hesitates to undress in front of him. Instead, she hides behind the headboard of her bed, with the bars of the headboard seeming to imprison her in shame, and the shadow of the bedpost falling on her like a phallic judgement. Hanging on the wall behind her is a crucifix that seems to loom over her, and her hands are clasped as if she were praying like a good Catholic girl. Nevertheless, Amira begins to disrobe, stripping off her pristine white top and taking down her bra very quickly and aggressively, fighting self-consciousness, and then sitting with her back to him on the bed as she slips off her panties and lies back in the nude, playing with the hair over her eyes as if to hide herself from the sight. But when Rocco then accuses her of flaunting her body and when he turns away to gaze at her mirror image (like the horrid Medusa reflected in a man's shield?) so that he no longer has to view her directly, Amira rolls onto her side to confront him with her full-frontal nudity while looking straight at him in defiance. The borders of the antique mirror frame Amira like a painting, raising her naked flesh to the level of an artistic nude. In fact, Breillat directed the actress to strike gracefully sensual poses and cinematographer Yorgos Arvanitis lit her body so that her skin would look both realistic and sublimely luminescent, as in Edouard Manet's *Olympia*, the notorious painting of a reclining nude courtesan whose effrontery scandalised viewers when she was first unveiled in 1865. As Charles Bernheimer describes the woman in the painting, 'She appears small and easily dominated, but also imperious and coldly disdainful. If her blatantly advertised readiness to be consumed as an erotic commodity seems to invite objectification, her taut, self-assured, commandingly resolute pose appears to defy any appropriative gesture' (Bernheimer 1989: 115). Breillat and Arvanitis based their representation of Amira on Manet's *Olympia* (among other artworks) so that she would appear to be both corporeal and sublime – 'la peinture vivante'[87] – and frame enlargements from the film were actually exhibited in an art gallery prior to the movie's release (Breillat in Tylski 2004).

But Rocco does not perceive the spirit shining through Amira's body for all he can see is her perishable flesh, a mortal weakness which threatens his own precarious sense of masculine strength and hoped-for transcendence of all things lowly and feeble. A poignant

87 'living painting'.

flashback shows us Rocco as a boy with long hair and red trousers seated on a tree branch, feeding grubs to a newborn bird and then placing it for protection in his shirt pocket. However, as the young Rocco climbs down from the tree, the bird is accidentally squashed. Horrified by the red seeping through his shirt pocket, the boy removes the bloody mess and hurls it to the ground, smashing it further with his foot. Having failed in his attempt at nurturing, the boy now tries to differentiate himself from the dying other, to distance himself from weakness. His androgynous potential is replaced by a hard and violent masculinity as Rocco becomes the man he is today, his close-cropped hair and cold white suit asserting a phallic dominance. It is mortally red flesh that Rocco sees when he looks at Amira's naked-ness, and for him 'la fragilité des chairs féminines impose le dégoût et la brutalité'.[88] While she is sleeping, Rocco uses lipstick to redden the 'lips' of her vagina, anus and mouth because this is the way he sees her, as a painted whore, a disgusting wound, someone worthy only of degradation. Like the director of a patriarchal porn film, he spreads her legs so that her body assumes lewd poses in her sleep, becoming a gaping obscenity, even though her limbs show a tendency to return to more 'infantile' positions as if to indicate her natural 'innocence'. After examining the red wound of her sex between her splayed legs like a doctor diagnosing an illness ('la fille est la maladie de l'homme'),[89] Rocco attempts to 'cure' her with degrading treat-ment, thrusting himself violently into her from behind, putting her out of his misery. Rocco grows hard here only because he feels he must dominate the 'female threat' (mortal weakness) which is all he sees when he looks at Amira. His vision of her is really just a projec-tion of patriarchal fears: 'ce désir ne venait pas de ce qu'il voyait mais de l'avilissement imaginaire qu'il lui faisait subir'[90] (Breillat 2001: 83). Rocco then subjects her to further phallic domination and degrada-tion by sticking the handle of a hoe into her behind – this after almost using the hoe's three-pronged fork to cut out the 'wound' of her sex by disembowelling her.

During another one of Rocco's examinations of Amira's body as she lies in bed, he probes her sex with his finger. This man in his

88 'the fragility of naked female flesh compels disgust and brutality'.
89 'the girl is the man's sickness'.
90 'this desire doesn't come from what he saw, but from the imaginary degradation he submitted her to' (Breillat 2006b: 68).

pious white suit with a shiny cross around his neck is horrified to see the blood of her menses on his finger, for such blood is the sign of a fallen nature and perishable flesh rather than the transcendent purity so prized by patriarchal religion. The camera cuts to a close-up of the crucifix hanging on the wall and moves slowly from the head of Christ down his bleeding body, before cutting to a close-up of Amira's face and then moving down her body to her menstruating sex. In this way, Breillat associates the feminine with the sacred, envisioning a kind of spirit that would embrace the suffering and mortal body rather than using brute force to crucify it: 'Le Christ que je filme n'est pas celui des églises. C'est le vrai Christ, en sang sur sa croix. La femme, elle-même, devient christique. Elle est clouée sur le lit, sous le regard de l'homme, qui peut être le regard du pharisien'[91] (Flach Film 2003). In another scene, Amira says that it must have been a man who designed the syringe-like applicator by which a woman can insert a tampon 'pour suppurer une plaie' while also 'en restant intacte de toute sa virginité'[92] since this way she does not have to touch or explore her genitals with her fingers, to defile herself – or access the core of her power.

Men may dread a bleeding woman for fear that her 'weakness' might spread to them like a contagious wound, but they may also fear her blood as the sign of her generative power, the superior ability of her sex to give birth. According to Simone de Beauvoir, 'C'est du jour où elle est susceptible d'engendrer que la femme devient impure. On a souvent décrit les sévères tabous qui dans les sociétés primitives entourent la fillette au jour de sa première menstruation. ... depuis l'avènement du patriarcat, on n'a plus attribué que des pouvoirs néfastes à la louche liqueur qui s'écoule du sexe féminin. ... A travers [le sang] s'exprime l'horreur que l'homme éprouve pour la fécondité féminine'[93] (Beauvoir 1949: 243, 244, 247). The varied evils for which menstruating women have been blamed include the power to make

---

91 'The Christ I film is not the one in the churches. This is the real Christ, bleeding on his cross. The woman herself becomes Christ-like. She is pinned to the bed under the man's gaze, which could be the gaze of the Pharisee'.

92 'to staunch a wound' ... 'preserving her virginity wholly intact'.

93 'on the day she can reproduce, woman becomes impure; and rigorous taboos surround the menstruating female. ... since patriarchal times only evil powers have been attributed to the feminine flow. ... Through menstrual blood is expressed the horror inspired in man by woman's fecundity' (Beauvoir 1978: 148, 149, 150).

'aigrir le vin, tourner le lait, pourrir la viande, les salaisons, le miel, les fruits'[94] (Chrystel Besses in Zabunyan 2003a: 54). In past times, patriarchal religion has viewed menstruating women as 'cursed' and has sought to distance itself from their 'unholy' taint: 'Dans le judaïsme tout contact avec la femme ayant ses règles est interdit et il lui est demandé de se purifier par un bain rituel. Tandis que certains musulmans du Caucase isolent les femmes ayant leurs règles dans une hutte construite à cet effet. Le christianisme ne lie pas perte de sang et impureté mais de vieilles traditions orthodoxes ne permettent pas aux femmes, pendant leurs menstrues, de communier. Il y a incompatibilité entre la sexualité féminine marquée par le sang et le sacré'[95] (Arlette Fontan in Zabunyan 2003a: 80). Amira poses a direct challenge to this view of her sex as unsacred when she places a bloody tampon in a glass of water and offers it to Rocco for him to drink. Here is a holy communion that includes the female body rather than abjecting it as profane. His drinking of her menstrual blood should be no more obscene than her mouthful of his seminal fluid, for true holiness subsumes sex and the body.

It is not just what flows from a woman's body that terrifies men but also what her sex takes in. In an earlier scene (prior to Amira's period), we see a giant close-up of Amira's vagina as Rocco's finger enters it and then the camera cuts away, as if giving the impression that he never comes out. The male desire to penetrate and possess a woman may be driven by a fear of being swallowed up, of losing himself inside her, as if he were to be reclaimed by his mother's womb: 'cette gangue ténébreuse que la mère a façonnée pour son fils et dont il veut s'évader, la maîtresse en referme autour de lui la glaise opaque dans les vertiges du plaisir. Il voulait posséder: le voilà lui-même un possédé'[96] (Beauvoir 1949: 265). Breillat modelled the close-up of

94 'wine turn sour, milk go off, meat putrefy, salting go bad, honey and fruits rot' (Chrystel Besses in Zabunyan 2003b: 54).

95 'In Judaism all contact with a woman is forbidden during her period and she is required to purify herself afterwards by ritual bathing. Certain Muslims in the Caucasus ... shut their women away in specially-built huts while they are menstruating. Christianity does not make a link between loss of blood and impurity but old Orthodox traditions prevent menstruating women from taking communion. There is an incompatibility between female sexuality, marked by blood, and the sacred' (Arlette Fontan in Zabunyan 2003b: 80).

96 'His mistress, in the vertigoes of pleasure, encloses him again in the opaque clay of that dark matrix which the mother fabricated for her son and from which he

Amira's sex on Gustave Courbet's 1866 painting *L'Origine du monde* (*The Origin of the World*) which has both naturalistic detail and mythic power in its magnified view of a woman's vagina. Breillat's close-up is not the 'beaver shot' of pornography that belittles and objectifies the female sex for male consumption, but a shot of woman as goddess with awesome creative and destructive power. As she lies there being examined by Rocco, Amira is reminded of a time when as a girl she spread her legs under a bush so that a group of boys could view her, with one boy using the arm of his glasses to probe her sex. Amira imagines that the boys were 'dégoûtés pour jamais du spectacle',[97] as if the distance and control they had sought to gain by gazing at her had become instead a dangerously close proximity in which they almost lost their little selves. Similarly, Rocco watches closely as a stone with a phallic shape is swallowed up by Amira's vagina in the same way that his sex could be consumed by her. This scene was inspired by the one in *L'Empire des sens* where, 'just before the man enters the woman, there's a shot of [a hardboiled] egg being swallowed by the vagina, which confirms her as the character with the power to murder, to kill' (Breillat in Whitely 2003). In between watching phallic objects disappear inside Amira's matrix as if they were nothing, Rocco often walks outside her house and stands overlooking the ocean. An over-the-shoulder shot shows Rocco gazing down at the ocean which fills the screen, as if he were losing himself in 'la mer/la mère' ('the sea/the mother'). Because Rocco has set himself up against 'fallen' nature, he can only view the physical world, including Amira's sexuality, as a threat to him: 'L'océan, malgré son nom trompeusement masculin, roulait dans l'ombre avec la régularité d'une chienne en chaleur, puisque cet océan, comme la femme, était un vide et pouvait ouvrir ses flancs pour étreindre jusqu'à disparitition totale'.[98] When Rocco takes up the garden tool to use against Amira, it (the handle of the hoe) is not only a substitute phallus he hopes will be strong enough to conquer her sex, it (the three-pronged fork) is also a trident which he wields as a kind of Neptune in an attempt to be god of the sea.

---

desires to escape. He wishes to possess her: behold him the possessed himself!' (Beauvoir 1978: 164).

97 'disgusted forever by the sight'.

98 'The ocean, despite its deceptively masculine name, rolled in the shadows with the regularity of a bitch in heat, for, like woman, that ocean was a void and could open its flanks and embrace you until your total disappearance'.

It is interesting to compare *Anatomie de l'enfer* with *La Maladie de la mort*, the 1982 Marguerite Duras fiction which Breillat had wanted to adapt to the screen but for which she was unable to obtain the rights.[99] Duras' text also concerns a man who watches a woman's naked body over several nights in a house by the sea, and like Rocco, the man struggles with his fear of the female sex and what comes out of it ('une eau gluante et chaude comme serait le sang') along with what can be taken in by it ('la mer noire', 'cela qui engouffre')[100] (Duras 1982: 40, 27, 29). As in Breillat, Duras' man is incited to murderous lust by the sight of the woman's nakedness, which connotes a weakness that he must distance himself from by dominating and demeaning her: 'Le corps est sans défense aucune, il est lisse depuis le visage jusqu'aux pieds. Il appelle l'étranglement, le viol, les mauvais traitements, les insultes, les cris de haine, le déchaînement des passions entières, mortelles'[101] (Duras 1982: 21). However, there are two important differences between Breillat's film and Duras' fiction that are worth remarking. First, while the book has the man hire the woman to allow him to look at her, it is the woman who pays the man to watch her in the film, for Breillat gives the woman greater agency and has her be the one to pose an active challenge to patriarchal gynephobia and her own internalised shame. Second, though both couples ultimately fail to sustain a connection, Amira and Rocco do achieve a degree of intimacy which eludes the man and the woman in Duras, particularly the man who remains too narcissistic to risk feeling for another: 'Quand vous avez pleuré, c'était sur vous seul et non sur l'admirable impossibilité de la rejoindre à travers la différence qui vous sépare'[102] (Duras 1982: 56).

99 Breillat's film may also have been influenced by three other Duras texts closely related to *La Maladie de la mort*: *L'Homme assis dans le couloir* (1980), *Les Yeux bleus cheveux noirs* (1986) and *La Pute de la côte Normande* (1986) (*The Seated Man in the Passage, Blue Eyes, Black Hair, The Whore of the Normandy Coast*). These Duras texts all contain autobiographical elements about her relationship with homosexual Yann Andréa, much as Breillat's film incorporates aspects of her own life with her homosexual first husband François Wimille.

100 'a hot sticky liquid like blood' ... 'the black sea' ... 'that which swallows up' (Duras 1986: 36, 22, 24).

101 'The body's completely defenseless, smooth from face to feet. It invites strangulation, rape, ill usage, insult, shouts of hatred, the unleashing of deadly and unmitigated passions' (Duras 1986: 16).

102 'When you wept it was just over yourself and not because of the marvelous impossibility of reaching her through the difference that separates you' (Duras 1986: 54).

Rocco's growing closeness to Amira can be gauged by the fact that on the first night we see him arriving by taxi and walking up to her house, then on another night he is shown just walking up, and on a further night he is depicted as already inside. Also, when he is in her bedroom, Rocco eventually moves from keeping his distance in an armchair, to examining her with a lamp in the bed, and finally to joining his body with hers in intercourse. In the scene where he grows hard and dominant by degrading her, we see him use the lipstick on her 'lips' and enter her from behind with his erection, but then the camera shows their faces as he is thrusting and, after his climax, he seems to search her face for a response while putting his hand tenderly on her arm. Soon thereafter, he is seated on the bed and weeping, his head drooping onto his shoulder as the camera moves down his body to reveal his flaccid male organ. As Pascal Quignard has written (in a book which has greatly influenced Breillat), 'Le sexe est lié à l'effroi. ... L'homme n'a pas le pouvoir de rester érigé. ... C'est pourquoi le pouvoir est le problème masculin par excellence parce que c'est sa fragilité caractéristique et l'anxiété qui préoccupe toute ses heures. L'éjaculation est une perte voluptueuse. Et la perte de l'excitation qui en résulte est une tristresse'[103] (Quignard 1994: 84–5). When Amira sees Rocco crying, she wipes the tears from his face and puts his arm around her neck to support and comfort him. In a later scene, after Amira has displayed her ability to swallow up the phallic stone with her sex (and then eject it), we see Rocco stroke himself to hardness and penetrate her in the missionary position, but what looks at first like an attempt at masculine dominance and female subjugation becomes something more reciprocal and compassionate. The 'pornographic' close-up of his erection yields to a long shot which includes both their bodies conjoining (on the right) and their faces gazing at each other (on the left) – a scene of physical and emotional intimacy. In meeting his gaze, Amira can be said to overcome some of the shame she has felt about her sex, and in regarding her tenderly (and also stroking her hair, cradling her head and kissing her on the lips after their climax), Rocco goes some way toward conquering his fear of coming inside her, of showing himself as something less

103 'Sex is linked to dread. ... The man does not have the power to remain erect. ... That's why power is the masculine problem par excellence because this is his characteristic fragility and the anxiety that disturbs his every hour. Ejaculation is a voluptuous loss. And the resulting loss of excitation is a sadness'.

than perpetually hard: 'Il faut transgresser l'effroi, la honte, les règles sociales'[104] (Breillat 2006a: 115). This scene between Amira and Rocco can be compared to *Dora et le minotaure* (*Dora and the Minotaur*), the 1936 Pablo Picasso painting in which the rampant bull/man seems about to violently mount the woman, and yet there appears to be a human tenderness in his beastly face, while the woman whose naked body is being assailed seems serenely unashamed and unafraid of animal passion: 'Face à la créature, mi-homme mi-bête, Dora se tient en arrière, et dans son regard on peut lire à la fois l'abandon le plus complet et une indomptabilité qui la rend maîtresse de son jeu'[105] (Amira Casar in Flach Film 2003).

This union of shameless female desire and masculine tenderness, this androgynous moment where each gender shares the other's attributes, does not last long. As Rocco withdraws from Amira after their mutual *jouissance*, the blood on his sex from her period triggers his worst fears of woman as a contagious wound, as if conjoining with her had led to engulfment and castration. (In Rocco's gynephobic mind, we are not far from the end of *L'Empire des sens* in which Sada strangles Kichi during intercourse and then cuts off his sex so that she can possess it forever.) A horrified Rocco is then quick to distance himself from Amira by accepting money for his nights with her, as though watching her had been a disgusting task that he had to be paid to do. Knocking back drinks in unison with another man at a bar soon thereafter, Rocco falls back into macho bragging about how hard 'je lui avais ... défoncé la chatte', with his misogynistic buddy adding that she must have been 'une pute comme les toutes'.[106] But Rocco's tearful response – 'Oui, mais la reine des putes'[107] – implies that he also admired and desired this brazenly sexual woman and that his degrading insults may be a cover for the sorrow he feels in being apart from her. Leaving all the money she had paid him behind at the bar, he returns the next morning to her house by the sea to reunite with her, but she is gone. At this point, Rocco seems to have a flashback in which he sees himself bearing down on Amira (last night?),

104 'It's necessary to transgress dread, shame, social rules'.
105 'Faced with this creature, half-man half-beast, Dora draws back, and in her look you can read both the most complete abandon and an indomitability which makes her the mistress of her game'.
106 'I'd ploughed her pussy' ... 'a whore like all the rest'.
107 'Yes, but the queen of whores'.

walking threateningly toward her as she backs away from him and then pushing her over a cliff into the ocean. Rocco had felt enough for her to save her from suicide, but did his fear of femininity finally drive him to kill her? If so, Amira's desire for a man who would look upon her with love rather than loathing could be said to have terminated in abject failure. But, as with the endings of several other Breillat films (including *Une vraie jeune fille*, *Romance* and *A ma sœur!*), it is possible to view Rocco's 'murder' of Amira as a fantasy whose significance is metaphorical rather than realistic. Earlier, she had told Rocco that, unlike woman who can give life, man 'donne la mort – et donc la vie éternelle',[108] and Amira is dressed all in white when Rocco pushes her to her death in the sea, leaving behind nothing but the empty and blood-stained bedsheet or 'shroud' which he cradles in his arms. Is Amira's death a ritual sacrifice to save Rocco's soul, to make him conscious that he crucified her, to bring him understanding of the value of what he has lost? In the film's last image (an extreme long shot), Rocco stands as a tiny upright figure at the top left, gazing down at the immense 'Amira' ocean spread out before him. Does he still feel threatened by so much life or can he finally look upon her with tender regard?

References

Audé, Françoise (1979), *'Tapage nocturne'*, *Positif* 224, 79.

Axe Films (1979), Dossier de presse: *Tapage nocturne*, Paris, Axe Films.

Beauvoir, Simone de (1949), *Le Deuxième Sexe*, vol. 2, Paris, Gallimard.

Beauvoir, Simone de (1978), *The Second Sex*, trans. H. M. Parshley, New York, Knopf.

Bernheimer, Charles (1989), *Figures of Ill Repute: Representing Prostitution in Nineteenth-Century France*, Cambridge, MA and London, Harvard University Press.

Bozon, Michel (2002), *Sociologie de la sexualité*, Paris, Nathan.

Breillat, Catherine (1979), *Tapage nocturne*, Paris, Mercure de France.

Breillat, Catherine (2001), *Pornocratie*, Paris, Denoël.

Breillat, Catherine (2006a), *Corps amoureux: Entretiens avec Claire Vassé*, Paris, Denoël.

Breillat, Catherine (2006b), *Pornocracy*, trans. Paul Buck and Catherine Petit, Los Angeles, Jovian Books.

Brouste, Judith, (1999), 'Le Sexe pur/Pure Sex': Interview de Catherine Breillat, *Art Press* 246, 22–7.

108 'gives death – and thus eternal life'.

Clément, Jérôme (2002), 'Catherine Breillat', *Les Femmes et l'amour*, Paris, Stock, pp. 267–300.

Clouzot, Claire (2004), *Catherine Breillat: Indécence et pureté*, Paris, Cahiers du cinéma.

Devanne, Laurent (2004), 'Catherine Breillat, cinéaste', *Kinok*, www.arkepix. com/kinok.

Diamond, Sara (1985), 'Pornography: Image and Reality', in Varda Burstyn (ed.), *Women Against Censorship*, Vancouver, Douglas & McIntyre, pp. 40–57.

Duchen, Claire (1986), *Feminism in France: From May '68 to Mitterand*, London and Boston, Routledge.

Duras, Marguerite (1982), *La Maladie de la mort*, Paris, Editions de Minuit.

Duras, Marguerite (1986), *The Malady of Death*, trans. Barbara Bray, New York, Grove Press.

Flach Film (1999), Dossier de presse: *Romance*, Paris, Flach Film.

Flach Film (2003), Dossier de presse: *Anatomie de l'enfer*, Paris, Flach Film.

Freud, Sigmund (1989), 'On the Universal Tendency to Debasement in the Sphere of Love' [1912], in Peter Gay (ed.), *The Freud Reader*, New York and London, Norton, pp. 394–400.

Goumarre, Laurent (2001), 'Catherine Breillat: Double remake', *Art Press* 272, 58–9.

Hughes, Alex and Reader, Keith (eds) (1998), *Encyclopedia of Contemporary French Culture*, London, Routledge.

Löwy, Ilana (2006), *L'Emprise du genre: Masculinité, féminité, inégalité*, Paris, La Dispute.

Lozerec'h, Brigitte (1984), *The Temp*, trans. Kathrine Talbot, New York, Dutton.

Lozerec'h, Brigitte (1995), *L'Intérimaire* [1982], Paris, Fayard.

McClintock, Anne (2004), 'Maid to Order: Commercial S/M and Gender Power', in Pamela Church (ed.), *More Dirty Looks: Gender, Pornography and Power*, 2nd edn, London, British Film Institute, pp. 237–53.

Milon, Colette and Renouard, Jean-Philippe (1999), '"Ne vois-tu pas que je brûle?": Entretien avec Catherine Breillat', *Vacarme* 9, Autumn.

Murphy, Kathleen (1999), 'A Matter of Skin: Catherine Breillat's Metaphysics of Film and Flesh', *Film Comment* 35:5, 16–22.

Oshima, Nagisa (1992), 'Theory of Experimental Pornographic Film', *Cinema, Censorship, and the State: The Writings of Nagisa Oshima, 1956–1978*, Cambridge, MA and London, MIT Press, pp. 251–64.

Pagès, Michèle (2001), 'Corporéités sexuées: jeux et enjeux', in Thierry Blöss (ed.), *La Dialectique des rapports hommes-femmes*, Paris, Presses Universitaires de France, pp. 219–38.

Phillips, Anita (1998), *A Defense of Masochism*, New York, St. Martin's Press.

Quignard, Pascal (1994), *Le Sexe et l'effroi*, Paris, Gallimard.

Réage, Pauline (1973), *Story of O*, trans. Sabine d'Estrée, New York, Ballantine Books.

Réage, Pauline (1975), *Histoire d'O* [1954], Paris, Jean-Jacques Pauvert.

Tylski, Alexandre (2004), 'Breillat, la peinture et *Anatomie de l'enfer*', *Cadrage*, April, www.cadrage.net.

Vasse, David (2004), *Catherine Breillat: Un cinéma du rite et de la transgression*, Issy-les-Moulineaux, ARTE, and Brussels, Complexe.

Vincendeau, Ginette (1999), '*Romance*', *Sight and Sound* 9:11, 51–2.

Whitely, John (2003), 'Film-makers on Film: Catherine Breillat', *Telegraph.co.uk*, 19 July, www.telegraph.co.uk.

Wilson, Emma (2001), 'Deforming Femininity: Catherine Breillat's *Romance*', in Lucy Mazdon (ed.), *France on Film: Reflections on Popular French Cinema*, London, Wallflower Press, pp. 145–57.

Zabunyan, Elvan et al. (2003a), *Cachez ce sexe que je ne saurais voir*, Paris, Dis Voir.

Zabunyan, Elvan et al. (2003b), *Keep This Sex Out of My Sight*, Paris, Dis Voir.

Zimmer, Jacques (ed.) (2002), *Le Cinéma X*, Paris, La Musardine.

Conclusion

With *Anatomie de l'enfer*, Breillat completed what she has called her 'décalogue', closing a cycle of ten films that are mostly about women's struggle to overcome shame at the sight of their own sexuality: 'Quand je dis que j'ai clos un cycle, je veux dire que je peux maintenant me regarder totalement en face. Je suis allée au bout de mes propres censures et je les ai vaincues. ... c'est important de mettre en œuvre l'identité sexuelle pour que toutes les femmes aient une identité sexuelle comprise, consciente et retrouvée. C'est parce que j'avais moi-même beaucoup de mal à supporter la vue d'un sexe féminin que j'ai fait *Anatomie de l'enfer*. C'était comme un exorcisme'[1] (Breillat 2006: 155, 107). By giving a form to forbidden things, by dealing explicitly with such issues as sexual shame, masochism and rape, Breillat has expanded the representational boundaries of mainstream cinema and led the way for other filmmakers to explore topics that were formerly taboo. Serving as a living link to an earlier generation of intrepid directors such as Bernardo Bertolucci with *Last Tango in Paris* and Nagisa Oshima with *L'Empire des sens*, Breillat now joins – and in numerous cases has directly inspired – a new generation of filmmakers who are pushing the limits by incorporating graphic sex and sexualised violence into 'serious' (not just 'pornographic' or 'exploitation') films. Sometimes grouped together as representatives of

1 'decalogue' ... 'When I say that I've closed a cycle, I mean that I can now look myself fully in the face. I have gone to the end of my own censorship and I have vanquished it. ... it's important to represent sexual identity in works of art so that women can understand, become conscious of and regain their sexual identity. It's because I myself had so much trouble standing the sight of the female sex organ that I made *Anatomy of Hell*. It was like an exorcism'.

'the cinema of abjection' or 'the new French extremity', these directors include many whose films have been strongly influenced by Breillat's work and particularly by *Romance*: Patrice Chéreau (*Intimacy*, 2001), Michael Haneke (*La Pianiste*, 2001), Bertrand Bonello (*Le Pornographe*, 2001), Gaspar Noé (*Irréversible*, 2002), Christophe Honoré (*Ma mère*, 2004), and Jean-Claude Brisseau (*Choses secrètes*, 2002 and *Les Anges exterminateurs*, 2006).[2]

Moreover, Breillat has been a leading light among an ever-increasing number of French female directors who are using the medium of film to explore women's desires. Continuing in the tradition of fore-mothers Agnès Varda and Marguerite Duras, Breillat's films have an affinity with those of her contemporary cinematic sisters, including Claire Denis, Virginie Despentes, Danièle Dubroux, Jeanne Labrune and Brigitte Roüan. Without the inspirational example of Breillat's courage (and international success), it is unlikely that we would have such women's films as Marina de Van's *Dans ma peau* (as audacious a directorial debut as Breillat's *Une vraie jeune fille*), Anne Fontaine's *Nathalie ...* (clearly influenced by *Romance*) and Laetitia Masson's *Pourquoi (pas) le Brésil?* (a movie like *Sex Is Comedy* about a female director struggling to make a movie about female desire).[3] As Breillat has said, 'For French spectators, women are taking power to talk about sex in a way that men don't' (Sklar 1999: 25). And French women are also writing about sex. It should be noted that Breillat is not only a filmmaker, but a figure of some prominence on the French literary scene, with eight novels, two published screenplays, a book of interviews and a collection of poems and plays to her credit. Breillat's texts – particularly her most radical work, *Pornocratie* (2001) – are strongly indebted to the writings of Marguerite Duras and Hélène Cixous, and Breillat can be seen as part of a growing group of women writers who are most unladylike in their sexually explicit confrontations with some of the darker aspects of passion. These authors include Virginie Despentes (*Baise-moi*, 1994), Marie Darrieussecq (*Truismes*, 1996), Catherine Cusset (*Jouir*, 1997), Christine Angot (*L'Inceste*, 1999), Camille Laurens (*Dans ces bras-là*, 2000) and Catherine Millet (*La Vie sexuelle de Catherine M.*, 2001).

Of course, one should not forget that each of these female authors

2 *The Piano Teacher, The Pornographer, Irreversible, My Mother, Secret Things, The Exterminating Angels.*

3 *In My Skin* (2002), *Nathalie ...* (2003), *Why (Not) Brazil?* (2004).

and auteurs has a distinct perspective on sexual experience. For example, although Breillat and Millet are often mentioned in the same articles – and 'the two Catherines' even appeared together at a 2001 Beaubourg colloquium entitled 'My Secret Life?' – there are significant differences between their works, despite the fact that both women were born in 1948, had a Catholic upbringing and are currently high-profile professionals (Millet is a distinguished art critic and the editor of *Art Press*). In her *Vie sexuelle*, Millet says that while undressing she adores gazing at her male partner's sex, she loves fellatio and she has never been a masochist. This is a far cry from Breillat's heroines who can barely look at their men, who struggle to give oral sex without feeling degraded and who often put themselves in humiliating positions. Remarkably (and somewhat incredibly), Millet seems to have absolutely no shame to overcome – 'j'étais en toutes circonstances, sans hésitation, sans arrière-pensée, par toutes les ouvertures de mon corps et dans toute l'étendue de ma conscience, disponible'[4] (Millet 2001: 43–4) – whereas the fight to liberate herself from sexual self-loathing is Breillat's great subject. Breillat has thus rightly called attention to the difference between Millet's work and her own: 'C'est l'énumération absolue, sérielle, autobiographique de la partouze, mais sans aucune progression. Sans qu'aucune désespérance n'intervienne. Je trouve cela fascinant, mais je ne le comprends pas'[5] (Clouzot 2004: 92).

Two other women with whom Breillat's name is often linked are Virginie Despentes and Coralie Trinh Thi, directors of the film *Baise-moi* (2000) based on Despentes' 1994 novel. When the right-wing 'family values' group Promouvoir pressured the government into branding this film with an X rating, which amounted to banning it, Breillat launched a protest petition which eventually led to the creation of a new '18+' rating that allowed the movie to be shown in mainstream theatres. But Breillat's anti-censorship defence of this film does not mean that she shares its creators' point of view. In *Baise-moi*, two women who have been sexually harassed, prostituted

4 'I was completely available: at all times and in all places, without hesitation or regret, by every one of my bodily orifices and with a totally clear conscience' (Millet 2002: 36).
5 'It's the absolute, serial, autobiographical enumeration of an orgy, but without any progression. Without any intervening despair. I find that fascinating, but I don't understand it'.

and raped by men turn the tables on their oppressors by going on a sex and murder spree, using males purely as objects of pleasure and shooting one man in the anus. The closest that Breillat's heroines have come to this kind of revenge is the largely symbolic deaths of the men at the end of *Romance* and *Une vraie jeune fille*. Breillat's heroines are often victimised, but they do not see becoming more violent than their oppressors as the solution. Neither as violently hyperactive as the women in Despentes/Trinh Thi's film nor as placidly passive as the narrator of Millet's book, Breillat's female characters resist falling into stereotypical gender roles whether these be submissively 'feminine' or aggressively 'masculine'.

Une vieille maîtresse (The Last Mistress)

Desire as a motivating force in the androgynous reinvention of gender roles remains a key theme for Breillat even as she inaugurates a new cycle of what are intended to be more accessible films with *Une vieille maîtresse*. Budgeted at seven million euros – which Breillat has said is more than the cost of her ten previous films combined – this new movie is her first period piece and her first literary adaptation from a novel not her own. Based on Jules Barbey d'Aurevilly's 1851 fiction of the same title, *Une vieille maîtresse* can be seen as an entry in the 'culturally respectable' heritage genre, 'prestigious but popular' films that are 'historical or literary in inspiration' and that 'place a premium on high production values' (Austin 1996: 144, 143, 142). It seems no accident that this is the first of Breillat's films to be selected for the official competition at Cannes, and viewers and critics have been exclaiming over the film as a feast for the eye and the ear with its elaborate costumes and sophisticated dialogue. In relation to other heritage films, *Une vieille maîtresse* is neither solemnly reverential like Jacques Rivette's *Ne touchez pas la hache* (2007) nor playfully postmodern like Sofia Coppola's *Marie Antoinette* (2006). Breillat steers a middle course, even in her treatment of sexuality, for the most part avoiding both frenzied couplings (like those in Patrice Chéreau's *La Reine Margot* (1994)) and metaphorical indirection (such as the thawing snow and the blooming flowers in Pascale Ferran's *Lady Chatterley* (2006)). Certainly, Breillat's film and Barbey's book are more passionately romantic and less wickedly witty than *Les Liaisons dangereuses*, even though Barbey was influenced by Pierre Choderlos de Laclos' 1782 novel, and Breillat's film has been compared to Stephen Frears' 1988 movie adaptation of Laclos. Breillat's hero, Ryno de Marigny, is a libertine but not a coldly calculating or manipulative one like Laclos' Valmont. Breillat also departs from some of the stylistic conventions of heritage cinema – the high angles and wide shots used to display lavish spectacle – by bringing her camera up close in order to emphasise the physical and emotional interactions between her characters. This breaking of convention is in keeping with the characters' own attempts to break free of social strictures to express their passionate individuality through intimate contact. Furthermore, though Breillat took pains to ensure the authenticity of most of the period dress, jewellery and interiors, she gave free reign to her imagination when it came to the extravagant costumes and coiffures of the heroine, Vellini, whose attire is as anachronistic as her passion is timeless.

Breillat's first costume film (set in 1835 Paris) nevertheless continues her exploration of patriarchal society's confinement of woman within the role of Madonna or whore. Ryno, a libertine without money or position, is betrothed to an aristocratic young virgin named Hermangarde whose sacred purity and social respectability are appealing. However, he is also tempted to renew his ten-year liaison with Vellini, a scandalous courtesan whose sensuality makes him burn with desire. As the novel's author once described this wife/mistress split, 'Le mariage a toujours une certaine pruderie ... C'est cela qui fait préférer, à une charmante jeune femme qu'on a épousée par amour, une vieille maîtresse devant laquelle on se permet tout'[6] (Barbey d'Aurevilly 1979: 9). Early in the film, when Ryno goes to say his last goodbye to Vellini, he ends up giving way to his animal lust for her on a tiger-skin rug and as she orgasms, a cut to another location shows us Hermangarde chastely garbed in white and engaged with her embroidery while she waits with her grandmother for her absent fiancé. As Vellini tells him about his impending marriage, 'Tu me reviendras, Ryno. ... Tu passeras sur le cœur de la jeune femme que tu épouses pour me revenir',[7] and sure enough, even after the newlyweds have gone to their conjugal

---

6 'Marriage always has a certain prudery ... It's that which makes one prefer, to a charming young wife whom one has married for love, an old mistress with whom everything is permitted'.

7 'You will come back to me, Ryno. ... You will trample upon the heart of the young woman you marry in order to come back to me'.

retreat in Brittany and Ryno has thrown a letter from Vellini into the fire, he has no sooner given the pure Hermangarde a chaste kiss on the forehead than he is off to meet Vellini again. He has taken his rifle as if to arm himself against her seductive wiles, but she grabs it and uses it to pull him to her, then forces him to take her into his arms in order to prevent her from throwing herself off a cliff into the sea. In this way, Ryno proves that his desire for Vellini is stronger than his wish to defend himself against her body, which in calling up his lust threatens to make him sexually dependent on her, menacing his proud masculine spirit. (By contrast, the gynephobic Rocco in *Anatomie de l'enfer* imagined pushing Amira over a cliff into the sea.) Yet despite his corporeal need for Vellini, Ryno is drawn to the socially approved femininity of his sainted wife, even if, as he admits to Vellini, proper ladies like Hermangarde are essentially frigid, keeping their legs and eyes closed during sex. Vellini's theory is that what Ryno really wants in a woman like Hermangarde is not her pure soul but her social standing and a properly passive female whom he can phallically dominate: 'Ça flatte ta petite fierté', she tells him, but 'c'est pas ça, l'amour!'[8]

This dialogue occurs during a sex scene in which Ryno rolls Vellini over so that he can be the one on top, but unlike Hermangarde's conventional femininity, Vellini's fierce independence is not so easily conquered and it is *her* sensuality that tends to ensnare *him*. When Ryno first lays eyes on Vellini sitting high in a carriage and licking an ice cream, he finds her 'laide' ('ugly') but only because such active appetite in a woman seems sinful and potentially overpowering to a man. As Breillat has noted, feminine beauty is actually something defined by patriarchal society according to what it wants – and doesn't want – to see in a woman: 'Quelle est la laideur de l'époque? C'est une question de sensualité. A un moment, Sophia Loren était laide, elle avait une trop grosse bouche. ... Jeanne Moreau était laide parce que trop sensuelle. Brigitte Bardot était vulgaire'[9] (Raya 2006). When the ideal beauty is a pure and docile innocent like Hermangarde, the sexually active and experienced Vellini can only be feared and condemned as 'ugly', for she is 'la *femme souveraine*, l'amazone qui prend et dont les désirs affirmés incarnent cette beauté tant récriée

8 'That flatters your tiny pride' ... 'that is not love!'

9 'What is "ugliness" at the time? It's a question of sensuality. At one moment, Sophia Loren was ugly, her lips were too large. ... Jeanne Moreau was ugly because too sensual. Brigitte Bardot was vulgar'.

dans le monde où on réprouve sous le nom de "laideur" la liberté affichée d'une femme, sa sensualité manifeste et son pouvoir sur les hommes"[10] (Breillat 2007: iv).

Ryno may be a notorious rake who has seduced a whole series of women, but the voluptuous Vellini threatens to captivate *him*. Breillat had originally considered casting popular French heartthrob Louis Garrel as Ryno, but instead she chose Fu'ad Aït Aattou, an unknown, first-time actor to play opposite the celebrated Euro-siren Asia Argento as Vellini[11] – an imbalance of star power which adds to the old mistress's dominance. And this mistress is not 'old' as in 'aged' (she is thirty-six), but rather in the sense of exerting a perennial hold over Ryno based on the ten torrid years they spent together, as if she were a primordial mother or sex goddess with blood ties to Ryno that are stronger than any he could ever establish with his belated younger bride. In one scene, Vellini is reclining like a queenly courtesan on a daybed in the same 'spiderweb' shawl and seductively languorous pose as the woman in *The Clothed Maja*, Francisco de Goya's 1805 painting. (This painting originally hung in the home of the Duke of Alcudia, who would use a pulley mechanism to reveal a painting of *The Nude Maja* behind it. The model for both paintings may have been the Duke's mistress.) An eternal woman of mystery, Vellini is frequently half-masked by fans and veils that incite Ryno's desire to see the face and flesh underneath. While seated in the carriage, she wears a black-lace mantilla over her head that partially covers her face, and when she goes to the opera, she hides behind a Spanish fan which she flutters just below the two strands of hair that form the shape of an inverted heart on her forehead. In these two scenes, Vellini looks exactly like the *femme fatale* Concha Perez (Marlene Dietrich) in *The Devil Is a Woman*, the 1935 Josef von Sternberg film which Breillat had Argento watch prior to filming *Une vieille maîtresse*. As Mary Ann Doane has noted about Dietrich's accessories, 'The tropes of the mask, fan and veil are here the marks of a dangerous deception or duplicity attached to the feminine' (Doane 1991: 49). Every time Ryno lets himself be drawn into the web of Vellini's fleshly charms, he fears

10 'the *sovereign woman*, the Amazon who takes and whose declared desires incarnate this beauty that is so loudly decried in a world where people reprove, under the name of "ugliness", a woman's assertion of liberty, her manifest sensuality and her power over men'.

11 Before Argento, rock star Madonna had been announced for the role of Vellini.

that he will be caught there forever, trapped in guilty pleasure with a sinful woman. Unlike the sacred heart of his pure bride, Vellini's heart is sensual and thus 'inverted', as in the sex scene where she is upside-down and Ryno's body forms an inverted cross with hers – the sign of the devil.

In fact, Vellini goes to a costume party disguised as the devil – not as a she-devil but as the devil himself, with talons or horns protruding from her shoulders. In actively expressing her desire as no 'good woman' is supposed to do, she becomes a phallic menace to Ryno in addition to the threat she poses of vaginal entrapment. At the costume party, she smokes a cigar like a man but blows a smoke ring whose O seems to encircle him – this right after the camera frames him as caught between her and her reflection in a mirror. When Ryno tries to abduct her from her horse in the woods, she whips his horse with her riding crop like a dominatrix, and when he fights a duel with another man over her, she comes cross-dressed in male attire as that man's second and would wield the pistol herself against Ryno if she could. After Ryno has been shot, she bends over his bed to lick his wound like a vamp, and later she will cut his face with a dagger and lick his blood off it.

But Vellini also declares herself 'vaincue' by Ryno's bullet wound, 'vanquished' by his weakness which brings out her tender love for him. Her licking of his wound could be seen as an act of primal care, a blood pact or pagan communion that unites them physically and emotionally. Earlier, Ryno had wanted to drink from her wine glass and thus showed a similar desire for sensual sharing rather than phallic conquering.[12] Ryno – with his full lips, delicate features and long curly hair – seems to have a 'feminine' side just as Vellini has a 'masculine' one, and a part of him seems to enjoy 'submitting' to her passionate lovemaking, at least in the times when he forgets his patriarchal paranoia about being emasculated. Ryno can dominate a docile soul like Hermangarde, but it is to the fiery spirit and carnal delights of Vellini that he keeps returning, ostensibly to conquer her but also to be conquered. In their coupling, Ryno and Vellini may come close to an ideal mixture of masculine and feminine and of body and soul, but society will not bless their unconventional passion and they are exiled to the Algerian desert. Here, without the protection and social

12 We recall Rocco and Amira drinking from the same glass of her blood in *Anatomie de l'enfer*.

stability afforded by the institutions of church and marriage, Ryno and Vellini's young daughter is stung by a scorpion and dies, and they nearly burn themselves up in a frantic but fruitless desire to conceive again.

From an extramarital passion with his mistress Vellini, whose strength and sensuality are condemned by society, Ryno turns to Hermangarde, who in being a 'virtuous woman' and 'the perfect wife' gives him a passionless marriage. It's not that the angelic aristocrat Hermangarde doesn't have a little bit of the devil in her, as evidenced by the avidity with which she herself throws open the church doors before her wedding, but her pure white wedding gown and virginal bridal veil weigh heavily upon her, repressing her desires, as if turning her into a marble statue of the Madonna. Even on their honeymoon in Brittany, Hermangarde sits there reading the Bible and feels that she can permit Ryno only the chastest of kisses for fear that her grandmother will see her unladylike behaviour. As a result, Ryno's love for Hermangarde is channelled more into idolatrous worship than libidinal passion, and without our seeing any sensual contact, she is suddenly and miraculously pregnant. Ryno then forbids her to engage in anything even remotely physical (such as riding her white horse in a churchly blue dress), and when we finally see the two in bed, Ryno's hand is on the pure white belly of this 'virgin mother' who is carrying his son.[13]

Trapped in the asexual gender role prescribed for her as patriarchal religion's holy vessel, Hermangarde can do nothing but watch Ryno's old mistress lure him away with the promise of primal pleasures and sinful delights. In one outdoor scene, the 'proper young wife' in her yellow bonnet looks down at a rock promontory and sees Vellini sitting there backgrounded by the sea. The 'little mother' is no match for the primordial mother's eternal pull, and unfortunately Hermangarde is 'la femme d'un amoureux de la mer'.[14] Later, after peering through the window of a hut by the sea and witnessing Ryno within Vellini's fleshly embrace, Hermangarde slogs back home through the mud in her green cloak and collapses on the marital bed, her pure virtue sullied by jealousy. When he returns home, a penitent Ryno tenderly

13 A similar moment occurs in *Romance* when Paul pats Marie's pregnant belly.
14 'the wife of a man in love with the sea'. As in *Anatomie de l'enfer*, Breillat often associates the sea ('la mer') with a primal female sexuality ('la mère' or 'the mother').

removes her shoes and stockings in what is the most sensual scene between them, except that she is unconscious – or pretending to be. When he then tries to move closer to her as they lie in bed, she pulls up a long white pillow between them. Expelling her sinful husband's unborn son in a miscarriage, Hermangarde purifies herself by sealing up her marble-white body and freezing Ryno out, maintaining an icy silence in his presence and wearing a blue-dagger pin where her heart would be.

In the last report we hear of Ryno after the married couple's return to Paris, he regularly attends the opera with his perfectly respectable wife, but he often leaves her behind in order to go sleep with his mistress. So Ryno does come back to Vellini, just as she had predicted, and there is some satisfaction in seeing that the independent and openly sexual woman has been vindicated and not demonised and abandoned in favour of the angelic but frigid wife. In getting a man while maintaining her independence, in finding a man 'feminine' enough to accept her 'masculine' traits, in being together with a partner at the end, Vellini realises some of the hopes of earlier Breillat heroines. But Vellini is still confined to the role of mistress, abhorred for her sensual ways and shunned by respectable society, much as Hermangarde remains trapped in her wifely role, respected for her virtue as long as she doesn't express any desires improper in a lady. And Ryno is compelled to shuttle back and forth between his wife and his mistress, splitting his life between them in a vain search for fulfilment, unable to find both sexual passion and social acceptance with any one woman. As Breillat has said, 'On est des êtres sociaux très fortement. Mais on est aussi des êtres amoureux, très fortement aussi. Donc il faut concilier ces deux choses'[15] (Tartan 2004). Sex and society have not yet been reconciled, though Breillat's films continue to show the way.

In October 2004, exactly one year before she started shooting *Une vieille maîtresse*, Breillat suffered a stroke in her home and then a major cerebral hemorrhage in the hospital. After a week in intensive care, she woke up to find the left side of her body paralysed. No one was sure whether she would be able to talk or walk again. Months of painful rehabilitation followed, during which she struggled to regain

15 'We are social beings, very strongly so. But we are also amorous beings, very strongly so. Therefore we must reconcile these two things'.

her motor functions and to relearn to speak, practicing her *o*'s and *i*'s every day. Throughout her ordeal, Breillat was surrounded by family and friends who helped her every step of the way: 'Mes maris, mes amies, des amis. Quand on réalise à tel point que les gens tiennent à vous, ça aide à remonter: on le fait pour soi et pour eux. Ça donne un sens à la vie'[16] (Breillat in Baecque 2006). Everyone encouraged her to direct again and, when she was finally well enough to begin *Une vieille maîtresse*, the actresses whom she had cast as the heroines of her previous films came back to her, rallying round her by taking bit parts in her film. In addition to the major role of Hermangarde filled by Roxane Mesquida (Elena in *A ma sœur!* and 'the actress' in *Sex Is Comedy*), small roles are played by Amira Casar (from *Anatomie de l'enfer*), Anne Parillaud (Jeanne in *Sex Is Comedy*), Sarah Pratt (Alice in *Brève traversée*), Caroline Ducey (Marie in *Romance*), Isabelle Renauld (Frédérique in *Parfait amour!*) and even Lio (Barbara in *Sale comme un ange*). With a stand-by director on call (as mandated by the insurance company) to take over in case she became totally incapacitated, Breillat began shooting. Even if she were not so gravely handicapped, making a heritage film would have posed extra challenges for a director used to low-budget contemporary films with smaller casts, but Breillat had a mattress brought with her to every new location so that she could lie down during lighting setups and costume changes. As can be seen from *Sex Is Comedy*, her film about her making of a film, Breillat directs with her body, and in the early days of shooting *Une vieille maîtresse*, she was constantly accompanied by a personal assistant who would help her to stand up, move hesitantly about, and strain to make arm gestures. But as filming continued, Breillat found herself performing more and more energetically, physically rehearsing with the actors, choreographing their grandest gestures and most complex moves. Her body uplifted by her spirit, she was doing things that she wasn't supposed to be able to do, inspired to direct another film that only she could make.

References

16 'My husbands, my girlfriends, friends. When you realise how much people are attached to you, that helps you to recover: you do it for yourself and for them. That gives a meaning to life'.

Austin, Guy (1996), *Contemporary French Cinema*, Manchester, Manchester University Press.

Baecque, Antoine de (2006), 'Breillat d'attaque', *Libération*, 28 June.

Barbey d'Aurevilly, Jules (1979), *Une vieille maîtresse* [1851], Paris, Gallimard.

Breillat, Catherine (2006), *Corps amoureux: Entretiens avec Claire Vassé*, Paris, Denoël.

Breillat, Catherine (2007), 'Préface', *Une vieille maîtresse* de Jules Barbey d'Aurevilly, Paris, Bartillat, pp. i–iv.

Clouzot, Claire (2004), *Catherine Breillat: Indécence et pureté*, Paris, Cahiers du cinéma.

Doane, Mary Ann (1991), *Femmes Fatales: Feminism, Film Theory, Psychoanalysis*, New York and London, Routledge.

Millet, Catherine (2001), *La Vie sexuelle de Catherine M.*, Paris, Seuil.

Millet, Catherine (2002), *The Sexual Life of Catherine M.*, trans. Adriana Hunter, New York, Grove Press.

Raya, Aurélie (2006), 'Catherine Breillat – Asia Argento – Sulfurieuses!', *Paris Match*, 27 July.

Sklar, Robert (1999), 'A Woman's Vision of Shame and Desire: An Interview with Catherine Breillat', *Cineaste* 25:1, 24–6.

Tartan (2004), 'Interview with Director Catherine Breillat', video supplement on *Anatomy of Hell* DVD, Tartan Video.

Filmography

All films scripted and directed by Catherine Breillat

Une vraie jeune fille (***A Real Young Girl***) (1976) 93 min., 35mm, col.

Production: Les Films de La Boétie, André Génovès
Screenplay based on the novel *Le Soupirail* by Catherine Breillat
Photography: Pierre Fattori
Editing: Annie Charrier
Sound: Bernard Mangière
Music: Mort Schumann, with words by Catherine Breillat
Cast: Charlotte Alexandra (Alice), Hiram Keller (Jim), Bruno Balp (le
    père), Rita Meiden (la mère), Georges Guéret (Martial), Shirley
    Stoler (l'épicière)

Tapage nocturne (***Nocturnal Uproar***) (1979) 94 min., 35mm, col.

Production: Axe Films, French Production
Screenplay related to the novel *Tapage nocturne* by Catherine Breillat
Photography: Jacques Boumendil
Editing: Annie Charrier
Sound: Alain Curvelier
Music: Serge Gainsbourg, performed by Bijou
Cast: Dominique Laffin (Solange), Marie-Hélène Breillat (Emmanu-
    elle), Bertrand Bonvoisin (Bruno), Joe Dallessandro (Jim), Domin-
    ique Basquin (Dorothée), Daniel Langlet (Bruel), Bruno Grimaldi
    (Frédéric), Bruno Devoldère (le mari), Maud Rayer (Léna), Hubert
    Drac (le metteur en scène), Annie Charrier (Annie), Gérard Lanvin
    (le loubard)

36 fillette (**Virgin**) (1987) 88 min., 35mm, col.

Production: French Production, CB Films, Sofica Cofimage, CNC
Screenplay related to the novel *36 fillette* by Catherine Breillat
Photography: Laurent Dailland
Editing: Yann Dedet
Sound: Jean Minondo
Cast: Delphine Zentout (Lili), Etienne Chicot (Maurice), Olivier
    Parnière (Bertrand), Jean-Pierre Léaud (Boris Golovine), Jean-
    François Stévenin (le père), Adrienne Bonnet (la mère), Stéphane
    Moquet (Gi-Pé), Berta D. Dominguez (Anne-Marie), Diane Bellego
    (Georgia), Christian Andia (le portier 'Opium'), Cécile Henry
    (Laetitia), Michel Scotto di Carlo (Stéphane), Anny Chasson (Mme
    Weber), Jean-Claude Binoche (M. Weber)

Sale comme un ange (**Dirty Like an Angel**) (1991) 105 min., 35mm,
col.

Production: French Production, CB Films, Ciné manufacture,
    Veranfilm
Screenplay related to the novel *Police* by Catherine Breillat
Photography: Laurent Dailland
Editing: Agnès Guillemot
Sound: Georges Prat
Music: Olivier Manoury
Cast: Claude Brasseur (Deblache), Lio (Barbara), Nils Tavernier
    (Didier Théron), Roland Amstutz (le commissaire), Claude-Jean
    Philippe (Manoni), Leila Samir (la danseuse arabe), Léa Gabrielle
    (Judy), Anny Chasson (Vishia), Brigitte Lecordier (l'inspecteur),
    Franck Karoui (Francky), Alain Schlumberger (Jeannot), Loretta
    di Cicco (Arlette)

Aux Niçois qui mal y pensent (1995) 22 min., 35mm, col.

Part of the anthology film *A propos de Nice, la suite*
Production: Margo Films, Georges Kapler
Photography: Laurent Dailland
Editing: Katya Chelli
Sound: Jean Minondo
Cast: Robert Benassayag, Marie-Jeanne Meillan, Yvette Wojtakboisson

Parfait amour! (*Perfect Love*) (1996) 113 min., 35mm, col.

Production: Dacia Films, CB Films, Georges Benayoun, La Sept
  Cinéma
Photography: Laurent Dailland
Editing: Agnès Guillemot
Sound: Jean Minondo
Cast: Isabelle Renauld (Frédérique), Francis Renaud (Christophe),
  Laura Saglio (Emmanuelle), Alain Soral (Philippe), Michèle Rème
  (la mère de Christophe), Delphine de Malherbe (Valérie de la Tour-
  nelle), Coralie Gengenbach (Bénédicte), Serge Toubiana (Louis),
  Marie Lebée (la juge d'instruction), Tom Rocheteau (Vincent),
  Alice Mitterand (Wanda)

Romance (1999) 98 min., 35mm, col.

Production: Flach Film (Jean-François Lepetit), CB Films, Arte France
  Cinéma
Photography: Yorgos Arvanitis
Editing: Agnès Guillemot
Sound: Paul Lainé
Music: D. J. Valentin, Raphael Tidas
Cast: Caroline Ducey (Marie), Sagamore Stévenin (Paul), François
  Berléand (Robert), Rocco Siffredi (Paolo), Reza Habouhossein
  (l'homme de l'escalier), Fabien de Jomaron (Claude), Emma Col-
  berti (Charlotte), Ashley Wanninger (Ashley)

A ma sœur! (*Fat Girl*) (2001) 93 min., 35mm, col.

Production: Flach Film (Jean-François Lepetit), CB Films, Arte France
  Cinéma, Urania Pictures, Immagine e Cinema
Photography: Yorgos Arvanitis, Olivier Fortin
Editing: Pascale Chavance
Sound: Jean Minondo
Music: 'Moi, je m'ennuie' and 'J'ai mis mon cœur à pourrir', words
  and music by Catherine Breillat
Cast: Anaïs Reboux (Anaïs), Roxane Mesquida (Elena), Libero de Rienzo
  (Fernando), Arsinée Khanjian (la mère), Romain Goupil (le père),
  Laura Betti (la mère de Fernando), Albert Goldberg (le tueur), Odette
  Barrière (une amie de la résidence), Pierre Renverseau (un ami de
  la résidence), Michel Guillemin (le gardien de la résidence), Claude
  Sese (l'officier de gendarmerie), Marc Samuel (l'inspecteur)

Brève traversée (Brief Crossing) (2001) 90 min., 16mm, col.

TV Série Arte 'Masculin/Féminin'

Production: Art Unité Fiction France, GMT Production, Jean-Pierre Guérin, Pierre Eid, Christophe Valette

Photography: Eric Gautier

Editing: Pascale Chavance

Sound: Yves Osmu

Cast: Sarah Pratt (Alice), Gilles Guillain (Thomas), Marc Filipi (le magicien), Laetitia Lopez (l'assistante du magicien), Marc Jablonski (le cuisinier du self), Christelle Dacosta (le douanier français), Nicholas Hawtrey (le vieil Anglais), Franck Lemaître (le serveur de la boîte), Philippe Quaisse (le photographe)

Sex Is Comedy (2002) 93 min., 35mm, col.

Production: Flach Film (Jean-François Lepetit)

Photography: Laurent Machuel

Editing: Pascale Chavance

Sound: Yves Osmu

First Assistant Director: Michaël Weill

Special Makeup Effects: Dominique Colladant

Cast: Anne Parillaud (Jeanne), Grégoire Colin (l'acteur), Roxane Mesquida (l'actrice), Ashley Wanniger (Léo), Dominique Colladant (Willy), Bart Binnema (le directeur photo), Yves Osmu (l'ingénieur du son), Francis Seleck (le directeur de production), Elisabete Piecho (la scripte), Diane Scapa (la chef décoratrice), Ana Lorena (une maquilleuse), Claire Monatte (une maquilleuse), José Cascais (l'accessoiriste), Arnaldo Junior (le chef électro), Julia Fragata (l'habilleuse), Elisabete Silva (la perchman)

Anatomie de l'enfer (Anatomy of Hell) (2003) 88 min., 35mm, col.

Production: Flach Film (Jean-François Lepetit), CB Films

Screenplay related to the novel *Pornocratie* by Catherine Breillat

Photography: Yorgos Arvanitis, Guillaume Schiffman

Editing: Pascale Chavance

Sound: Carlos Pinto

Cast: Amira Casar (la fille), Rocco Siffredi (l'homme), Pauline Hunt (doublure d'Amira Casar), Jacques Monge (le pilier de bar), Claudio Carvalho (l'enfant oiseau), Carolina Lopes (la petite fille), Diego Rodrigues, Joao Marques, Bruno Fernandes (les enfants docteurs),

Alexandre Belin, Manuel Taglang (les amoureux du terrain vague), Maria Edite Moreira, Maria Joao Santos (les pharmaciennes), la voix de Catherine Breillat

Une vieille maîtresse (**The Last Mistress**) (2007) 104 min., 35mm, col.

Production: Flach Film (Jean-François Lepetit), CB Films
Screenplay based on the novel *Une vieille maîtresse* by Jules Barbey d'Aurevilly
Photography: Yorgos Arvanitis
Editing: Pascale Chavance
Sound: Yves Osmu
Cast: Asia Argento (Vellini), Fu'ad Aït Aattou (Ryno de Marigny), Roxane Mesquida (Hermangarde), Claude Sarraute (la marquise de Flers), Yolande Moreau (la comtesse d'Artelles), Michael Lonsdale (le vicomte de Prony), Anne Parillaud (Mme de Solcy), Jean-Philippe Tesse (le vicomte de Mareuil), Sarah Pratt (la comtesse de Mendoze), Amira Casar (Mademoiselle Divine des Airelles), Lio (la chanteuse), Léa Seydoux (Oliva), Nicholas Hawtrey (Sir Reginald), Caroline Ducey (la dame de Pique), Jean-Claude Binoche (le comte de Cerisy), Thomas Hardy (le valet de Mareuil), Jean-Gabriel Mitterrand (le valet de Ryno), Eric Bouhier (le chirurgien), Frédéric Botton (le cardinal de Flers), Patrick Tétu (Père Griffon), Isabelle Renauld (l'arrogante)

Select bibliography

See also the references at the end of each chapter.

Texts by Catherine Breillat

(1968), *L'Homme facile*, Paris, Christian Bourgois; reprint (2000), Paris, J'ai lu; English trans. (1969), *A Man for the Asking*, trans. Harold J. Salemson, New York, William Morrow. A novel.

(1970), *Le Silence, après ...*, Paris, François Wimille. A novel.

(1971), *Les Vêtements de mer*, Paris, François Wimille. A collection of poems and plays.

(1974), *Le Soupirail*, Paris, Guy Authier; reprint (2000), *Une vraie jeune fille*, Paris, Denoël. A novel.

(1979), *Tapage nocturne*, Paris, Mercure de France. A novel.

(1985), *Police*, Paris, Albin Michel; reprint (1985), Paris, J'ai lu. A novel.

(1987), *36 fillette*, Paris, Carrere. A novel.

(1991), 'Une vraie jeune fille', *Cahiers du cinéma* 443/444, 12.

(1993), 'Nagisa Oshima: *L'Empire des sens*', *Cahiers du cinéma*, hors-série: *100 films pour une vidéothèque*, 50–1.

(1994), 'Un jour j'ai vu *Baby Doll* ...', *Positif* 400, 13–15; English trans. (1995), 'One day I saw *Baby Doll* ...', in John Boorman and Walter Donohue (eds), *Projections 4½: Film-makers on Film-making*, London, Faber and Faber, pp. 28–32.

(1996), 'L'Eternelle Histoire de la séduction', *Cahiers du cinéma* 499, 26–7. On João César Monteiro's *God's Comedy*.

(1997), 'J'aime trop la littérature pour l'opposer au cinéma', *Magazine littéraire* 354, 40–1.

(1998), 'La Vérité sans fard: L'Autobiographie vue par les cinéastes', in Alain Bergala (ed.), *Je est un film*, ACOR (Association des cinémas de l'Ouest pour la recherche), pp. 37–8.

(1999a) (ed.), *Le Livre du plaisir*, Paris, Editions 1; reprint (2001), Paris, Le Livre de poche. An anthology of mostly male writings on sex, edited and annotated by Breillat.

(1999b), *Romance: Scénario*, Paris, Cahiers du cinéma.

(1999c), 'Le Tombeau de Stanley Kubrick', *Positif* 464, 46.

(2001a), *A ma sœur!: Scénario*, Paris, Cahiers du cinéma.

(2001b), *Pornocratie*, Paris, Denoël; English trans. (2006), *Pornocracy*, trans. Paul Buck and Catherine Petit, Los Angeles, Jovian Books. A novel.

(2001c), 'Shohei Imamura: Rire jaune', *Positif* 490, 13–19. Breillat interviews the director of *Warm Water under a Red Bridge*.

(2002), 'Guilty Pleasures', *Film Comment* 38:1, 8. On Elia Kazan's *Splendor in the Grass*.

(2003a), 'Témoignages', *Cahiers du cinéma* 576, 42–4. On Maurice Pialat.

(2003b), 'Le Film qui m'a inventée', *Cahiers du cinéma* 582, 66–7. On Ingmar Bergman's *Sawdust and Tinsel*.

(2004), 'De l'importance d'être haï', *Trafic* 50, 109–16.

(2005), 'Ciné-Manga', *Cahiers du cinéma* 600, supplément, 24.

(2006a), *Corps amoureux: Entretiens avec Claire Vassé*, Paris, Denoël.

(2006b), 'La Censure, pour se cacher de soi-même ... ', in Eric Alt (ed.), *Le Sexe et ses juges*, Paris, Syllepse, pp. 69–73.

(2007a), 'Préface', *Une vieille maîtresse* de Jules Barbey d'Aurevilly, Paris, Bartillat, pp. i–iv.

(2007b), *Bad Love*, Paris, Léo Scheer. A novel.

Texts on Breillat's films

Breillat, Catherine and Denis, Claire (1999), 'Le Ravissement de Marie', *Cahiers du cinéma* 534, 42–6. A revealing conversation between Breillat and one of the contemporary female directors she most respects.

Brinkema, Eugenie (2006), 'Celluloid Is Sticky: Sex, Death, Materiality, Metaphysics (in Some Films by Catherine Breillat)', *Women: A Cultural Review* 17:2, 147–70. Provocative psychoanalytic feminist study of *Une vraie jeune fille, Romance* and *A ma sœur!*

Brouste, Judith (1999), 'Le Sexe pur/Pure Sex: Interview de Catherine Breillat', *Art Press* 246, 22–7. Interview on *Romance*, with bilingual text.

Clément, Jérôme (2002), 'Catherine Breillat', *Les Femmes et l'amour*, Paris, Stock, pp. 267–300. An in-depth interview with Breillat on the subject of gender, in a collection which also includes interviews with Elisabeth Badinter and Catherine Millet.

Clouzot, Claire (2004), *Catherine Breillat: Indécence et pureté*, Paris, Cahiers du cinéma. A volume in Cahiers du cinéma's prestigious 'Auteurs' series (and thus a milestone of recognition for Breillat as a member of the canon of great auteurs), this chronological survey of her films presents valuable behind-the-scenes information and an extensive interview with the director.

Constable, Liz (2004), 'Unbecoming Sexual Desires for Women Becoming Sexual Subjects: Simone de Beauvoir (1949) and Catherine Breillat (1999)', *MLN* 119:4, 672–95.

Felperin, Leslie and Williams, Linda Ruth (1999), 'The Edge of the Razor', *Sight and Sound* 9:10, 12–14. Interview with Breillat on *Romance*.

Gillain, Anne (2003), 'Profile of a Filmmaker: Catherine Breillat', in Roger Célestin, Eliane DalMolin and Isabelle de Courtivron (eds), *Beyond French Feminisms: Debates on Women, Politics, and Culture in France, 1981–2001*, New York, Palgrave Macmillan, pp. 201–11. Career overview that considers the question, what kind of feminist is Breillat?

Goudet, Stéphane and Vassé, Claire (2001), 'Une âme à deux corps', *Positif* 481, 26–30; partial English trans. (2004), 'One Soul with Two Bodies', trans. Royal S. Brown, booklet insert, *Fat Girl* DVD, Criterion Collection. Interview with Breillat on *A ma sœur!*.

Hottell, Ruth A. and Russell-Watts, Lynsey (2002), 'Catherine Breillat's *Romance* and the Female Spectator: From Dream-Work to Therapy', *Esprit créateur* 42:3, 70–80.

Ince, Katherine (2006), 'Is Sex Comedy or Tragedy?: Directing Desire and Female Auteurship in the Cinema of Catherine Breillat', *Journal of Aesthetics and Art Criticism* 64:1, 157–64.

Jousse, Thierry and Strauss, Frédéric (1991), 'Entretien avec Catherine Breillat', *Cahiers du cinéma* 445, 76–8. Interview on *Sale comme un ange*.

Krisjansen, Ivan and Maddock, Trevor (2001), 'Educating Eros: Catherine Breillat's *Romance* as a Cinematic Solution to Sade's Metaphysical Problem', *Studies in French Cinema* 1:3, 141–9.

Le Pallec-Marand, Claudine (2006), 'L'Age de femme du cinéma: Intégrale Catherine Breillat', *Critikat*, 17 October. Career overview that looks at Breillat's representation of female sexuality on film and that is highly critical of *Romance* and *Anatomie de l'enfer*.

Le Pallec-Marand, Claudine (2007), 'Maman et putain transfigurées: *Une vieille maîtresse*', *Critikat*, 29 May.

Macnab, Geoffrey (2004), 'Sadean Woman', *Sight and Sound* 14:12, 20–2. Interview with Breillat on *Anatomie de l'enfer*.

Maddock, Trevor H. and Krisjansen, Ivan (2003), 'Surrealist Poetics and the Cinema of Evil: The Significance of the Expression of Sovereignty in Catherine Breillat's *A ma sœur*', *Studies in French Cinema* 3:3, 161–71.

Martin, Adrian (2000), '"X" Marks the Spot: Classifying *Romance*', *Senses of Cinema* 4. Probing analysis of the censorship controversy surrounding *Romance* in Australia.

Murphy, Kathleen (1999), 'A Matter of Skin: Catherine Breillat's Metaphysics of Film and Flesh', *Film Comment* 35:5, 16–22. Consistently revealing and provocative survey of Breillat's films through *Romance*.

Phillips, John (2001), 'Catherine Breillat's *Romance*: Hard Core and the Female Gaze', *Studies in French Cinema* 1:3, 133–40.

Prédal, René (2001), 'De la place du sexe dans les rapports amoureux, ou pouvoir et désir féminin chez Catherine Breillat', *Contrabande* 6, 27–38.

Price, Brian (2002), 'Catherine Breillat', *Senses of Cinema*, November. A career overview, especially interesting for the connections it makes between Breillat's films and other related film styles and movements.

Puaux, Françoise (2001), 'Entretien avec Catherine Breillat', *Le Machisme à l'écran*, *CinémAction* 99, 165–72. An interview containing some of Breillat's most trenchant comments on masculinity.

Rouyer, Philippe and Vassé, Claire (2004), 'De l'évanescent qui n'est plus de l'ordre du charnel', *Positif* 521/522, 36–40. Interview with Breillat spanning her directorial career.

Sineux, Michel (1991), 'Je raconte l'âme et la chair des gens', *Positif*

365/366, 16–18. Interview with Breillat on *Police* and *Sale comme un ange*.

Sklar, Robert (1999), 'A Woman's Vision of Shame and Desire: An Interview with Catherine Breillat', *Cineaste* 25:1, 24–6. Interview on *Romance*.

Spoiden, Stéphane (2002), 'No Man's Land: Genres en question dans *Sitcom, Romance* et *Baise-moi*', *Esprit créateur* 42:1, 96–106.

Strauss, Frédéric (1996), 'Entretien avec Catherine Breillat', *Cahiers du cinéma* 507, 23–9. Interview on *Parfait amour!*

Tarr, Carrie with Rollet, Brigitte (2001), *Cinema and the Second Sex: Women's Filmmaking in France in the 1980s and the 1990s*, New York and London, Continuum. An important discussion of Breillat within the context of other contemporary female directors.

Vasse, David (2004), *Catherine Breillat: Un cinéma du rite et de la transgression*, Issy-les-Moulineaux, ARTE, and Brussels, Complexe. A published dissertation, this highly sophisticated study takes a thematic approach to Breillat's films with an emphasis on mythic rites of passage.

Vincendeau, Ginette (1989), 'The Closer You Get ... ', *Monthly Film Bulletin* 661:56, 41–2. Interview with Breillat on *36 fillette*.

Vincendeau, Ginette (2003), 'What She Wants', *Sight and Sound* 13:5, 20–2. Excellent piece on gender, *Sex Is Comedy* and other films about filmmaking.

Wells, Gwendolyn (2002), 'Accoutrements of Passion: Fashion, Irony, and Feminine P.O.V. in Catherine Breillat's *Romance*', *Sites: Journal of Contemporary French Studies* 6:1, 51–66.

Williams, Linda (2001), 'Cinema and the Sex Act', *Cineaste* 27:1, 20–5. Important discussion of *Romance* and *A ma sœur!* in relation to other sexually explicit art films, by the author of *Hard Core: Power, Pleasure, and the 'Frenzy of the Visible'*.

Williams, Linda Ruth (2003), '*Sex Is Comedy*', *Sight and Sound* 13:8, 56–8. Insightful review that discusses Breillat as an auteur.

Wilson, Emma (2001), 'Deforming Femininity: Catherine Breillat's *Romance*', in Lucy Mazdon (ed.), *France on Film: Reflections on Popular French Cinema*, London, Wallflower Press, pp. 145–57.

Index

Note: 'n.' after a page reference indicates the number of a footnote on that page. Note: page numbers in *italic* refer to illustrations.